MW01644142

RELENTLESS

The Making Of An Investigative Reporter

By

Stephen Cain

Dedication

To Pat and our seven now adult children: Mike, Jim, Sue, John, Jeff, Tim, and Beth. You make the world a better place.

Table of Contents

Reviews: 1
Forward 3
Chapter 1 A Kid Writes Soberly About Gay Birds 6
Chapter 2 The Striking Workers Were Pawns 9
Chapter 3 Under Police Interrogation 12
Chapter 4 The Day President Kennedy Was Assassinated 15
Chapter 5 Too Poorly Educated For Ann Arbor 18
Chapter 6 A Brutal Confession 21
Chapter 7 Taylor, Burton, And Sweet Revenge 24
Chapter 8 One Of Our H-Bombs Is Missing 26
Chapter 9 My Mother, Lindbergh, And A Silly Toy Save The Whales 29
Chapter 10 The Women Who Helped Pave The Way 32
Chapter 11 A Barefoot Boy From Southern Indiana 37
Chapter 12 When Abortion Was Illegal 42
Chapter 13 No Money, No Heart 46
Chapter 14 The Bomber Had A Crush On Me 49
Chapter 15 My Connection To The Storied Past 55
Chapter 16 Finessing A Racist Newspaper Policy 58
Chapter 17 Master Of The Universe, Not! 62
Chapter 18 I Hang The Wrong Men Out To Dry 63
Chapter 19 Jack Daniels To The Rescue 68
Chapter 20 Kicking A Hornet's Nest 70
Chapter 21 Tear Gas, Pepper Spray, Billy Clubs, Bricks 74
Chapter 22 Blood Disappoints One, Enriches Another 77
Chapter 23 Sesame Street And A "Disloyal" Doctor 81

Chapter 24 Apollo 11's Unreported Brush With Death 83
Chapter 25 A Dead-End Metaphor 88
Chapter 26 Six Armed Men, One Turned And Fired 91
Chapter 27 A Lesson From A Colleague 95
Chapter 28 A Phony Medical Student Guesses Right 97
Chapter 29 She Falsely Confessed To Infanticide 102
Chapter 30 An Inspired And Shameless Con Job 107
Chapter 31 "Super Breeze" Borrows A .40, Hunts Me 110
Chapter 32 Peter Posey and Henry the Cigarette Eater 115
Chapter 33 Manipulating justice to save a junkie 121
Chapter 34 He Watched The Waters Take His Mother 125
Chapter 35 I Savage A Rival Reporter 129
Chapter 36 Old Crow Survives A Pipeline 132
Chapter 37 Gallows Humor Keeps Us Sane 136
Chapter 38 I Play At Being Lt. Colombo 138
Chapter 39 I Violate A Journalistic Standard 140
Chapter 40 A Manipulation Had Unintended Consequences 144
Chapter 41 The Malpractice Crisis And Rescuing A Friend 146
Chapter 42 Four Outlaw Bikers Framed For Murder 148
Chapter 43 L.D. Bickford Was The Wrong Killer 152
Chapter 44 "Mr. And Miss Butt" Break A Conspiracy 155
Chapter 45 A Betrayal, My Pride, A New Murder 159
Chapter 46 They Ran Afoul Of Corrupt Feds 162
Chapter 47 Stan Swinton Knew Everyone 165
Chapter 48 Cognitive Dissonance 167
Chapter 49 Putting Myself In Harm's Way 171
Chapter 50 Harmonica Man Fades Away 175
Chapter 51 The Detroit News Turns Cowardly 179
Chapter 52 A Father Of Integrity And Courage 186
Chapter 53 The Dairyman And The "Retards" 191

Chapter 54 A Lasting Impression 195
Chapter 55 Choosing What's Right 197
Chapter 56 Lora, The Girl With The Forward Look 200
Chapter 57 Indulging A Hard Edge 204
Chapter 58 Not Everything Academic Is Brilliant 209
Chapter 59 Socrates vs. The Jesuit 216
Chapter 60 The "Barons Of Pot" Overreach 218
Chapter 61 "Mad Dog" Merkle And The Pot Genius 225
Chapter 62 A Billion-Dollar Doper Scams The Feds 229
Chapter 63 State Shrink Seduces Pedophile Killer 235
Chapter 64 Exposing A Deadly, Fetid Nursing Home 241
Chapter 65 Too Many Failures Enable A Rapist 247
Chapter 66 Spicing Up The Police Briefs 253
Chapter 67 I Jerk My Publisher's Chain 255
Chapter 68 I Censor Myself 257
Chapter 69 "Baby Jessica" Custody Turns Ugly 260
Chapter 70 Two Women Build A Good Life 268
Chapter 71 When I'm My Own Worst Enemy 272
Chapter 72 Life After Newspapers 276

Reviews:

"Relentless" is a gritty, hard-hitting and yet poignant collection. Part murder mystery, part urban lore, the stories are an unforgettable peek at street life as seen through the sensitive eyes of Stephen Cain. A former investigative reporter, Cain is a passionate and skilled writer with a gift for capturing the depth of human emotion -- from anguish and defeat to determination and triumph. He shares them all in this descriptive, hauntingly beautiful blend of politics, crime and his own personal pursuit for justice. Readers who dare to pick up "Relentless" will enter a world that few have experienced and even fewer have escaped. It's an enticing drama … that just happens to be true.

— Denise Crittendon, retired reporter and editor, author of "Where it Rains Color"

Any of these enterprising news stories could be a book or TV miniseries but here Steve Cain has summarized each in perfect detail. "Relentless" is a history of Ann Arbor and Detroit as much as a memoir. For Steve it has always been just the facts, but facts no one else seemed to be able to uncover.
— Joan Lowenstein, attorney, former adjunct professor of journalism

Stephen Cain, member of the Michigan Journalism Hall of Fame, had a thing for underdogs during decades of reporting for The Detroit News and The Ann Arbor News. From getting four outlaw bikers off death row to working undercover exposes, he poked at injustices and made them right.

— Ric Bohy, retired journalist, author of "Flirt"

What Stephen did as an investigative reporter is beyond amazing. Readers will be mesmerized. Most don't have a clue these days what newspapers used to be able to do. Most impressively, while he gives the reader a glimpse of the darker side, he preserves the humanity of everybody he writes about, from the highest to the lowest.
— Jeff Gaynor, educator, elected official

Steve Cain and and I were colleagues, the young stars at The Detroit News in the late 1960s. His book is emblematic of his work, insightful, well written, and fully aware of the settings.
— William Connellan, former journalist, university administrator

Steve Cain was an old-school investigative reporter. He wrote interestingly and accurately about several of my major cases, as would befit a reporter nominated twice for a Pulitzer. I look forward to reading a full account of the stories although I know the ending of some.
— Greg Stejskal, FBI special agent (1975-2006), columnist

A captivating memoir from an ace reporter who covered so many important hard-news stories. The award-winning scribe paints a fascinating, intimate look inside the golden age of newspapering, the newsroom tensions, and the powerful stories he wrote.
— Patty LaNoue Stearns, journalist, editor, author

"Relentless" is the account of how Steve Cain built his career. Story after story that others might overlook, he dug until the truth was known. Would that young writers followed this model instead of following the same story every other dog in the pack is covering. He showed the way time after time.
— Maureen McDonald, journalist, Michigan Journalism Hall of Fame committee

"Relentless" is a feast of tales from a Michigan newsman who seems to have done it all. A self-described "adrenaline junkie," Stephen Cain took risks — necessary and unnecessary — in pursuit of hidden truths. He kept his cool while reporting on some of southeast Michigan's most compelling and occasionally dangerous stories. To get the inside story of institutional abuse at a mental institution, Cain, under an assumed name, had himself committed as a patient. He worked undercover four times, succeeding thrice. Cain's crisply written memoir takes the reader on a perilous, hellacious, and often hilarious journalistic journey.
— Jack Kresnak, retired journalist, author "Hope for the City."

Forward

He thought of her as "Tweety," his made-up name for the woman he'd murdered.

Her real name was Theresa Gallagher, but he didn't know that. He was a Nowhere Man: poorly educated, unemployed, a few minor scrapes with the law, not even a tough guy. He was still in his early twenties, but like so many folks with no prospects and living on the fringes in the late 1960s, he ended up squatting in Detroit's Cass Corridor. The area north of downtown, south of Wayne State University, and west of Woodward Avenue has since been scrubbed, gentrified, and renamed Midtown.

Imagine tumbling down a stairway and sprawling at the landing with nowhere further to fall. Back in the day, that was the Cass Corridor. It was a refuge for whores, hippies, and stumble-down alcoholics. It was an area of boarded-up brick apartment buildings and abandoned Queen Anns and Victorians stripped of their stained glass, crown moldings, and cast iron radiators.

For Theresa, life was a struggle. Her father worked when he could, but that wasn't often because he drank a lot. There were just the two of them in a one-bedroom apartment, also in the Cass Corridor. She slept on the sofa. He had the bedroom. She worked at a nearby service station, paid most of the rent, did most of the cooking. I was never able to get him to tell me what had happened to his wife. He did give me a picture from Theresa's high school graduation two years earlier. It showed a trim but fairly homely young woman with a bowl haircut more typical of guys. But she had a nice smile. That was how she greeted the world. It was the smile that got her killed.

The Nowhere Man told the Detroit Police he really liked her smile, that she would wave to him when he walked past. He had a gun with him that day. He was showboating. He took it out, waving it around, thinking he would impress her. The gun discharged, a single shot, killing her. It wasn't a robbery, just a stupid accident. He stood around in shock waiting for the police. I wrote the story, handed in her picture. They ran in The Detroit News the next day under the headline "A Friendly Wave and Death Results."

In four decades of newspapering, I had written some 12,000 byline stories. I helped get four outlaw motorcyclists off death row in New Mexico, freed a Midland, Michigan, woman serving a life sentence after being falsely convicted of starving her infant daughter to death, and saved a heroin addict from certain conviction in the robbery-murder of a Brinks guard. I did four under-cover investigations, won three dozen news writing awards in the state, was twice nominated for the Pulitzer, and was voted into the Michigan Journalism Hall of Fame. Virtually all of those stories were versions of Joe Friday's "Just the facts, Ma'am." They were short on atmospherics, largely devoid of adverbs, and revealed no hint of who I was as a human being or how I saw the events I was writing about. That was journalistic convention. But I let emotion creep into the Tweety story. That's why I remembered it so vividly. That should have told me something.

I loosened up in my writing during my subsequent years at the Ann Arbor News, but ran afoul of the editor and took early retirement in late 1998. I enrolled in Eastern Michigan University and completed the last two years of my bachelor's and all the coursework for my master's in an insanely intense nineteen months.

I had been doing a lot of posting on Facebook and collected a large number of friends and followers. With the 2016 election of Trump, I started posting daily screeds on his awfulness. My youngest daughter Beth challenged me to take a one week vacation from politics and fill seven days with stories of my adventures and misadventures in journalism. I got a lot of positive feedback, and seven swelled to seventy one.

Perry Plouff, a friend from Saline, Michigan, did an initial editorial run-through, catching an embarrassing number of errors and highlighting passages that lacked clarity. Ann Arbor's Elizabeth Hurwitz, an elder law attorney and screen writer whose judgment I valued, said I needed to put more of myself into the stories so the readers could view the events through my eyes, know what I was thinking and feeling as well as the life experiences I brought to the telling. The idea of stripping off my cloak of invisibility was pretty scary, but it made sense because it's never "just the facts Ma'am." Mary Marsh Matthews, a friend and retired professional copy editor, did a masterful job of whipping the manuscript into decent shape.

My first name for the stories, read mainly by my friends, was "Cain's Chronicles." As the audience expanded, I changed the name to the more descriptive "Relentless — "The Making of an Investigative Reporter."
I've always had a love-hate relationship with the term "investigative

reporter." Particularly when I was younger, I thought it terribly presumptuous and preferred just to call myself a reporter. There are the obvious traditional investigative pieces — my freeing a woman wrongly convicted of murdering her baby or Pro Publica's masterful expose of undisclosed gifts (soft bribes, really) to Supreme Court Justice Clarence Thomas. But I contend that all really good reporting is investigative. I would argue that it's not just settling for a racially tinged account of young Blacks beating and robbing an elderly White woman but looking beyond to how pushing a freeway through a historic Black community destabilized a peacefully integrated neighboring community. I was relentlessly driven to look behind the curtain, so with that as the criterion, I'm fine with calling myself an investigative reporter.

The resulting book is a collection "war stories" from the second half of the 20th Century — the last golden age of newspaper reporting — an account of an approach to journalism is less widely practiced in the age of the internet, a personal memoir, and social history.

Chapter 1 A Kid Writes Soberly About Gay Birds

Mostly, I was a storyteller. My first venture into anything that could be called journalism was a literal recounting of the "birds" part of the "birds and the bees." It was unintentionally hilarious because I was only ten years old at the time and dead serious. My medium was "The Junior Scientist," a newspaper I put out four to six times a year from fourth grade through sixth grade, when the circulation peaked at about 150. I would dictate the stories to my mother, who would type them up. My father would run the copies on the mimeograph machine in his Department of Conservation office at the University of Michigan. I wanted to be a scientist like my father.

The summer of the birds, my father was conducting a seminar at the U-M Biological Station, known by students and faculty as the "Bug Camp," at Douglas Lake in the northern part of Michigan's Lower Peninsula. On some evenings I would tag along with the graduate students to a country tavern outside Indian River where, after last call, they would join the locals in closing the place with an inebriated rendering of "Good Night Irene." On other evenings, rather than leave me alone in the cabin, my parents would take me to faculty lectures.

The talk by a professor of ornithology told of how he and his students solved the mystery of cliff swallow reproduction. Other than where they chose to nest, the biggest difference between barn and cliff swallows was that cliff swallows averaged 30% more eggs per productive nest. One theory was that the greater number of eggs made up for more pressure from predators. It didn't check out.

The professor said that the cliff swallows would segregate themselves by sex prior to mating. All the male swallows would wash in one pool, the female swallows in another. His graduate students put red dye in one pool, blue dye in the other. Then they sat with binoculars watching the birds nest in the side of a gravel pit. It turned out that nearly a third of the nesting pairs of cliff swallows were red-red or blue-blue. The heterosexual mating pairs had been compensating for the egg deficit from the gay birds. Even back then, I knew a good story when I stumbled across one.

There were also ordinary stories, like fossil hunting along the AuSable in Ontario and in the limestone quarries in Sylvania, Ohio. My father subscribed to the "Bulletin of the Atomic Scientists," so I wrote about the doomsday clock. I thought people were foolish for building fallout shelters. I was mad at the government for not figuring out how to get rid of the bombs and wrote a passionate editorial against paying farmers not to grow crops while people were starving in India.

My interest in writing took a five-year vacation, resuming my junior year of high school when I joined the staff of "The Broadcaster," the once-a-month student paper at University High School, the U-M's since shut down laboratory school for teacher training. Wes Maurer, chairman of the U-M Department of Journalism and a friend of my parents, decided that made me a candidate for his summer program at the university for high school journalists. With the program under my belt, I served as co- editor of "The Broadcaster" my senior year. The paper was literate but painfully dull. We never picked a fight, never stoked a controversy, and I never did anything irregular until the last hour of the last day of the school year.

I had taken a proof copy of the final issue to the office for the principal to review. Most of the paper consisted of pictures from the senior picnic. Mr. Fox, the principal, said it was okay. I started for the door only to be stopped by Miss Lane, one of the teachers. There was a picture of her sitting sideways at a picnic table, surrounded by senior girls. She was wearing shorts. Her legs were crossed modestly. "You may not show my legs", she said. I argued, but the principal backed her.

The paper was printed by letterpress on glossy paper. The pictures were in tin engravings mounted on wood blocks. There was barely enough time to run the press and deliver the copies before school let out for the year. There was no way the picture could be replaced. I mounted the plate on a router and carefully took out her legs. Then, in a fit of inspiration, I routed out her shorts up to the edge of her nether region, leaving nothing but white space to tease the imagination. I dropped the papers at each classroom and headed quickly out the door. If there was any fallout, it never reached me.

The next fall, I enrolled in Amherst with the intent of becoming a geologist. Did fine in history, English, and political science but flunked German and calculus. Amherst had been written up in The New York Times for starting something it called its " underachiever program. " It didn't want bright students who coasted along on "gentleman C's." I became the college's second underachiever. The freshman dean said I could come back for my sophomore year if I successfully completed ten credit hours of calculus and physics in summer school. I returned to Amherst just long enough to get off academic probation and quit.

I took a job peddling Collier's Encyclopedias door-to-door in Toledo but couldn't maintain the con. I sold only one set of books. The bosses withheld half my commission. They made the mistake of leaving me in charge of a training class of new recruits while they went to lunch. I left with all the recruits, locking the door on the way out.

I fled back to Ann Arbor. I had no qualifications for a regular job. I got a copy of the Michigan Publisher's Yearbook and drew a fifty-mile radius around Ann Arbor with the intent of calling on editors of weekly papers. My first interview was with Jack Hoffman, editor of The South Lyon Herald and protege of the U-M's Wes Maurer. He hired me at $55 a week.

Chapter 2 The Striking Workers Were Pawns

WHITMORE LAKE — There was a pall hanging over the O & S Bearing and Manufacturing plant in Whitmore Lake. The striking workers gathered around the nighttime fire in a rusted fifty-five-gallon drum, were glum about their prospects. They were bored and talking too much for their United Auto Workers International rep's peace of mind. Inside the plant, the next day, the O & S president, worried about the future of his company, was chatting with me more than his outside labor negotiator would have wished. I was working for The South Lyon Herald and its Whitmore Lake News edition. This was my first honest-to-God hard news story, and I was learning on the fly.

The company's workforce was predominately old, took home paychecks enhanced by their seniority, and allegedly didn't work as fast as younger folk. The workers felt threatened. The company felt squeezed. I'd talk with the workers, then ask the company about the workers' concerns, take the company's comments back to the workers, and so on. The workers claimed the company's hired gun hoped to make his reputation by sticking it to them. My sense was they were probably right. The hired gun argued that the UAW's international rep, who supposedly had been demoted for some unspoken earlier failure, hoped to draw a better assignment by hammering the company. I sensed he was probably right.

I fell into a pattern that I would follow for the rest of my career. I tried to focus on what really mattered to the people I was interviewing and ignoring bullshit, ignoring what seemed aimed mostly at scoring points on the other side, ignoring the canned talking points. The company's labor negotiator, for example, claimed that an earlier personnel director had made a practice of hiring ex-cons, implying that this somehow degraded the workforce. But he then said that was off the record, so I figured he was simply trying to poison me against the workers. There's an old journalistic trope that you weren't doing your job unless both sides were mad at you. I thought that was stupid. I preferred that people felt they were treated fairly, even if they were unhappy with what I wrote.

A state mediator in Detroit eventually worked out a contract that didn't gore either side too badly. It preserved the status of existing workers but allowed the company to hire new workers at lower pay. What I hadn't realized until decades later was that this two-tier approach prefigured the

UAW's later job-saving contracts in the auto industry. The O & S workers ratified their contract, and I went on to other stories. A couple of weeks later, I got a note from the mediator telling me he had used my stories as a roadmap to bring the sides together. To be told that what you did actually meant something was a serious affirmation for a nineteen-year-old kid.

In South Lyon, I went on to do weekly "Meet Your New Neighbor" columns. That felt like an incredible comedown for the only child of high-achieving parents. I was raised with my father's graduate students. Thirteen of the twenty-five boys in my high school class had IQs of 135 or better (I had swiped the test scores). My former classmates at Amherst were mostly products of East Coast prep schools and destined for the elite. The new neighbors in South Lyon and Whitmore Lake were mostly working-class high school graduates. I went from never seeing myself as the smartest guy in the room to a world where I often was. Hoffman insisted on the stories, so I interviewed the newcomers to find out who they were, where they had been, what they had done, and, most importantly, what their hopes and dreams were. I did the new neighbor stories for the better part of a year. I discovered that if I really probed and listened, I could find out something interesting about almost everybody and have a great time doing it. The best lesson from Jack Hoffman's assignment was understanding that seeing myself as the smartest guy in the room would be fatal to becoming the kind of journalist I wanted to be.

My favorite story from that year was the dedication of the small, white clapboard Pentecostal Church of the Apostolic Faith, Bethlehem Temple, in rural Salem Township, outside of South Lyon. The building housed a small display of Civil War memorabilia, including a drum and a tintype of a young Black bugle player. The pastor told me the neighborhood had been a terminus of the underground railroad. There were only six or eight African-American families in the congregation, but the tiny church was packed with Black and White Pentecostals who poured in from as far away as Arkansas.

In the front of the church, off to the left, were two twelve-year-old trumpet players, twin Gabriels, really. They were that superb. Then, The Reverend Lee Sizemore, a wallpaper hanger from Northville, Michigan, began his sermon. He would speak for a bit. The last line of that part of his sermon would be the first line of the next gospel song, accompanied by the trumpets. The last line of the song would be the first line of his continued sermon, and so on. The bravura performance blew me away.

After the sermon concluded, the visitors began testifying, rising one after another to enthusiastically praise the new church. Each testimony was rewarded with hearty "Amens." I had a knot in the pit of my stomach when I realized I was about to be called on. I had just enough time to compose my praise. I wasn't up to the standards of the Pentecostals but good enough to earn a respectable chorus of "Amens."

Then, The Rev. Sizemore called on the South Lyon superintendent of schools, the only outsiders other than myself and the date I had brought the dedication. He was caught flat-footed, hemmed and hawed in his praise, and was rewarded with tepid "Amens." I omitted that from my story. I saw no reason to shame him.

Chapter 3 Under Police Interrogation

There is a persistent fantasy from another era that big city reporters dream of retiring to the relaxation of running a country weekly where they would be their own boss. Long before I became a big city reporter, I learned that the reality is different. I don't know how Jack Hoffman managed before he hired me. He was still working full time after I came on board, and I was putting in far more than forty hours a week writing stories for South Lyon and its Whitmore Lake edition, taking pictures, hand-setting my own headlines on a Ludlow machine at the printing plant in Northville, delivering bundles of newspapers to stores in Whitmore Lake, and sometimes collecting overdue ad bills.

The papers were printed on Thursdays, so Wednesdays meant working late to put it to bed. I needed another two hours after everyone else had left to finish up my stories. It was about 1:30 a.m. on a Thursday morning when I finally bailed out of the office, took the Pontiac Trail from South Lyon to Ann Arbor, and turned east on Fuller Road past the University Hospital and the Veterans Administration Hospital. A slow-moving freight heading toward Detroit on the far side of the Huron River beat me to the crossing on Geddes Road. I waited and waited. It slowed to a halt, sat there for about five minutes, then started up again with sequential clanks as the couplings tightened between each of the freight cars. I saw the lights of a car coming down the steep hill on Geddes. The headlights flashed periodically through the gaps between the boxcars. Then the headlights disappeared.

The instant the caboose passed (there were still cabooses in 1960), I raced across the tracks before the crossing lights stopped. Those headlights were from an Ann Arbor Police car that had backed onto Huron River Drive. I cursed my impatience as he pulled in behind me and turned on his flashers. There's no shoulder on that section of Geddes. I drove slowly to the top of the hill and pulled into the driveway that served my parents' house and two other residences. I stopped halfway down the driveway. The officer ordered me into the back seat of his cruiser. I asked to inform my parents in case they woke up and saw my empty car. He refused. I thought that was extreme for running a signal light, but I didn't protest.

At the station downtown, they sat me down in a room with a table and a bunch of chairs and actually tilted a desk lamp so it shone directly into my eyes. One man did the questioning while other officers rotated in and out of the room. My interrogator was precise and seemingly emotionless. The other officers had lips drawn tight and glared. He asked who I was, where I'd come from, what route I had followed, whether I had seen anyone, had stopped, and had anything happened along the way. It was the same thing over and over again. I answered every question, repeatedly asking what had happened and what I had supposedly done. He refused to answer. I demanded that he let me call my parents. He refused. I figured it was probably a hit-and-run, and I should be okay. They would check my decrepit 1950 Chevy, and there would be no evidence that I hit anybody.

I was White, a journalist of sorts, an upper-middle-class son of a university professor in a university town. I had been picked up once for fireworks when I was in high school, once for egging a car full of kids from a different high school. I was pretty sure no record existed. What could go wrong?

They left me alone in the room for what seemed like an hour. Finally, the officer who had arrested me came in to say I was being released and drove me home. He refused to say what it had been about. This was all pre-Miranda: No right to silence, no right to a phone call, no right to an attorney. I felt abused.

I waited until morning to tell my parents. My father called Peter Darrow, attorney, chair of the Washtenaw County Democratic Party, and friend of the family. Darrow had sold me my Chevy for $75. It had been his mother's. Two days later, Peter came out to the house with a chilling story. It seems a young woman had been out with her boyfriend, and they had made love. She had badly overstayed her curfew and was petrified that her father would beat her when she finally got home. She had run into the VA Hospital on Fuller, claiming she had been kidnapped and raped and had just escaped. With my being held up by the train, the timing was perfect. I was the only young man anywhere in the area whom the police had encountered.

So why did they let me go? It turned out they pressed the girl about what her assailant was wearing. She said Levis and a T-shirt. I was wearing a dress shirt, sports coat, and slacks. There was no change of clothes in my car. They confronted the girl. She eventually confessed to cooking up the story.

I stewed about it for a long time. What if I had been a poor Black kid, and they had held a line-up rather than challenging her story? She would have known that they had arrested a "suspect." I would have had perhaps one chance in six of being picked out if the police had played it straight. But police didn't always play it straight, particularly when they were sure they had their man.

I was working for The Ypsilanti Press in 1966 when the U.S. Supreme Court, by a 5-4 vote, decided in Miranda v. Arizona that an accused felon had the right to an attorney and the right not to incriminate himself. I wrote up my personal story as a sidebar to the historic ruling.

For years, the Miranda decision had been widely attacked by law and order types for supposedly handcuffing the police and coddling criminals. But I have come to believe that Miranda was one of the best things that could have happened to good cops. My reasoning is straightforward: When you can't count on sweating a confession out of a suspect, you have to conduct an actual investigation, and this has made officers better investigators. That doesn't mean that "Central Park Five" miscarriages of justice won't happen. As my later work would demonstrate, too many police, prosecutors, and judges remain agents of injustice, serving their own ends.

I finished up my year under Hoffman's tutelage, enrolled at the U-M, quit going to half my classes midway through the semester, and then quit entirely. I started getting letters from my draft board that I stuck in a drawer unopened. I got a call at home from Prof. Maurer. He had set up a journalism internship program at The Grand Haven Daily Tribune on the west coast of Michigan. He offered me a choice: He could enroll me in the internship with a tuition waiver and a draft deferment, or I could report for a pre-induction physical. He never told me his connection to my draft board. I never asked. I got in my car (I'd traded up to a 1957 Chevy) and drove to Grand Haven.

Chapter 4 The Day President Kennedy Was Assassinated

GRAND HAVEN —The bells on the Associated Press teletype machine were clanging nonstop, like what you hear when a train approaches a dangerous crossing. I thought the machine was jammed. It wasn't. It was a couple of minutes after 1:30 p.m. on November 22, 1963. A two-word message printed out: "KENNEDY SHOT." I ran back to the press room of the Grand Haven Daily Tribune. For the first and only time in my life, I shouted: "Stop the presses!"

Nothing can adequately prepare you for a moment like that. I was a 22-year-old intern whose job included serving as wire editor and covering the Spring Lake City Council. The only other people present who had anything to do with the news operation were Almon McCall, the elderly editor, and Tad Poole, the city editor and principal reporter. The sports editor and photographer had gone home for the day.

McCall and Poole lapsed into a fugue state, unable to think or act, repeating over and over how awful it was. I was dead calm and plunged into action. I can't pretend it was some kind of heroic competence. Looking back, I think it was a form of emotional denial, finding something productive to do so I could postpone feeling the pain. It was the same way when my father died. I wrote a story on the Ann Arbor Hash Bash and his obit before I began to grieve.

Grand Haven is Dutch Reform country, which made me a stranger in a strange land. Bored and lonely, I would spend some evenings in the back booth of a diner, chatting up a waitress friend while she was between customers (we would become Facebook friends fifty-eight years later). During warm summer nights, I would sleep on a lightly visited section of Lake Michigan beach south of Grand Haven's lighthouse. I also hooked up with a pool shark — imagine The Fonz without the charm — who found it difficult to get a game because of his reputation. I, on the other hand, was "Starfish." A fish is a mark, and a starfish is a hustler's wet dream. With my Princeton haircut and black horn-rim glasses, speaking the King's English, and wearing a sports coat, I could walk into any seedy bar in Western Michigan and be challenged to a game. I would insist on doubles and bring in the shark. It's how I earned the money to pay for Pat's engagement ring.

To my great good fortune, the balance of my social life involved joining the printers' bowling team. Because I started off with a low average, practiced like mad, and improved week over week, I was an asset to the team. They paid me back many times over. None of the guys in the back shop had more than a high school education, but they read everything. Not a week went by in which they didn't save me from some error.

They held me in some regard because I could read mirror-image type and also because I didn't pretend to know everything. As a kid, I'd heard that Leonardo DaVinci wrote his lab notes in mirror-image script to hide them from the Inquisition. I taught myself to do that and took my notes in mirror image throughout junior high. And at the weekly papers, I'd learned to hand-set my own headlines. All that equipped me for the day Kennedy died.

I sent one of the printers rummaging around a storage room. He found some 216-point types. I had two headlines set in the three-inch-high type: "Kennedy Shot" and "Kennedy Dead." AP provided member papers with several hundred standing obituaries of prominent people. I found Kennedy's in the file, updated it, and had one of the printers begin setting it in type.

A second printer tore out an inside page so we'd have space for the obit. An hour passed between the first bulletin and the announcement of the president's death, but I was operating on the assumption, almost from the beginning, that the shots were fatal.

Poole and McCall were standing over the teletype, reading the bulletins as they came over from Parkland Hospital in Dallas. I assured them I was taking care of things. Returning to the back room, I took half the stories from the front page and simply threw the type in a bin to be melted. I took the rest of the stories, cut them in half, and wrote new headlines. Three-quarters of the original front page was chopped away and waiting.

I put the fastest typesetter on the newest of our two Mergenthaler typesetting machines and had him set the AP copy in two-column measure as I tore it off the teletype, paragraph by paragraph. The type slid down into a tray to the left of the keyboard. As soon as it was cool enough, I scraped it and took it over to the guy putting together the front page. I was standing too close when the Mergenthaler spit hot lead that landed on my left shin. I carried that burn scar with pride for more than two decades before it faded to invisibility.

By some miracle — and for this, I credit the guys in the back shop with the greatest part — we managed to keep all the additions, corrections, and substitutions straight. The story read as if we had taken all day to put it together. Later in the afternoon, one of AP's best writers did a brilliant write-through, but it was too late for us.

In the years before offset printing, specialized cardboard was used to take an impression of the front page's lead type. A curved lead plate was made from the cardboard. The plate was then loaded on the press to do the actual printing. The total elapsed time from the "Kennedy Dead" bulletin to the start of presses was a shade more than thirty minutes, which was remarkable for a small paper in the era of hot type.

Our press run was normally about 10,000 and was almost complete when I stopped the press. The pressmen asked me how many more to print. I told them to do another 10,000. No one questioned me. When the last paper came off the press, the publisher — McCall's older brother — asked me how many extra copies I had ordered. When I told him, he sighed and asked rhetorically, "That many?" It turned out we could have sold twice that number.

I returned to my desk and wrote an editorial for the next day. Then I grieved.

Chapter 5 Too Poorly Educated For Ann Arbor

Midway through the internship, I gave up on trying to socialize in Grand Haven and started commuting weekends to Ann Arbor. I rekindled my friendship with Pat Laughna, whom I had been dating off and on since our junior year of high school. I used the pool hustling money to buy a ring and asked her to marry me. She said she would, but I had to formally ask her father for permission. That was a challenge. Robert Laughna, the imposing former vice president of Chrysler Corp., head of a major trucking company, and a successful investor, was not eager to see his only daughter married just then and had offered to send Pat to Europe for a year.

The first time I asked Pat out on a date, I picked her up at her apartment. It was a nice apartment. Later, I learned her family owned the building. I was met at the door by Pat's petite mother. There was a normal sofa in the living room and a chair with a three-foot-wide seat. I asked her whose chair that was. "My husband's," she said. "Does he fill it?" I blurted out. "Pretty much," she said. When Mr. Laughna came in, I asked, "What time would you like your daughter home, sir?"

He had played tight end for the University of Illinois, stood six-foot-three, weighed about 350 pounds, had a near-eidetic memory, and could be charming or intimidating. The secretary-treasurer of a Teamsters Union local had once tried to solicit a bribe for labor peace. Mr. Laughna had thrown the man through his office door, breaking his collarbone. My prospective father-in-law had immediately called Jimmy Hoffa (who was about to be indicted by the feds in Tennessee), told him about the extortion threat, said he knew was the last thing that Hoffa needed or wanted with the heat on, and knew that he would take care of it. Hoffa did.

I didn't think Pat's father would turn me down out of hand. That would jeopardize his relationship with his daughter. But I knew he would test me pretty severely. I tried to think of everything he might throw at me and how I could respond. After some small talk, I asked for permission to marry his daughter. Then he threw me a curveball: "What does my money mean to you?" I was ready for that one. Pat was starting out as a home economics teacher. Newspaper reporting was all I wanted to do. Neither was a high-paying profession. I noted that Pat's favorite movie was "Cheaper by the Dozen." She wanted a large family. We could handle the basic needs. "If you could help with college," I said, "we could have the size family Pat wants." He may not have been enthusiastic, but I did get his blessing.

For the rest of my newspapering career, I learned to prepare meticulously for important interviews, playing out questions and answers in my mind.

Pat and I were married at St. Francis Catholic Church in Ann Arbor, with the reception at the Barton Hills Country Club. Following a honeymoon in Washington, D.C., I resumed taking classes at the U-M. I declared a major in journalism and did spectacular well in that subject, but quit attending my other classes for reasons I have never fully understood. I ended up dropping out of college for the third time.

I went down to The Ann Arbor News to seek a reporting job. I had taken a news writing course from City Editor Elwood Louella, who had been teaching part-time at the U-M. I was his A+ student, and he had asked me several times to apply to the paper when I graduated. But he was under treatment for lung cancer and had taken a leave of absence. I was interviewed instead by News Editor Dave Tefft. He turned me down with these words burned into my memory: "It is beneath the standards of The Ann Arbor News to hire someone who is not a college graduate. We are the newspaper of a university town, you know."

Although down in the dumps from my serial educational screw-ups and Tefft's dismissiveness, I put on a brave face and went to see Paul Tull, the owner of the weekly Saline Reporter. He had no openings at the paper but hired me to do the writing for several factory publications he put out. I did that for several unsatisfying months and applied to The Ypsilanti Press, which had been purchased by Booth Newspapers, owner of The Ann Arbor News.

Jim Brown, the editor, was happy to take me on if I passed muster with Booth's consulting psychologist. The shrink administered the Minnesota Multiphasic Personality Inventory. It was a cakewalk. In six years at the U-M's lab school, we were given batteries of tests, sometimes twice a year. We learned how to make ourselves test normal. After the MMPI, the psychologist took me to lunch at a Dearborn Country Club. As we were ordering, he asked me if I wanted a drink. He was staring at me in anticipation. It was another test. I declined but said if he was drinking, I would join him with a glass of wine. He passed on a drink. I got the job.

Brown assigned me to cover Washtenaw County. That was perfect. My depression was replaced by anger. I made a vow to myself: I would go into Ann Arbor once a month and find a story that The Ann Arbor News didn't have. Each piece had to meet two additional criteria: The story needed to be of interest to Ypsilanti readers, and it had to be so good that The News would regret not having it.

My first opportunity came via Albert H. Wheeler, the U-M Medical School's first Black-tenured faculty member, founder of the rights organization that became the local chapter of the NAACP, and chairman of the Washtenaw Office of Economic Opportunity, the centerpiece of President Lyndon 'Johnson's war on poverty. He would go on to become Ann Arbor's first Black mayor.

I approached Dr. Wheeler to do a story on the OEO. His dilemma at the time of our discussions was how to bring the most War on Poverty money to Ann Arbor and Ypsilanti and put it to good use. A singular commandment from Washington was that there had to be "maximum feasible participation of the poor" in the governance of the OEO as well as the creation and operation of the anti-poverty programs. Two decades later, it would be called "empowerment," and it was something Wheeler believed in wholeheartedly. Wheeler needed the U-M's White academic professionals who volunteered to work with the OEO. They had the expertise in designing programs and writing grant applications, and they believed they knew best. The story I wrote was about Wheeler's successful juggling act and how he used the White expertise while keeping control of the programs in other hands. It won the Michigan Associated Press's top news writing award for small papers.

Wheeler decided I was worth his time and invited me back to his office in the Medical School for extended talks on what it was like to be Black in America. My parents were utterly egalitarian, and I had about as little racial baggage as possible for a White kid growing up in the 1950s and early 1960s. But my education at Wheeler's hands was far more valuable to me than any award.

Chapter 6 A Brutal Confession

It happened in the large open room on the second floor of the Ypsilanti City Hall sometime in the afternoon of August 11, 1931. Harry Bennett, Henry Ford's thuggish director of security, put the Black man's penis on the edge of the table and repeatedly smashed it with a nightstick.

That man, David Blackstone, was in no condition to confess then or several hours later in court. But pals Fred Smith and Frank Oliver, with Bennett looming over them and a lynch mob of 10,000 to 15,000 howling for their deaths, needed no further inducement to admit their roles in the most horrendous murders in Washtenaw County history.

Blackstone and his two White companions "officially" confessed to the Flaming Torch Murders at 5:35 p.m. They were arraigned at 6:40 p.m., convicted of first-degree murder in a Washtenaw County Circuit Court bench trial in Ann Arbor, and sentenced to mandatory life in prison at 8:56 p.m. They were driven through the gates of Southern Michigan Prison in Jackson at 11:36 p.m.

My involvement with the Flaming Torch Murders, as with many of the better stories I've done through the years, stemmed from a friendship. The late Henry Conlin, then a private attorney but later a Washtenaw circuit judge, was a jovial glad-hander and one of my father-in-law's best friends. Pat and I saw a lot of Conlin and his wife, Dorothy. My father-in-law gave us the boxer pup he had spontaneously named "Henry" when the Conlins had shown up unexpectedly at his Orlando home and asked the name of the dog.

Pat and I were at a dinner that included the Conlins. Henry Conlin was chatting about being hired by the family of Frank Oliver in 1967 in a last-ditch effort to get the Flaming Torch killer's conviction on four counts of first-degree murder commuted. I don't know if the attorney was angling for me to do a story. I never asked, but I rose to the possibility like a brook trout to a mayfly. Ever since I was a kid, I have had a visceral hatred of two things in this world: Bullies and injustice.

Blackstone, Smith, and Oliver, who had been drinking in a southside Ypsilanti speakeasy, went looking for someone to rob. They found two teenage couples in a lover's lane, robbed them, and then killed them. Smith and Oliver testified they decided to kill the four because they had been recognized. One of the teen boys had been shot, the others bludgeoned. The two White defendants claimed that Blackstone had raped one of the girls. Smith and Oliver said they drove the bodies around for a while, parked the car, doused the four with gasoline, and set them ablaze.

Blackstone was in no condition to give his version of events. His confession was a grunt that Washtenaw Circuit Court Judge George W. Sample accepted as his admission to the crimes. Details of the statements that Smith and Oliver gave in court were inconsistent and didn't track with independent information on their movements that night, but it didn't matter to the judge.

The burning car had been visible from Bennett's fortified castle on the Huron River. He and several of his men joined the subsequent investigation, which involved the Washtenaw County Sheriff, Ypsilanti Police, Michigan State Police, and Wayne County authorities. Bennett's exact role was never explained, although he did transport the defendants from Ypsilanti to the county jail in Ann Arbor in the face of the mob. After the convictions, he personally drove the trio to Jackson with two cars full of his heavily armed men providing security.

Blackstone was transferred to the state's maximum security prison in Marquette, in Michigan's Upper Peninsula, where he was reportedly fed to a rock crusher. His death certificate stated merely that he died of heart failure. Smith also died in prison but of natural causes.

Oliver petitioned for a new trial in 1950, arguing that he had confessed as the result of being beaten, that he had no legal representation, hadn't understood the proceedings against him, and that it had been a hurry-up trial in the face of a lynch mob that threatened even the court. All of that was true, but Judge James R. Breakey Jr., Sample's successor, denied the petition. He ruled that Oliver's 18-page confession to the court showed that he was both guilty and had his faculties about him.

Fast forward to 1967. Oliver, a one-time sign painter, was now 55. With the help of his family and after taking a correspondence course, he was licensed as a nursing home administrator and had an out-of-state job waiting for him if his sentence was commuted, according to Conlin.

He told Conlin about Bennett's beating of Blackstone and added one other salient fact: Oliver said he and Smith were told that, unless they confessed and pled guilty in court, they couldn't be protected from the lynch mob, which had made four separate attempts to get at the defendants. A rope with a hangman's noose had been thrown over the branch of a tree outside the courthouse. And this was in progressive Michigan, not Mississippi burning.

Conlin got the commutation for his client, I think in part because the governor preferred not to have the state's historic dirty laundry aired. Oliver died a free man several years later.

Chapter 7 Taylor, Burton, And Sweet Revenge

Annette Hodesh was tall, statuesque, and strikingly beautiful enough to have been a model for Peter Arno's elegant New Yorker cartoons. She was also an excellent cook who had trained at Le Cordon Bleu in Paris. Annette and her husband Bob, then editor of The Continental and former editor of The Ford Times, had joined several other couples for a cocktail party on the flagstone patio of my parent's house on Geddes Avenue on the outskirts of Ann Arbor.

I was reporting for The Ypsilanti Press but never passed up an opportunity to bartend at my parents' gatherings. Martinis were the drink of choice, and almost everyone wanted their martinis dry. I had read that Churchill had made his seven-to-one, gin-to vermouth. That was the ratio I used.

Annette, a marvelous raconteur, was telling about the time she was cooking for Elizabeth Taylor and Richard Burton during the filming of "Who's Afraid of Virginia Woolf?" in Northampton, Mass. It was a story I wanted to retell. I approached Annette and Bob at the end of the cocktail party. She had signed a nondisclosure agreement that barred her from revealing household secrets. But since she didn't have any nasty things to say about the Burtons at home, she figured there would be no harm in talking with me.

Annette had gone back to see her mother in Northampton, Massachusetts., the home of Smith College. On a lark, she answered a classified ad in the Daily Hampshire Gazette. Ernest Lehman, who wrote the screenplay based on Edward Albee's great stage play, was seeking a cook. Annette was hired and began preparing his meals. The Burtons liked her cooking so much that they pulled rank and brought Annette to their rented house.

Annette's story was full of charming details about two of the most famous and glamorous people in the world. They typically slept late and then lingered over breakfast. Late one morning, they spotted some workmen doing street repair outside and invited them in for melon wrapped in Italian prosciutto ham.

I made the rank amateur move of leading off my story with Lehman before turning to the Burtons. The Associated Press picked it up as a member contribution and, thankfully, rewrote it with the Burtons first. That AP story, with a Ypsilanti dateline and my byline, appeared in more than a thousand daily newspapers. It set the 1966 national record for the most usage of an Associated Press member contribution. I checked The Ann Arbor News each afternoon to see if and how they used my story. Several weeks later, my story showed up on the inside Women's page. They had removed the Ypsilanti dateline, my byline, and the AP bug, publishing it as if it was their own piece.

This was my final victory and sweet revenge. As I recounted earlier, my response to The Ann Arbor News' dismissive refusal to hire me was to scoop them every month for as long as I was in Ypsilanti. The News' sleazy response to the Taylor-Burton story allowed me to let loose my anger. I still came up with stories the larger and richer paper to the west didn't have, but I did it out of pleasure, not compulsion.

Several years after I had moved on to The Detroit News, I dropped in on Ann Arbor News Editor Art Gallagher to ask for permission to examine his paper's clipping files for a story I was researching. We were chatting amiably when he mentioned how much he'd hoped that I would have applied to The News. I told him my Tefft story.

Chapter 8 One Of Our H-Bombs Is Missing

The Ypsilanti Press was a great place to work in the middle to late 1960s. The three editors I reported to—first Jim Brown, then Tom Mercy, and finally Jim Treolar—were all competent, liked me, and were quite happy to turn me loose when my other work was done. That other work involved covering county government, writing and editing the Saturday arts page, and running the city desk on Mondays because City Editor Joe Owsley worked on Saturdays. Owsley was supposed to make staff assignments for the coming week on each Saturday. He was usually overwhelmed, so it fell to me on Mondays. Joe convinced himself I was angling for his job, but I assured him I never wanted to be anything but a reporter looking for the next story.

The next story was the Lockheed EC-121 Warning Star, the military version of the four-engine prop Super Constellation, that flew into Willow Run Airport in late January 1968 and taxied over to the University of Michigan's Willow Run Labs. The first I heard about it was when eleven naval aviators checked into Bill Anhut's Huron Inn and, noticeable in their uniforms, started wandering around Ypsilanti because most didn't have anything else to do. The airmen were vague about where their craft was based, what its normal duties entailed, and what it was doing at the Willow Run Labs.

I have always been obsessively curious, which is the main reason I became a reporter. It's the only profession that pays you to poke around in other people's business whenever the spirit moves you. The first part of my research was easy. The Navy and Air Force primarily used the EC-121 as a radar surveillance aircraft to supplement the Distant Early Warning Line, the Cold War DEW Line that was supposed to tell us if the Soviets were attacking over the North Pole. In addition, some of the aircraft were outfitted for storm and iceberg monitoring. I presumed that would include infrared remote sensing gear that could spot icebergs through cloud cover because of their different heat signature from the ocean waters around them. There would be no more Titanics on their watch.

A year earlier, I had interviewed long-time Willow Run Labs Director Dr. William Brown for a feature story. I called to ask him what was going on with the Navy plane, but he was mum. Through the Saturday arts page, I got to know one of the senior research scientists who was also active in community theater. He wouldn't tell me anything, either. Several days went by. It was obvious to me that the aircraft was being outfitted with some kind of futuristic electronic gear, probably something still under development, but I didn't know what or why.

The Labs had a reputation for developing the most advanced infra-red remote sensing in the world. It was the 1960s, and U-M's student radicals were organized to protest the university's conduct of military research. A prime target for the radicals, the Labs were in the midst of a very public effort that would result in reinventing themselves as ERIM, the Environmental Research Institute of Michigan. That meant publicizing all the ways that the remote sensing capabilities it was developing for the military could be used for such laudatory purposes as monitoring the spread of pollution or measuring the health of crops.

(In a curious side note, my father, as a master's degree student at the University of Chicago in late 1920, had gone up in a biplane to photograph and analyze crops. It was the first-ever use of aerial photography for environmental studies).

I had been enrolled in a program for budding science writers and was flooded with press releases. I remembered one that announced the Labs had developed airplane-based sensors that could track whales at considerable depth by their body heat. So why would the Navy want something like that and be so hush hush about it?

On January 21, 1968, a fire had broken out in a B-52 loaded with four 1.1-megaton hydrogen bombs. It tried to land at the Thule Air Base in Greenland, but the fire spread too fast. The crew was forced to eject. The pilotless aircraft crashed onto the sea ice of North Star Bay, only seven-and-a-half miles west of the air base. Conventional explosives in three of the bombs detonated, spewing radioactive material over a large area. Extreme heat generated by 225,000 pounds of burning jet fuel melted the sea ice. The wreckage and the fourth bomb sank to the sea floor.

The Danes were seriously upset. By treaty, Greenland was supposed to be a nuclear-free zone. Congress was pissed as well, and the military was seriously embarrassed because they couldn't find the fourth bomb. I imagined that someone who knew of the infra-red gear's iceberg and whale-spotting magic thought perhaps it could find the missing bomb on the ocean floor. It seemed plausible.

The morning of the day the plane was scheduled to leave, I called the Willow Run Airport tower. I said I was Lieutenant So-and-So. In my gruffest voice, I asked if the flight plan had been filed. The tower gave me the ETA in Thule. As I hung up, it occurred to me that posing as a military officer might have broken some federal law, so I didn't include my call in the story.

The piece I wrote was speculation. I didn't consider it a big deal. But some folks in Washington did. Several days later, two middle-aged men in blue suits with short-cropped hair dropped in on my then-editor, Tom Mercy. They inquired about the story but left without talking to me. Mercy didn't say which agency they represented, and I failed to ask him.

Early the next week, I got a call from Dr. Brown, who said the agents had turned his lab upside down, trying to find out where the leak had come from. Brown said he explained to them that there was no leak. "Cain's a bright fellow," he said he told them, "and put it together from stuff that was public knowledge."

When the security team left, their one order was that Brown change the padlocks on all the file cabinets. I think this was an early version of the security mindset that decided, after one failed shoe bomber, we would forever have to take off our shoes before boarding a commercial flight.

As for the fourth bomb, a Danish investigative team concluded it was still on the ocean floor. The Americans have never said.

Chapter 9 My Mother, Lindbergh, And A Silly Toy Save The Whales

My mother's insistence on straying from the beaten path, Charles E. Lindbergh's flash of brilliance, and a silly plastic-and-metal toy from an alley in a working-class neighborhood of Tokyo combined to save the world's whales.

A theory says that the flapping of a butterfly's wings in Tahiti night results in a hurricane that devastates New Orleans, but who believes a major development in the world of humanity could result from such an obscure sequence of events?

That obscurity was lucky for the whales.

It was early August, 1968. I was in my third year at the tiny Ypsilanti Press, waiting for the Detroit newspaper strike to end so I could begin a waiting job at The Detroit News. My parents came back from Tokyo with an improbable but true story.

My father, Stanley A. Cain, was on leave from the University of Michigan to serve as Stewart Udall's assistant secretary of the interior, overseeing the national parks and sport and commercial fisheries. My mother, Louise, had written the document that created the U-M's Center for the Education of Women and served briefly as its director before joining my father in Washington.

They became close friends of the irrepressible Hubert Humphrey, who adopted conservation as his cause after President Lyndon Johnson exiled his vice president from mainstream Washington politics. Johnson named Humphrey to serve as the U.S. representative to the International Whaling Commission, which was meeting at the Imperial Hotel in Tokyo. My father was his second. Louise and Humphrey's wife, Muriel, flew over with them.

The commission was established in 1946 to set quotas by treaty on the number of whales each whaling nation could harvest annually. The latest renewal of the treaty was due to expire, and discussions on the new quotas had been stalled for four or five years. The commissioners were still at loggerheads as they ended the last full day of their meeting. The final half-day was just to draft a joint statement and adjourn.

The mood was glum that night at a U.S. Embassy reception. Failure to reach a treaty would mean the resumption of unrestrained whaling. Modern technology for tracking and killing whales meant certain extinction of some species of these magnificent creatures whose brains are up to six times the size of ours and whose languages in song we barely understand.

Earlier that day, my mother had asked to see something of Tokyo beyond the bright lights and famous gardens and temples. Mrs. Clinton E. Atkinson, wife of the embassy's fisheries attache, was dispatched to be her and Muriel's guide. As the ladies wandered the byways, they encountered a man selling clever toy whales from a card table in an alley. My mother and Muriel each bought two. My mother brought one to the embassy reception that night and showed it to Lindbergh, who was there as the representative of the International Union for the Conservation of Nature. Disgraced for his earlier Nazi leanings, the Lone Eagle sought a quiet redemption in his work on behalf of the world's creatures.

The silly toy was a sensation. It was a six-inch blue-black plastic whale on wheels with a large hinged metal jaw. Inside the whale was a light green metal fish, also on wheels. A thin nylon cord linked the tail of the fish to the whale's gullet. As you pulled the two apart, the nylon cord wound up a spring that drove the fish's wheels. When you released the two, the fish would go scampering across the floor, winding up the cord and pulling the whale ever closer. When the whale reached the fish, the whale's mouth would fly open, and the fish would disappear inside.

Lindbergh got a Tokyo street map, questioned the ladies as to where they had encountered the toy man, and dispatched an embassy aide on a late-night mission. The aide found the man, bought out his supply and brought them back to the embassy. Lindbergh had them wrapped and placed in front of each delegate's chair so they would see them in the morning,

"Several of the commissioners opened up the wrapped boxes and ran the toys on the table," my father recalled. "Everybody laughed." The ice was broken. The U.S., Canada, and Russia each agreed to give up a few whales for their shore-based factories, something they had not been willing to do for years. A draft treaty was quickly wrapped up. The whales were saved.

Every time I see the beautiful Pacific Life television ad showing mother-and-child whales and hear the announcer say, "Fifty years ago, humpback whales were nearly extinct," I feel a touch of familial pride.

Chapter 10 The Women Who Helped Pave The Way

Being the only child of brilliant parents was both a curse and a blessing. The curse was my fear that I would never measure up. The blessing was a vibrant set of experiences.

In my mid-teens, I mostly perceived the curse. My intuitive mother picked up on my massive self-doubt, but I wouldn't talk to her about it. She packed me off to see a man who, reputedly, was the most highly regarded child psychiatrist at the U-M. It was a disaster. All I wanted were answers. Are my kind of doubts common? Are other kids going through the same thing? But he turned everything back on me: "Is that what you feel? Is that important to you?" And that's how it went for two very frustrating sessions.

On our third visit, I said, "I think I know what you are doing. If you answer my questions, I might or might not accept what you say. But if I arrive at the truth myself, then it's mine." He responded with yet another question. I said, "Look, I really do know what you are doing. You want me to look deeply within myself and discover that I'm really a pretty good guy. But what if we go through this process, stripping away all my defenses? I'm left looking at the core of who I am, and I really am a can of worms. What have you done for me?" He asked, "Is that what you believe?" "No," I said and walked out, feeling somewhat better.

I would go on to sabotage my first three ventures in higher education. But there was a point when I came to realize that I was a better writer than either of my parents. I always knew my father was a great man. That boost of self-confidence also gave me the freedom to appreciate the incredible depth of my mother.

Several years following my early retirement, my wife, Pat, and the other women who ran the Catholic parish education programs in Western North Carolina were meeting with Father Frank Cancro, their advisor, to plan a retreat for their volunteer teachers. I tagged along as Pat's driver. I'm not sure how it started, but over lunch, everyone took turns relating the most embarrassing thing that had ever happened to them.

My parents had built a new house on the outskirts of Ann Arbor when we came back from Brazil in 1956. My bedroom doubled as my mother's library. She had a master's in Middle English from Mount Holyoke, had headed the English Department at Dickinson College in Carlisle, Pennsylvania, and later taught English at the University of Tennessee, where she met my father.

I was a voracious reader, and at 15, when I ran out of my books, I started on hers. After exhausting Steinbeck and Hemingway, I turned to Lawrence Durrell's Alexandra Quartet and D.H. Lawrence's "Lady Chatterley's Lover." I picked up Sir Thomas Malory's "Le Morte d'Arthur," but it was in Middle French.

Then, I discovered Henry Miller's "Tropic of Cancer" and "Tropic of Capricorn." In one of them, there is a scene where the narrator takes this absurd Hindu gentleman to a Paris whorehouse. They make their selections and go off to their respective rooms. The narrator hears an uproar and emerges from his room to see screaming whores beating on the Hindu and driving him from the bordello. He can't imagine what could possibly have shaken up a French whore until he sees, floating in the bidet outside the Hindu's room, a single perfectly formed turd.

I must have laughed out loud because, the next day at breakfast, my mother correctly guessed which of her books I was reading and even the scene I had encountered. In relating my embarrassing story over lunch with the group, I admitted I could not remember which of the tropics I had been reading. "Oh, it was Cancer," said the priest. Or perhaps he said Capricorn. I still get them confused.

So here's a bit about Louise Gilbert Cain.

In 1952, my mother, as president of the League of Women Voters in Michigan, had been tasked with accompanying the wife of the Indonesian ambassador to the United States, including to a conference in the U-M's Michigan Union. They were blocked at the front door and told that women were allowed in only through a side entrance. They went around to the side.

It was the first time I'd ever seen my New England-bred and totally composed mother spitting mad. She never told me exactly what happened next, only that she had a pointed conversation with a U-M executive officer. But the practice wasn't changed for another four years.

On April 23, 1951, Governor G. Mennen Williams appointed Blair Moody, a Detroit News reporter when the paper was owned by Moody's uncle, William Scripps, to fill the unexpired term of Senator Arthur Vandenberg. Moody ran for reelection in 1952 but lost to Charles E. Potter in the Eisenhower sweep. My mother resigned as the League's president in late 1953 to run Blair Moody's campaign in the Democratic primary for the U.S. Senate. He was opposed by Patrick McNamara, a union member supported by both the AFL-CIO and United Auto Workers. Moody died suddenly in July 1954. The liberal wing of the party contemplated backing my mother to oppose the more centrist McNamara, but she demurred. McNamara went on to win in November.

My mother managed Adlai Stevenson's 1956 presidential campaign in Michigan. She also ran for the Ann Arbor City Council from the then-heavily Republican old Fifth Ward. Playing poker with my father's graduate students, I dragged each pot for twenty-five cents and contributed several dollars to her campaign. I also got my picture in The Ann Arbor News wearing a sandwich board promoting her candidacy. She lost by seventy-five votes.

My mother came to regret her only success in politics. She wanted to end the U-M Board of Regents' good old boys club. She recruited Irene Murphy, sister of the late Michigan Governor Frank Murphy. She engineered Irene's Democratic nomination and ran her successful campaign. Irene, who always called me "Stevie" (I hated the diminutive), abused my parents' hospitality.

While the men in my parents' circle in the 1950s and 1960s were the primary breadwinners and uniformly high achievers, the women were in many ways at least as remarkable. My father had taught me to mix a mean martini. I bartended their many cocktail parties, which gave me a ringside seat to observe a great confluence of academics, liberal politics, social activism, and what later came to be called feminism.

The women of Ann Arbor — including many of my mother's friends — served as Neil Staebler's organizers and shock troops as they wrested control of the Michigan Democratic Party from the Teamsters Union. The circle of friends included Carol Ludington, who graduated from Vassar and moved to Ann Arbor to be my mother's administrative assistant in the Michigan LWV. She followed my mother into politics, served on Staebler's Democratic State Central Committee, and eventually ran a successful statewide spring campaign. She married Professor of Anthropology Frank Livingston, whose research on sickle cell anemia remains the best proof of human evolution. Dorothy McGuigan, the wife of Staebler principal aide Bernard "Mac" McGuigan, taught business writing at the U-M and authored the 1970 book "A Dangerous Experiment: Women at the University of Michigan."

Robert Lansing was one of the founders of the Institute for Social Research at the U-M. His wife, Marjorie, turned to Eastern Michigan University, where she served from 1966 to 1986 as a professor of political science. Her landmark 1970 book, "Women and Politics: The Invisible Majority," introduced the concept of the gender gap. Taffy Larcom, who was married to Ann Arbor's highly regarded City Administrator Guy Larcom, was an EMU professor of journalism from 1969 to 1979. My father, after eleven years as chairman of the U-M's Department of Conservation, recruited Lyle Craine to be his successor. His wife, Asho, served in the League of Women Voters, was a founding member of the local Gray Panthers, and was a peace activist, poet, and memorialist.

My mother wrote a proposal for creating the U-M's Center for the Education of Women and briefly headed it before John Kennedy nominated my father to serve as Assistant Secretary of the Interior. She chose to go with her husband to Washington. My mother turned the CEW over to Jean Campbell, who ran it from 1964 to her retirement in 1985. But when Jean's husband, Angus Campbell, another of the founders of the Institute for Social Research, came up for a sabbatical, Jean took a leave from the CEW to be with him. Although these were not the women of "Mad Men," their careers were not yet accepted as co-equal with those of their husbands.

The last of that group of fabulous women, Eunice Burns, died on October 20, 2016, at the age of ninety-three. She had served three terms on the Ann Arbor City Council beginning in 1962, ran unsuccessfully for mayor, and served as executive assistant to the U-M's Dean of Education.

Following my father's mandatory retirement from the U-M, my parents moved to Santa Cruz, California, where my father established College VIII on the UCSC campus in 1972. My mother was a founding member and later president of the university's Friends of the Farm and Garden, the support group for the most highly regarded agroecology program in the country. She was also something of a den mother to the two dozen or so Farm and Garden apprentices who lived in teepees on campus. She tapped into her expanding network of friends to find part-time work for the apprentices.

When the successor to UCSC Chancellor Dean McHenry was threatening to end the apprenticeship program because it wasn't "academic," my mother wrote an academic program for the apprentices and took it to my father, who approved it.

The Friends imported an English master stonemason to build the gatehouse to the Farm and Garden that would also serve as a meeting place and educational facility. They named it after my mother.

My mother died in October. 22, 1993, after a long struggle with cancer. She was eighty-two. Friends, apprentices, and family gathered on the patio of my parent's house overlooking Santa Cruz and the Cowell Redwood Forest and told Louise Cain stories. I had written a eulogy—writing is what writers do—but I choked up halfway through. My son Jim put his arm around my shoulder, took the paper, and finished up for me. During her final weeks, I flew out from Ann Arbor while my eldest son, Mike, came in from Hawaii. Mom had sought reassurances over and over again that she had lived a good life. "Yes, Mom. It was a perfect life."

Chapter 11 A Barefoot Boy From Southern Indiana

I grew up wanting to be like my father: A great scientist and an inveterate storyteller. He was an ecologist. I was intending to be a geologist. I got the storytelling part, but midway through my sophomore year at Amherst, I realized I liked people better than rocks and gave up on geology. Even though I ended up in journalism, I couldn't escape from — and ended up far the better for — a thousand dinner table conversations reflecting the ecologist's way of looking at how things are interconnected. Most journalism has a bias for seeing events in terms of linear cause and effect. My bias since childhood has been for context, and interconnectedness. I think that made me a better, although sometimes longwinded reporter.

My father, Stanley Adair Cain, graduated from Butler University in 1924 and got his master's and then his doctorate from the University of Chicago in 1930. He was an old Socialist in the day, voting five times for Norman Thomas for president. He would become a world authority on plant ecology and was one of the founders of the scientific study of the interrelationship between man and the environment. He was a man of sophistication and wit, but he loved to salt his conversation with country stories and the occasional Hoosierism.

There was my father's great-uncle Lemuel. The youthful Lemmie had limited his bathing to an occasional summertime dip in the old swimming hole. Lemmie's teacher, distressed with his ripeness, went to see the young man's father with the polite request that Lemuel acquaint himself with a bar of soap. "Lemmie ain't no rose," the father responded. "Learn him, don't smell him." Lemuel Cain, like my father, was a barefoot boy from Southern Indiana. Lemuel became a reporter for the St. Louis Post-Dispatch around 1900.

If my dad was particularly pleased with something, he might say, "Ain't had so much fun since the hogs et my little brother." If he was mildly vexed with me, he might say, "Shape up, Steve, or I'll tear off your arm and beat you over the head with the bloody stump." I have no idea how a Southern Indiana saying would come to echo Beowulf dispatching Grendel. For all his loquaciousness, what my father never did was talk seriously about where he came from or how he became the man I knew growing up.

I had some playmates, but mostly, I tagged along after my father's graduate students, who taught me bridge, chess, and poker when I was eight, and I read whatever I could get my hands on.

As I've said earlier, my bedroom doubled as my mother's library. There was a Webster's Dictionary (copyright 1936) whose cover, embossed in gold lettering, read "Louise Gilbert Marston." Gilbert was my mother's maiden name. It was also, also my middle name. Who was Marston? Was I not my father's son? Was I actually born before 1941? Most adults don't know how to talk to kids and thought they were complimenting me by saying how mature I looked. I stewed on this for months before I asked my mother who Marston was. Marston was Charlie Marston, my mother's first husband, a professor of entomology at the University of Tennessee who died of a brain aneurysm in the late 1930s.

My mother hastened to add that my father had been married before, to Lillian for nine years before they divorced, childless. Lillian, in my mother's telling, was the daughter of my father's high school biology teacher, the man who mentored him, directed him toward science, and apparently helped pay his tuition at Butler. My mother said my father married Lillian out of gratitude.

Sometime in his mid-twenties, while still in graduate school, my father discovered and fell in love with the Great Smoky Mountains. He spent the next two decades unraveling one of the most complex plant ecologies in the world. What had happened in the mountains was this: At the end of the Wisconsin glaciation period, as the ice retreated about 15,000 years ago, cold weather plants were left behind on the upper elevations of the Smokies while warmer weather plants thrived on the lower elevations. They were mixed together in the mid-elevations.

He analyzed soil types, elevation, temperature, precipitation, groundwater, steepness of slope, orientation to the sun, and every other factor that determined what grew where, how the different plant communities came into being, and how they developed. His work culminated in the 1944 publication of The Foundations of Plant Ecology, the seminal work in the field. He even discovered a new species of grass that was named for him, Calamagrostis Cainii. The original sample he collected is in the University of North Carolina herbarium.

My father taught at the University of Tennessee from 1935 to 1946, laid out a number of the trails built by the Civilian Conservation Corps in the Smokies, and became a friend of the mountain men, a number of whom would make a few dollars guiding groups of school teachers each summer. He told the story of walking silently up a trail to the summit of Mt. LeConte, encountering a group of teachers and their mountain man guide. The guide picked up a few blades of grass and announced, "This is Pinus Pinaceae" (actually the scientific name for a pine). He knew the sound of Latin because my father was forever identifying plants by their scientific names. The guide had simply plucked a couple of Latin words. Catching sight of my dad, he added slyly, "Leastwise, that's what I calls it."

In 2005, a decade after his death, I contacted the archivist at Great Smoky Mountains National Park to see whether they had any record of my father's time in the park. It turned out they had a marked-up manuscript copy of a guide to an ecological trail my father and his graduate students had built in the mid to late 1930s. The trail was laid out so it would take the hiker past more than a dozen distinctively different forest communities, each marked with a discreet wooden sign and described in detail in the guide's text. I set out to rediscover the trail, but the wood markers were long gone. His trail map was in pencil, and it was not to scale. The trail itself was overgrown beyond recognition because the Park Service never maintained it, and the trees were seventy years older. I'm fairly sure I found three of the stops.

My father went from Tennessee to the Cranbrook Institute of Science, and then onto the University of Michigan. In 1950, he founded and was chair of the U-M's Department of Conservation at the U-M. He remained its chairman until 1961.

He was also a member of the International Phytogeographic Expedition. Every four years, the world's leading plant geographers would troop off to some corner of the globe to look at plants. My father had been with them on a trip to Borneo, and another to Finnish Lapland. In 1952, twenty-seven of them gathered in Ireland.

My father was the only American and only scientist of Irish extraction, although he had no clear idea of where in Ireland his ancestors had come from. The others were all European and claimed they could trace their lineages to Charlemagne. The great game was to find a headstone with my father's surname. Somewhere in County Cork, the two Germans came running down from a hill overlooking an ancient manor house, shouting, "We found it. We found it!" There on the summit was a headstone that read: "1766-87, To Cain, the best bitch a man ever had," honoring the lord and master's hunting dog. My father would trot out the story on St. Patrick's Day to answer an ersatz Irishman's bragging.

On his return trip, he took a four-engine Constellation from Shannon to Gander, Newfoundland, where the plane was to refuel and continue on to Idlewild. They were past the point of no return when they ran into a ferocious storm over the North Atlantic. Gander was socked in, so they diverted to Idlewild, which was within the plane's fuel margin of safety. As the plane was being buffeted, he said five nuns across the aisle had their Rosaries smoking. If there was a God, my dad reasoned, He couldn't save the nuns without saving Cain. So he took out his Olivetti typewriter and wrote a speech he was scheduled to give the following week. I was sometimes successful in emulating my father's calm fearlessness.

My father was originally nominated by John Kennedy to serve as Stewart Udall's Assistant Secretary of Interior for fish and national parks, but Lyndon Johnson was president by the time the Senate finally got around to confirming him in 1965.

It was in Washington that he and Bob Teeters, one of his former graduate students, invented what would become environmental impact statements. The U.S. Army Corps of Engineers had dredged virtually every harbor and navigable river that needed dredging and had run out of projects that could be justified on a cost-benefit basis. But if the outdoor recreation value of a proposed project could be counted, the Corps could have more things to do. My father sent Teeters to work for the Corps. Teeters would evaluate Corps proposals, modify them to be more environmentally friendly if necessary, calculate their recreational value, and send his report on to my father. If the Interior signed off on them, the Corps got to do more work. This type of report, given the formal name of Environmental Impact Statement (EIS), became a legal requirement under the provisions of the National Environmental Policy Act of 1969.

My father was elected to the National Academy of Sciences the following year. The academy's testimonial reads: "Under Cain's persistent urgency, the Department of the Interior realized the importance of preserving the nation's environment, and it adopted the role as the protector of the nation's natural resources."

My father owed the last chapter of his professional career to Dean McHenry, the founding chancellor of the University of California at Santa Cruz. McHenry brought my father out to UCSC to consult on laying out the new campus so it would do the least possible violence to its coastal redwoods setting.

When my dad reached mandatory retirement at the U-M, McHenry hired him to establish College VIII in 1972, develop a curriculum focused on ecology and environmentalism, and hire its original staff. He also taught there until 1980, when Alzheimer's began to take its toll.

Back in the late 1960s and early 1970s, most universities still imposed required mandatory retirement rather than sorting through which professors still had all their marbles and which didn't. McHenry's genius was to search the country for the top professors in each academic field who had reached forced retirement but still had undiminished intellects. McHenry would bring them to UCSC under three-year contracts. Some of the nation's best post-docs would follow them for the chance to study with the "great men." Under McHenry's leadership, UCSC, within a decade of its founding, became one of the top 10 universities in the country in National Science Foundation funding.

On Sept. 15, 2016, College VIII, whose alumni include many of the nation's leading environmental professionals, was renamed Rachel Carson College as a testimonial to its environmental activism.

Chapter 12 When Abortion Was Illegal

Our first child, Michael, was born December 31, 1965, with a bilateral cleft lip and palate, a disfigurement so severe that, had he been born several decades earlier, he might not have survived. Pat, my wife, had been born with a single cleft that had been skillfully repaired at the Mayo Clinic in Rochester, Minnesota. Her parents immediately called Mayo following Mike's birth. The clinic folks told them that the world's foremost cleft reconstructive surgeon, Dr. Reed Dingman, was on the faculty of the University of Michigan with his practice in Ann Arbor. He accepted Mike as a patient and performed, within weeks, the first two of more than a dozen surgeries. They were transformative.

Pat and I were taught how to feed Mike using a modified turkey baster with a soft rubber tube on the end. That was critical because he couldn't get suction to the nurse. We loved him, hugged him a lot, and he thrived.

I've always been driven to know the why of things. It saturated the atmosphere of my growing up. Curiosity dominated the lives of my ecologist father and his ever-present graduate students, and I wanted to be like them. If Mike's cleft was a genetic gift from Pat, that raised questions about our desire to have a large family. The research I found didn't suggest a particularly strong genetic link, but there had been a German measles (rubella) outbreak the previous spring. A woman who contracted a clinical or subclinical German measles infection during the first trimester of her pregnancy had an elevated risk of giving birth to a baby with a cleft, a congenital heart defect, or profound deafness. Mike, given a thorough physical, was in perfect health except for the cleft.

Pat's brother, Bob, had come down with meningitis prior to his second birthday, and it nearly killed him. The treatment left him with only three percent hearing in one ear, less in the other. His parents decided to mainstream his education rather than send him off to the Michigan School for the Deaf in Flint.

I knew the school had room for only about thirty new students a year. I wondered if the state was making preparations for a potential influx of deaf kids from the rubella epidemic, an influx that would overwhelm the school. I wondered how many there might be in the pipeline. The Centers for Disease Control was no help. Michigan didn't collect data on birth defects. Ohio gathered some data, but not enough to help. I called Dr. Gordon Brown, the father of a high school friend and one of the epidemiologists who had worked with Dr. Tommy Francis in organizing and evaluating the field trial of 1.8 million children that proved the success of Dr. Jonas Salk's polio vaccine.

I told him I was trying to get an estimate of the number of children with birth defects that resulted from the German measles outbreak the previous spring. I asked if he had any idea what percentage of fetuses were damaged in women who contracted German measles in their first trimester. His answer was burned into my memory: "That's the wrong question for two reasons, Steve. I know it's horrible to say, but the first is that the rotten fruit tends to drop from the womb. The other is that we perform so many abortions." Oh.

This was seven years before Roe v. Wade. Abortions were illegal. He wasn't talking about a women at home with a bent coat hanger or some back-alley abortionist, but doctors at one of the nation's leading research hospitals. Was this really a story I wanted to write? Pat is Catholic. While not slavish to everything that comes out of the Vatican, she is strong in her faith. My plunging into such a volatile story would ask for a lot of forbearance from her. I believe very strongly in a woman's right to choose. Suppose I nailed down the story, hardly a given. Would hospital-based abortions be shut down and the doctors prosecuted? I decided that, if I was serious about being a journalist, I couldn't back out of a legitimate story because it didn't fit comfortably with my personal beliefs. But at least I could do it on my own terms.

It took a lot of calls and a lot of persuading, but I got three ob-gyns to go on the record acknowledging that abortions were performed as an unwritten institutional practice at U-M Women's Hospital in Ann Arbor and in Detroit at Henry Ford, Harper, and Sinai hospitals. The doctors admitted they were breaking the law but said they were acting as a matter of conscience under their Hippocratic Oath commitment to treat. The operations were billed mostly to Blue Cross and Blue Shield as dilation and curettage and paid without question.

I had approached each of the doctors with the assurance that the story needed to be told, and that I understood their commitment to their patients and their courage in acting on their patients' patients' behalf. I noted that there was legislation pending in Lansing to legalize abortion, but it seemed likely to fail because there were not enough people willing to take a stand on its behalf. I pointed out that the only women in Michigan able to get clean, safe abortions were those fortunate enough to have personal physicians with privileges at the state's premier hospitals, women who tended to be upper middle class. The vast majority of the state's women, the less advantaged, were out of luck. I think it was the equity argument that won them over.

I went to then-Michigan Attorney General Frank Kelley, a Catholic, who recognized a hot potato he did not want to juggle. He set me up with his Jewish deputy, who gave me a long explanation of prosecutorial discretion, asserting that there were more urgent matters on the attorney general's plate. He used the example of a State Police trooper seeing a whole line of speeding cars but being able to pull over only one or two. I also interviewed several legislators on opposite sides of the abortion bill as well as Eleanor O'Brien, board chair of Planned Parenthood of Mid-Michigan, the measure's primary advocate. She also made the equity argument.

My stories ran in all nine Booth Newspapers: The Grand Rapids Press, Muskegon Chronicle, Bay City Times, Flint Journal, Jackson Citizen-Patriot, Kalamazoo Gazette, Saginaw News, and Ann Arbor News in addition to The Ypsilanti Press. I expected The Detroit News and Detroit Free Press to pick up the story, that the Detroit TV stations would jump on the bandwagon, and that it would become a big deal in the state. What actually happened was that everyone outside of Booth simply ignored the story. Part of the quiet may have stemmed from the fact that I had kept my prose deliberately non-inflammatory. Also, Evangelical Christians hadn't yet discovered abortion as a wedge issue around which they could mobilize.

There was virtually no pushback against my revelations. To the best of my knowledge, the doctors and hospitals went on as they had been. I did get a brief note from one of the doctors I'd quoted saying he enjoyed the articles and would continue to enjoy them as long as he stayed out of jail. I was of two minds: Disappointed because a reporter likes to think his work made a real-world difference, and relieved because I didn't want to be the agent that harmed something I believed in. The abortion bill failed in the Legislature, and abortion remained a felony in Michigan until Roe v. Wade.

The abortion stories, however, did change my life. They won the Michigan Associated Press annual news writing contest's top award for small papers. It was the second time in three years I'd taken home the top award. And I got a call from Detroit News Managing Editor John O'Brien [Eleanor O'Brien's husband] offering me a job at half again more than I had been earning in Ypsilanti. The day I showed up to start, The News and Free Press were shut down by a strike. O'Brien said the paper would honor its commitment and take me on at full pay but asked if I could keep working temporarily in Ypsilanti. I spent nearly another year in Ypsi.

Chapter 13 No Money, No Heart

The University of Michigan Hospital decided Philip T. Barnum of Kalamazoo, Michigan, could go ahead and die. Barnum, 49, had advanced cardiomyopathy, degeneration of the heart muscle, and was given only weeks to live, a couple of months at most. He had been admitted to the U-M's Clinical Research Unit and was slated to become the state's first heart transplant recipient if a suitable donor could be found in time. But the money for the research unit had run out.

There were eighty-three Clinical Research Units around the country. All were totally dependent on federal funding. They were intended to focus on research, with treatment being an incidental consequence. By federal regulation, the units were not allowed to use third-party funds such as insurance monies or private pay. They were supposed to get a supplemental appropriation, but we were deeply mired in the Vietnam War. It was a question of guns or butter, and guns won. About half of the units across the nation had already closed, and the others were to follow shortly. With the closing of Michigan's CRU, there was no place for Barnum and no protest from the U-M.

On December 3, 1967, Dr. Christiaan Barnard, at Groote Schuur Hospital in Cape Town, South Africa, performed the world's first heart transplant. Louis Washkansky lived eighteen days. There was another in Texas, also with poor results. The problem was the body's rejection of foreign tissue. The chairman of the U-M's Department of Thoracic Surgery had written an editorial in the Archives of Surgery decrying the circus atmosphere in South Africa and Texas, suggesting medicine wasn't advanced enough to make heart transplants good medicine. With one of his own surgeons preparing to do an operation he had publicly decried, the chairman was silent on the closing of the Clinical Research Unit.

It was early fall of 1968, the beginning of my second week at The Detroit News. The News had hired me to work on general assignment and to supplement medical writer Jean Pearson, a lovely lady and well-respected among her colleagues but a dull writer. I had been a part-time science and medicine writer at The Ypsilanti Press. In January, I'd done an in-depth feature story on Dr. Donald R. Kahn, an associate professor of thoracic surgery at the U-M, who had done promising research on tissue rejection and was prepared to do a heart transplant. I got a call on that Tuesday tipping me off to the fact that the Clinical Research Unit had been shut down the week before, dooming Barnum.

For Wednesday's front page story, I detailed all the background on the closing of the research unit. The story boiled down to one fact: No money, no heart. The headline read: "Transplant or death - U-M patient's crisis." My colleague, John Peterson, drove to Ann Arbor to interview Barnum's wife, Aileen, and their daughter, Nancy. "I'd give my own heart," Aileen Barnum told him.

My Thursday's front page story was a total capitulation. Hospital officials said the transplant would go forward if a suitable donor could be found, and the U-M would worry about the money later.

Friday's front page story was about an anonymous donor who had pledged $20,000 to pay for a transplant. I was told privately that the money came from Upjohn Pharmaceutical, which was based in Barnum's home town and had close ties to the U-M Hospital. I couldn't confirm it for the record.

Saturday's front page story, thanks to quick work by The News' Washington Bureau, announced a policy change from the National Institutes of Health that allowed the temporary use of third-party funds and enabled clinical research units across the country to reopen.

Then, on Sept. 20-21, a 22-person team headed by Dr. Kahn gave Barnum a new heart. I had half the front page of Sunday's paper. The other half, except for a small standing feature, was taken up by a picture and story I did on "President" Dave Valler, who talked about and would later be arrested, charged, and convicted with of eight anti-establishment bombings in the Detroit area.

Dr. Kahn, in a remarkable gesture, went public with a plea for doctors to work more closely with the press and credited both me personally and The News with rescuing the transplant program and helping save Barnum's life. Barnum lived until Dec. 10, 1969. During his additional fifteen months of life, he got to see Nancy graduate from high school and his son marry. Dr., Kahn was made a full professor.

Doctors across the world have made stunning progress in developing drugs to combat tissue rejection. By 2023, there were about 3,500 heart transplants a year worldwide, almost half performed in the United States. The average survival is fifteen years.

I was one of the youngest reporters at The Detroit News, the tenth largest newspaper in the country, and I was on fire.

Chapter 14 The Bomber Had A Crush On Me

In the world of Richard Nixon, J. Edgar Hoover, and the Weather Underground, Dave Valler was an absurdity: A darling of the weekend hippies with flyaway blond hair, the White Panther candidate for president, and a full-time stoner.

Dave was also the leader of a prolific bombing conspiracy and would later betray his old colleagues. Befriending him became my window into federal law enforcement gone wrong.

For me, it started with one of the stupidest assignments in the annals of newspaper journalism. It was either that or someone was taking one of The Detroit News' newest hires down a peg or two for having had three consecutive top of front page stories the previous week.

It was the fall of 1968. There had been a series of eight dynamite bombings in the Detroit metro area, including the CIA office on South Main Street in Ann Arbor, the University of Michigan Institute of Science and Technology on the North Campus, the South Lake School District Board of Education office, the East Detroit draft board, and a couple of Detroit Police cars parked in precinct lots. The Detroit Free Press had labeled them "hippie bombings."

Right when I came to work that morning, an assistant city editor told me to take a photographer and go around to the bombing sites to see if I could find anyone who had seen someone with long hair running away just before the blasts. Then we, too, could call them "hippie bombings." Of course, the bombings were all post-midnight, and I was working days. I was too new and too stunned to protest, so I grabbed a photographer and started the canvass. By the time I came to work the next morning, I was seriously bent out of shape by the assignment. There was a fifty-member federal task force on the case, yet I was supposed to find a trace of someone with long hair at the wrong time of day.

I was reasonably familiar with the Students for a Democratic Society and the Weather Underground, but this didn't have the earmarks of a serious protest. Besides, I couldn't imagine Ann Arbor-based radicals caring about East Detroit or the South Lake schools. What I could imagine was a bunch of hippies in a Cass Corridor commune who had come across a cache of dynamite, sitting around getting stoned, debating what they should blow up next.

I told the photographer he was free for the day, headed up to the Cass Corridor, the decrepit neighborhood south of the Wayne State University campus, and simply began stopping guys with long hair. I identified myself as a Detroit News reporter, noted that the bombers were being really careful not to hurt anyone, and asked, who the hell could say what was being protested? Was it the war in Vietnam, racism, capitalism, Amerika with a "K?" Can you imagine a sophisticated veteran reporter doing anything so idiotic? If I'd told the city desk what I was doing, they would have wanted to send me back to Ypsilanti.

About the fourth or fifth long-hair I stopped said, "Go find President Dave. He's the darling of the weekend hippies. He'll talk about anything." I dropped any mention of the bombings and began asking after President Dave, the self-styled White Panther candidate for president whose platform was the Black Panther ten-point program, plus such things as free government dope and fucking in the streets. The White Panthers were an Ann Arbor-based, sometimes radical counter-culture organization put together by John Sinclair, legendary rock impresario, poet, and maven of marijuana.

I said I was tired of Richard Nixon versus Hubert Humphrey and thought Dave would make an excellent story. I got pointed to a crash pad in an abandoned building off Canfield. It was boarded up. Across the street, I went up to a middle-aged man in a wife-beater undershirt with an impressive beer belly, rocking on his porch. He cursed the absent hippies except for President Dave, who he said was pleasant and would stop to chat. We had talked for a while when he suddenly said, "There's Dave," pointing out a slender young man with long, blond hair strolling down the street.

I fell in alongside Dave, told him who I was, and he agreed to talk about his campaign. After several hours and many cups of coffee at Johnny's, a Wayne State campus hangout, I made a tearful confession that, while I really cared about his campaign, I was also interested in the bombings.

We talked quite a bit more. He said the bombings were, indeed, a protest against the war and racism. I said I couldn't print that unless I could establish his credibility. It was an interesting negotiation with someone who was seriously stoned. In the end, we agreed that, for the record, he would neither confirm nor deny that he was the bomber but conceded that it would be reasonable for the police to suspect him. I told him I needed proof that he was the bomber, but I would keep that secret. He told me he bought the dynamite at a hardware store in Midland, explaining to the proprietor that his father intended to blow up some stumps on his farm outside of town.

I told him no one would believe me unless he went with me to The News. We stopped at his latest crash pad, where he got another hit of LSD. He said it was his three hundredth or so in the last two years. I had him sit for a studio portrait at The News. Several of the photographers stuck their heads into the studio to gawk at the long hair. It was shortly before 5 p.m. when I took Dave downstairs to meet Assistant Managing Editor Boyd Simmons. We walked into his office. "Hi Boyd, I'd like you to meet Dave Valler, President Dave. He's the bomber." Boyd, the old pro, maintained an admirable poker face. We chatted pleasantly for about ten minutes, and I drove Dave back to the Cass Corridor.

I called the Midland hardware store in the morning, pretending to be Valler's father's accountant. I said I needed to verify the dynamite purchase for tax purposes. I got the confirmation. It still took The News a couple of weeks to get up the courage to run the story, and then only after I took Simmons out to interview Dave's parents in Dearborn. Also, the Detroit Police confirmed privately to the editors that Valler was their prime suspect. The headline over Valler's picture screamed, "Is This the Bomber?"

It ran the same Sunday as my story on Philip Barnum's heart transplant at the U-M, one of the first in the country. The two stories took up the entire front page except for a small standing feature. At the Monday morning editors' meeting, Editor Martin Hayden berated Managing Editor John O'Brien and Assistant Managing Editor Boyd Simmons, saying, "I give you the largest reporting staff in the state, and you turn the paper over to a green kid!" O'Brien told me later that this was Hayden's way of finding out how good they thought I was, testing whether they would defend me. They did. Also, that morning, I was told I had to go over to Detroit Police headquarters and tell the Red Squad commander that I had nothing to tell him. For the sake of our police police-beat reporters, I had to let him vent on me. Vent, he did.

In the end, eighteen young men and women were implicated in the bombings, some just complaining about what they would like to see blown up, others actually going along with Dave on the bombings. Dave pled guilty in state court and was sentenced to twenty-five years in prison. He sobered up, decided drugs had ruined his life, and went on to become a law-and-order advocate. Dave was the perfect illustration of what longshoreman-philosopher Eric Hoffer called the "transferability of extremism." Hoffer wrote about atheists who became born-again Christians, former Communists who became the darlings of the House Un-American Activities Committee, and their ilk. To my dismay, my editors ordered me to go to Jackson Prison and write a story on Dave's conversion into what they saw as a right-thinking young man. With Dave now rehabilitated, The News' Sunday Magazine hired him to write a column titled "From 1600 Cooper Street," the prison's address.

Unbeknownst to me at the time, Valler completed his about about-face by becoming a government informant. He told a Federal Grand Jury in Detroit that White Panther President John Sinclair, White Panther Minister of Defense Pun Plamondon, and party member Jack Forrest had carried out the September 29, 1968, CIA office bombing. The feds decided that I was the only non-hippie, non-law enforcement person, who could credibly testify about Dave's mental acuity at the time of the bombings. U.S. Attorney Ralph Guy had been colluding with my editors, some of whom were perfectly happy for me to testify.

I was tipped off that a grand jury subpoena was coming. I traded seats at the Michigan-Michigan State football game with a Spartan friend, but Simmons, my own editor, tracked me down on the MSU side of the stadium and served me with the subpoena. Otherwise, he said, the feds would have confronted me at home in front of my family.

I spent two hours after the game convincing Managing Editor O'Brien that I wouldn't even go into the grand jury room to tell them I wouldn't testify. I reminded him that, on behalf of The News, I had been dealing with radicals, dopers, criminals, and other miscreants based on my absolute pledge that "I won't testify for you or against you, no matter what." I told O'Brien about covering an anti-war demonstration during which I was being stalked by a guy carrying a length of steel rebar pressed to the side of his leg. I spotted the counter-culture's Peter Werbe, a friend who has kept the faith to this day. Peter told the guy I was okay. The stalker dropped the rebar and wandered off.

O'Brien said that I wouldn't have any legal protection for refusing to testify. I said I would write stories from prison until they were forced to let me go. I said I had a wealthy father-in-law who would support my wife and kids and that the name of The News would be mud in the world of journalism for not backing its own reporter. He believed me. One of the other editors went to the feds, said I would not testify, and that The News felt compelled to back me. I was told to tear up the subpoena.

Interestingly, the White Panthers and their friends believed my word was good. Even though they held me partially responsible for President Dave as a turncoat, they were still willing to talk to me. John Sinclair's brother gave me my first joint.

The feds went ahead with their indictment of Sinclair, Plamondon, and Forrest. Sinclair was already in state prison by then, serving a nine-and-a-half to ten-year sentence for giving a Michigan State Police undercover officer two joints. Forrest was arrested in Ann Arbor. Plamondon went underground, becoming the first hippie to make the FBI's Ten Most Wanted list before his subsequent arrest in Northern Michigan for littering. He'd thrown an empty beer can out of the car. A routine license-and-registration check showed who the State Police had bagged. He would later consider making the most-wanted list a badge of honor.

The trio drew a crack defense team that included, including William Kunstler of Chicago Seven fame and Detroit's Hugh "Buck "Davis. They peppered U.S. District Judge Damon J. Keith with motions, including a demand for any any government intercepts of the defendants' conversations.

It turned out that the government had been monitoring the Black Panthers in Oakland, California, and had recorded calls Plamondon had made to them. Judge Keith demanded the government turn over the transcripts. The government refused, citing national security. Judge Keith ruled that the government's illegal political surveillance had invaded the defendants' right to privacy and dismissed the charges. The government appealed

Keith's ruling, citing national security, but lost 2-1 in the U.S. Court of Appeals and 8-0 before the U.S. Supreme Court in what was one of the most important rights cases of the decade.

In 1983, fifteen years after the bombings, I was reading "The Puzzle Palace," James Bamford's masterful expose of the National Security Agency. I put a couple of Bamford's nuggets together with information I had gathered and realized why the government was so adamant about not releasing its Panther intercepts. It wasn't the tapes themselves that the government wanted to keep secret, but the fact that the Nixon Administration had been using the NSA to illegally eavesdrop domestically. Meanwhile, Judge Keith had been promoted to the Court of Appeals. I called him at his chambers in Cincinnati and filled him in on the solution to the mystery behind his most famous case. We also discussed that the FBI had been illegally wiretapping two phones at the White Panther headquarters on Hill Street in Ann Arbor during his trial. The FBI shut down the Ann Arbor taps on the day after the feds had been forced to reveal the existence of the Black Panther intercept.

Sinclair, Plamondon, and Forrest filed suit against the federal government for the Ann Arbor taps. Discovery revealed, for example, that the FBI intercepted 276 conversations dealing with the bombing conspiracy trial, including 88 between defense lawyers and members of the defense committee. I had also called Hill Street during the period of the taps, but I'm pretty sure my conversations were innocuous. Ultimately, U.S. District Judge George LaPlata of Ann Arbor dismissed the case against the government.

Two decades after the bombings, Valler, out of prison, dropped in to see me at The Ann Arbor News, where I had moved after The Detroit News had censored my investigative piece on the Teamsters vice president who controlled the distribution of the paper. To my chagrin, I learned that I was not as clever as I thought I had been all those years ago. It seems that Dave was gay and had had a crush on me.

Chapter 15 My Connection To The Storied Past

My byline at The Whitmore Lake News and South Lyon Herald was Steve Cain. It was the same during my University of Michigan intern year at The Grand Haven Daily Tribune and again when I dropped out of college for the third time and was hired by The Ypsilanti Press.

During my first weeks at The Detroit News, I had a dizzying run of across-the-top front-page bylines with my heart transplant and hippie bomber stories. Managing Editor John O'Brien called me into his office. "You're going to be editor of this paper someday," he said. "You should have a more distinguished byline."

I immediately changed my byline to Stephen Cain, even though I was more comfortable with informality. The idea of becoming an editor, however, was a nonstarter. Reporters have the most freedom and fun, and they don't have to spend years as someone else's vassal before landing the top job. I wasn't going to tell John that. I thought he walked on water. He was one of those rare people who had survived a sometimes rocky career with his integrity intact. Besides, I saw him as my link to newspapering's storied past.

John took Pat and me out to a Detroit steakhouse in 1970 to celebrate some award I'd won. We were joined at our table by the owner, an elderly friend of John's who had operated a speakeasy that John frequented during Prohibition. They traded stories. The speakeasy had a magnificent mahogany bar on wheels. When the police staged their obligatory raids, the officers would smash a few bottles but were careful not to touch the bar. After the cops padlocked the front door, the proprietor would push the bar through a side door to an adjoining room and be ready to open the next evening.

On July 31, 1975, the day after Jimmy Hoffa disappeared from Machus Red Fox Restaurant in Bloomfield Hills, I paid a social call on John. It was a Mob hit, he said, explaining that Detroit Mafia big men Tony and Billy Jack Giacalone were seen uncharacteristically glad-handing at the Southfield Athletic Club at the precise time of Hoffa's disappearance, giving them an iron-clad alibi. Some days later, it was revealed that Hoffa had expected to meet Tony Giacalone and New Jersey mobster Anthony

Provenzano at the restaurant, but they had never showed. Provenzano never even left New Jersey.

John recalled that, during Prohibition, the owners of the 15,000-seat Olympia Arena would give reporters and cops free tickets for the Friday night fights. One night during the undercard, at precisely 8 p.m., a fight broke out among the patrons at ringside. A man stood up on a chair, waving his arms, shouting, "Break it up! Break it up!" The man was the most notorious southwest Detroit bootlegger, a man who brought speedboats full of whiskey from Canada to the mouth of the Rouge River under the protection of Harry Bennett, Henry Ford's corrupt and violent director of security. There were probably a thousand men at Olympia that night who realized that, somewhere Downriver, a rival was being executed at that exact time. It turned out that three men were assassinated.

In 1929, John had joined the staff of The Detroit Times as a cub reporter, becoming one with the hard-drinking Runyonesque characters who made the Hearst paper the most entertaining reading in the city at the time. In 1932, John and best friend, Martin Hayden, who much later would later become editor of The Detroit News, decided to attend the University of Michigan together. "But John didn't have enough money," Hayden recalled. "He decided to get himself fired so he could collect severance pay. The only human being who didn't like John was the Times' city editor. It was arranged that John would deliberately not show up for work, and all of his friends would turn him in. But the city editor himself got drunk and didn't show up for work." John waited in Jimmy King's Saloon across the street from The Times until the editor showed up sober enough to fire him, and the two young men went off to room together at Michigan.

Following graduation, John worked briefly for his uncle, who was Michigan's attorney general. He then went off to become a successful dog tout in Florida, recommending various greyhounds to bettors even though he'd never seen a dog run. During World War II, he was a sergeant in a Mobile Army Surgical Hospital unit run by his brother-in-law and served throughout the Italian campaign. He had to be ordered to accept a lieutenant's bars.

After the war, he returned to newspapering. William Randolph Hearst picked John to head a successful campaign to establish the interstate highway system in the 1950s. He went on to become executive editor of

Hearst's Pittsburgh Press. But he got tired of fighting Hearst's New York office every time he wanted to pay a columnist $5 more, so he quit to become an editorial writer and columnist for Hayden at The News.

In 1965, John began a four-and-a-half half-year reign as managing editor of The Detroit News. It was a great time for reporter-writers. The best pure writer in those days was Al Stark, who would, from time to time, get stinking drunk, write an angry letter of resignation, drop it on John's desk, and go home to sleep it off. A sobered-up Al would come in the next day, hem and haw, and ask John whether he'd left something on his desk the previous night. John would play dumb, and Al would wander off, relieved. Stark eventually dried out and was made an assistant city editor.

Following his official retirement, John would commute by train from his home in Ann Arbor to hand deliver the weekly column he wrote for the The News. Paul Poorman, John's hard-driving successor as managing editor, once asked John the secret of his success. John answered, "Hire good people, pay them well, and get out of the way." Poorman rarely got out of the way. Another time, Poorman asked John why he bothered to come in in person. "For laughs," said John, who quit his Detroit News column after several years.

John's wife Eleanor died in 1982. He came out of retirement again to write a weekly column for The Ann Arbor News. My favorite piece of his was a gentle joshing of strident feminists who had taken to calling their opponents "male chauvinist pigs." He traced the term to Nicholas Chauvin, an excessively patriotic and possibly fictional soldier and uncritical fan of Napoleon. Kevin McCarthy, a friend and owner of Gibb's Wide World of Wines on a bombed bombed-out stretch of Gratiot Avenue on Detroit's east side, was able to come up with two bottles of Chateau Chauvin, a grand cru classe de Saint Emilion. I gave one bottle to O'Brien in honor of his column, saved the other for myself.

Following his death in 1985, old friends and colleagues gathered for a memorial service in the Michigan Union's Kuenzel Room to swap O'Brien stories. Of the several dozen in the room, I was the youngest at forty-four. There was sadness in realizing how much of newspapering's institutional memory had been lost.

Chapter 16 Finessing A Racist Newspaper Policy

In Detroit's Grayhaven neighborhood, it's called the "steal and stomp." That was the lead of a provocative 1969 story I wrote that set in motion a series of events that got The Detroit News out of a racist trick bag it had fabricated for itself.

During the Detroit newspaper strike of 1967-1968, the startup Detroit American newspaper became fabulously successful financially by providing racially tinged reporting to the city's still substantial but shrinking White population. The centerpiece of the paper's coverage of the city was the daily police blotter that listed every street crime and identified the race of the perpetrator, even if race was the only salient description the victim could supply.

When the strike ended in August, 1968, The Detroit News began its own similar police blotter. The protest was immediate and intense, from Mayor Jerome Cavanagh to the pastor of the smallest storefront church. Big-city papers refuse to be bullied, even when they're wrong. Editor Martin Hayden dug in his heels.

Most of the reporters hated the blotter, and we did everything we could to avoid being assigned to crime stories involving race. I was one of The News' first hires after the strike and, at twenty-seven, was one of its youngest reporters when my luck ran out. Two young Black men had broken into the Grayhaven home of a White widow in her eighties. They stole her valuables, tied her up with an electrical cord, and beat her with a hammer, leaving her in critical condition.

I drove out to Detroit's far east side the next morning, desperate to find a non-racist way of telling the story. I started knocking on doors, talking to anyone willing to talk with me.

Grayhaven, I learned, had been a fairly typical White working-class neighborhood of well-kept homes and lawns. Integration had come without panicked White flight because the Blacks who moved in, mainly auto workers with middle-class incomes, also valued well-kept homes and lawns. What changed was the unintended consequence of the federal Urban Renewal Program and freeway construction that eradicated Detroit's historic Black Bottom along with other poor, predominately Black neighborhoods. Many of the dislocated migrated to Grayhaven.

Single-family homes became multi-family as their owners sold and fled to the suburbs. Crime exploded, and both Black and White long-time residents felt they were under siege from the newcomers.

A Black auto worker told me about the burglary of his home. The following Sunday in church, he saw someone else's children wearing his kids' clothes. He said the men of that family were bad people, and that he would be beaten or worse if he did anything. about it. He said Blacks, as well as Whites, were victims of what he called the "steal and stomp" in Grayhaven.

I had a story I could live with. I dodged the racist bullet, but what about next time? The answer seems pretty obvious in hindsight: Change the focus to the criminal justice system—police, prosecution, and corrections— to where the system works, where it breaks down, and how people are affected. Add to that the roles of education, the economy, jobs, racial attitudes, and the instability caused by urban renewal and freeway construction. Decades later, these were critical elements of what would be called Critical Race Theory. The News actually had a well-informed urban affairs writer, but he had the a reputation in the city room for turning out dull thumb-suckers, and so was marginalized.

I recruited fellow reporter John Peterson, who also hated the racial blotter approach to crime coverage. We worked up a list of some two dozen hard-edged stories and took them to Assistant Managing Editor Boyd Simmons. He refined the list and gave John and me three each to do. We worked around our other assignments. With those six stories written and edited by Simmons, I cynically outlined an editorial that The News could write about them. The series would be called "Crime: The Search for Solutions." The News would take credit for forcing the Black community to confront the reality of Black street crime. Having done that, The News could drop the blotter and take an in-depth look at the problem. Simmons took it to Hayden, who jumped at the opportunity to save face.

We were delighted to be out from under the police blotter. I earned a lot of credit with Hayden, but I still ended up having to do crime and courts stories for a very long time.

One of those stories took me to the courtroom of Detroit Recorders Court Judge Thomas L. Poindexter and earned me the enmity of the

Detroit Police Tactical Mobile Unit. The four-man TMU cars were also called "clean-up units," and the men cultivated their reputations as tough guys. More than half-a-dozen TMU search and seizure cases, all involving poor Black defendants, had been gathered for preliminary examinations on the same day in front of Poindexter, a conservative, White, old-school jurist.

Virtually all of the police testimony followed the same script: "We were driving south on [street name] when we observed a car with a burned-out right rear taillight." They always "observed" rather than "saw." "As we approached the car, I observed the driver stoop as if to place some unknown object under the front seat. As the driver exited the car, I observed in plain view the corner of a packet I knew from past experience was likely to contain an illicit narcotic." Sometimes, it was the corner of a gun that was supposedly sticking out from under the front seat. It was amazing that the drivers never managed to get their dope or gun all the way under the front seat.

What in fact, had happened was that the TMU pulled over cars of young Black males for shakedown searches. If they found a gun or dope, one of the officers broke out the right rear taillight with his billy club. Why the right rear taillight, you may ask? When police pull over a car, one officer approaches the driver. A second stations himself at the right rear so as to have the drop on the driver or passengers if they tried anything. The officer at the right rear breaks the light if the other officer finds something.

The traffic violation (broken taillight), furtive gesture (the stoop), and "in plain view" statement all fulfill U.S. Supreme Court standards to establish reasonable cause for lawful searches. Poindexter, confronted with such a concentration of obvious perjury and a reporter sitting in the front row taking notes, dismissed all of the cases. I wrote up the story, labeling the practice "The TMU Stoop."

In Recorder's Court, the vast majority of cases that did get through preliminary examination were settled with guilty pleas to reduced charges. Of the cases that went to jury trial, however, increasing numbers were resulting in not-guilty verdicts. I dug into the figures and confirmed the obvious: Black juries were reluctant to convict Black defendants on cases that depended solely on the testimony of White officers.

As part of the "Crime: The Search for Solutions," I took a look at the various criteria used in determining police promotions. It turned out that one of the factors was the raw number of arrests an officer made, not good arrests, just numbers. Moreover, there was no mechanism for subtracting bad arrests, the ones almost certainly based on perjury. I went to then-Police Commissioner John Nichols and argued that this promotion system was a massive incentive for police perjury. I suggested this was part of why Black juries were poisoned against White officers. He refused to acknowledge his officers were a problem.

The general reputation of White officers in the Black community was not good, and it was not just their reputation for perjury. I was riding with a pair of veteran White officers in the Tenth (Livernois) Precinct when they got a call to take a burglary report from an elderly Black woman. It was raining. They walked into her living room with wet shoes. One of them addressed her as "Auntie." The officers were inconsiderate and patronizing. I searched her face for some reaction, but she kept it carefully blank.

In the fall of 1973, Nichols launched a law-and-order campaign for mayor. Mayor Roman Gribbs, in an effort to keep the Detroit Police Department out of politics, fired Nichols in September. In November, State Senator Coleman A. Young narrowly defeated Nichols in a bitter contest and began instituting a series of police reforms.

Nichols moved to suburban Oakland County, where his law-and-order stance made him the county's top vote vote-getter in three of his four successful campaigns for Oakland County sheriff.

Chapter 17 Master Of The Universe, Not!

There is a quote from Mike Ditka, the great former linebacker and coach, that I should have had tattooed on the inside of my eyelids: "Success isn't permanent, failure isn't fatal." I had written a string of sensational front-page stories, collected three merit raises in one year, and was beginning to think of myself as a master of the universe.

The tip had all the earmarks of an urban legend. It came to me from a member of the "Clinton Street Bar," one of those lawyers who operated out of their briefcases and made their livings as appointed counsel for poor defendants in the old Detroit Recorder's Court on Clinton Street. But the man had been credible in the past. He told me of a heroin-addicted prostitute who had been called for jury duty and ended up on the trial of her supplier.

The woman was real. I tracked her to a bar in the Greektown area of downtown Detroit. In an afternoon of extended drinking with me buying, she acknowledged that she was a lady of commercial virtue. But I couldn't tease her legal name out of her or anything that might let me track her encounter with the court.

She wore a low-cut top, was generously endowed, and spent most of our interview leaning forward with her elbows on the table between us. She was smoking Kool cigarettes, blowing smoke in my face, and making a game out of deflecting my questions. I wasn't drunk, but I wasn't sober either. And I was a bit turned on in spite of myself.

I had quit cigarettes two weeks before and was still in withdrawal. I grabbed one of her cigarettes. That was it. I was back smoking again and left without my story. I probably could have tracked her through her street name or the lawyer-tipster, but I was so disgusted with myself that I moved on, sadder, wiser, and addicted. It would be many years before I would permanently wean myself from cigarettes.

Chapter 18 I Hang The Wrong Men Out To Dry

We all would like to be the hero of our own story. I might entertain that delusion if I could forget Peter H. Denton. On March 27, 1969, I wrote a front-page story in The Detroit News falsely branding the University of Michigan student as the possible killer of U-M law student Jane Louise Mixer, the third of the seven infamous "Michigan Murders" that had terrorized young women in the Ypsilanti-Ann Arbor area.

The first thing that happened on the day of publication was that Dwight David Eisenhower, thirty thirty-fourth President of the United States, died peacefully at Walter Reed Hospital. That pushed my story off the front page and onto the classified ad jump page, thankfully, as it turned out. Then I got a call from an Ann Arbor Police command officer telling me that Denton, active in radical student politics at the U-M, had been under police surveillance when Mixer had disappeared the week before. I was so chagrinned at the realization that I'd been sold a bill of goods by a state psychiatrist, the source that got me involved in the story, that it never occurred to me to question whether the police were, in fact, telling me the truth. They weren't.

Then, as the bodies piled up, I did an interview with confrontational Black activist Charles Thomas Jr., knowing my story would cause the authorities to look at him as a possible suspect. He, too, turned out to be innocent. The Thomas case raised serious ethical questions that I didn't consider at the time.

Mary Terese Fleszar, nineteen, an accounting student at Eastern Michigan University, disappeared on July 9, 1967. Her nude body was found in an abandoned Superior Township farm on August 7. She had been beaten and stabbed thirty times. Her feet had been severed just above the ankle. One forearm, and the thumb, and the ends of the fingers on her other hand were missing.

On June 30, 1968, Joan Elspeth Schell, twenty, an EMU art student, disappeared. Her body was discovered on a rural Ann Arbor roadside on July 5. She had been raped, stabbed 25 times, and was found with her mini-skirt tied around her neck. There were several other factors that indicated Fleszar and Schell were killed by the same man. I'd covered those first two murders as a reporter for The Ypsilanti Press before moving to The Detroit News.

The third victim, Mixer, twenty-three, had posted a note on a U-M Law School message board seeking a ride home to Muskegon on March 20, 1969. Her partially nude body was found the next day in Denton Cemetery on Denton Road in Wayne County, just east of Ypsilanti. She had been shot twice with a .22 and garroted with a nylon stocking, not her own.

Four days later, the body of sixteen-year-old Romulus resident Maralynn Skelton was found on Earhart Road, several hundred yards from where Schell's body was found. She had been tortured and suffered extensive blunt-force trauma. A garter belt had been tried around her neck, and a branch had been inserted in her vagina. She had been hitchhiking in the Ann Arbor area when she disappeared.

I was at my desk in Detroit when I got a call from Dr. Ames Robey, head of the Center for Forensic Psychiatry at Ypsilanti State Hospital, a man I had dealt with several times in the previous two years. He wanted to talk. He had been medical superintendent at Massachusetts' Bridgewater State Hospital for the criminally insane when confessed Boston Strangler Albert DeSalvo, a murderer named George Nasser, and then-Harvard student Peter Denton had all been patients. DeSalvo, serving a life sentence for a series of rapes, had confessed to Nasser that he was the strangler, but he was never charged with any of the ritual murders of thirteen Boston-area women between 1962 and 1964. Some people in Massachusetts law enforcement believed Nasser to be the actual Boston Strangler. There were others, including Dr. Robey and Cambridge Police detectives, who favored Denton as the strangler.

Dr. Robey, who was intimate with Denton's mental problems, made a persuasive case, based on his supposed expertise. Then there was the "coincidence" of Mixer's body having ended up on the opposite side of Ann Arbor from where she was headed, in the obscure Denton Cemetery on the obscure Denton Road. I checked Dr. Robey's background, interviewed a senior Cambridge detective who had worked on the strangler case, and reached Denton in Ann Arbor by phone. He hung up without commenting. But I did not call the Ann Arbor Police. I figured they would just try to put a lid on my story and didn't see how putting the spotlight on Denton would compromise their investigation. I had talked myself out of making the check that would have saved my bacon. In Denton's case, my enthusiasm for a sensational story outweighed my normal skepticism and my compulsion to check everything, particularly so-called expert opinion.

The day after my story, The Ann Arbor News, under Bill Treml's byline, republished Dr. Robey's comments from my article without attributing them to The Detroit News. He also omitted Denton's name. Treml did quote Ann Arbor Police Chief Walter Krasny as saying, "This man is being checked out along with several others. He is no better a suspect than anyone else." There was no blowback on my Denton story. I figured I got off easy for screwing up and vowed to myself to be far more careful in the future, not allow myself to fall in love with a particular outcome.

On April 16, the stabbed, slashed, and tortured body of Dawn Louise Bascon, sixteen, of Ypsilanti, was found on the side of a road outside of Ypsilanti. She had been strangled with an electrical cord. On June 9, the body of Alice Elizabeth Kalom, twenty-one, a U-M graduate student, was found in a gravel pit in Northfield Township. She had been shot in the head.

I got a call at home from Dr. Donald J. Holmes, an associate professor of psychiatry at the U-M and a friend. He said he had a problem, and wondered whether if I could help. He said one of his patients was the live-in girlfriend of Charles Thomas and had come to the psychiatrist seriously frightened. During their love-making, the young woman said, Thomas had railed against Washtenaw County Sheriff Douglas Harvey, asserting that the killer of the White girls was too smart for the bumbling Harvey to catch. Thomas didn't say he was the killer, the young woman said, but she was left the impression that he might be.

Thomas, a former Marine and civil rights activist who had had several brushes with the law, was the organizer, chairman, and principal member of The Committee to Recall Sheriff Harvey. I met Thomas at the apartment he shared with the young woman. He was quite happy to be interviewed about his views of Harvey and the sheriff's role in the Michigan Murders investigation. And he was pleased with my subsequent article in The Detroit News.

Whatever interest the authorities may have had in Thomas disappeared on July 27, when the body of EMU student Karen Sue Beineman, eighteen, of Ypsilanti, was found in a wooded gully along side Huron Parkway in Ann Arbor. She had been beaten, tortured, raped, and strangled. From the day Beineman's body was found, suspicion focused on John Norman Collins of Ypsilanti. The case came together with amazing speed, and he was arrested on July 30. Charged only with the Beineman killing, he was convicted of first-degree murder on August 19, 1970, and sentenced to mandatory life in prison. The authorities closed all but the Mixer case, convinced Collins had killed the other five.

And there things rested for me until I did several Google searches while writing the "Relentless" stories . One search turned up a long entry from blogger and author Gregory Fournier, a former Ypsilanti schoolteacher who had reviewed the Ann Arbor Police's Mixer case file before it went into cold storage. It turned out that Denton had been the target of off-and-on police surveillance because of his association with John Sinclair's White Panthers, but not when Mixer disappeared. I'd been played a second time, first by Dr. Robey and then by the police.

March 28, 1969, the day after my story had appeared, Ann Arbor Police Lieutenant Eugene Staudenmaier showed up at Peter Denton's Ann Arbor apartment and asked to interview him. But Denton, according to Fournier, said that he was preparing to go to Detroit to meet lawyer Ernest Goodman to start a lawsuit against Robey for my article (no suit was ever filed).

The blogger said members of the Massachusetts Attorney General's staff had come to Ann Arbor in April to give Denton a polygraph examination. When the police confirmed that Massachusetts had cleared Denton of involvement in the Strangler Case, they dropped him as a suspect in Mixer's murder.

The Ann Arbor Police also interviewed Robey but kept him in the dark about what they knew, Fournier said. They did, however, discreetly check out the psychiatrist since he had been both associated with the Strangler case and been here for all the Michigan murders.

Postscript #1 — Charles Thomas went on to form the Washtenaw County Black Economic Development League, which was funded by the Inter-Faith Coalition of Congregations. He provided genuine services for minority youth, worked on behalf of affordable housing, and received several commendations. We had a number of friendly encounters during the years. After Thomas died in 1994, a scholarship for African-American youth was established in his name at Washtenaw Community College.

Postscript #2 — Massachusets DNA tests released on July 19, 2013, confirmed that DeSalvo, who was murdered in prison in 1973, was the actual rapist and killer of Mary Sullivan, the last of the Boston Strangler victims.

Postscript #3 — Cold case DNA tests and strong circumstantial evidence revealed that Gary Earl Leiterman, a retired male nurse who had been working in Ann Arbor in 1969, was the real killer of Jane Mixer. He was convicted of first-degree murder on July 22, 2005, and sentenced to life in prison.

Postscript #4 — Dr. Ames Robey was fired by the Michigan Department of Mental Health in 1975. He had friends in the Legislature, and a House committee held a hearing on his discharge. During a recess, Dr. Robey took me aside to tell me that the man who fired him, Mental Health Director Dr. Donald C. Smith, was having an affair with a senior aide, the wife of Wayne State University State Medical School Dean Dr. Robert D. Coye. Robey didn't know that Coye was a long-time friend of mine.

Enunciating my words with cold precision. I told Robey I didn't know whether his "tip" was revenge or part of a blackmail scheme. I said that, if his slander ever became public, no matter how, I would hang him out to dry. Robey shied back from me as if he had been scalded, huffed that he was merely trying to do me a favor, and scurried back into the hearing. I never heard another word about the Coyes. Robey eventually sued the state for wrongful discharge but settled for $15,000 in back pay, less than his legal expenses. He moved back east and died in 2004.

Postscript #5 — A U-M Graduate School Board of Inquiry found Denton guilty of disrupting a class in 1970, fining him $100. I found no further trace of him but haven't looked too hard.

Chapter 19 Jack Daniels To The Rescue

I kept an unopened pint of Jack Daniels Black Label in the belly drawer of my desk at The Detroit News. I never drank at the office, but I liked to fantasize that I was heir to the hard-bitten old-timers of Hecht and MacArthur's "Front Page." I ended up cracking the bottle, but not in the way I'd imagined.

They were mostly known as the "Michigan Murders," the killings of seven young women in the Ann Arbor area. I had labeled them the "Co-ed Killings" as a reporter at The Ypsilanti Press and continued some reporting on them when I moved on to The Detroit News in early 1968.

Some months before the last killing, a frantic editor came by my desk at The News. The Associated Press had just moved an item that a young man in the custody of the Metropolitan Nashville Police Department had confessed to the killings, and I was to fly there immediately. He gave me a wad of cash. I grabbed a couple of reporters' notebooks and pens, and an envelope of clippings on the murders, shoved the bottle into the inside breast pocket of my sports coat, and headed for Detroit Metro Airport.

The Nashville department's detective bureau was a zoo when I arrived in the mid-afternoon. Two television cameras were set up, and several print reporters were wandering around. The chief of detectives, a captain, was in a surly mood. He said Washtenaw County authorities were in transit (Prosecutor William Delhey had dispatched his lead investigator), and there would be no announcements until after they had had a chance to confer.

My father had been a professor at the University of Tennessee back in the 1940s, and my mother taught English there. My childhood was in the Smokies. I used that as a basis for small talk, also letting the captain know that I had the Jack Daniels. He invited me into his office on the condition that I wouldn't ask him about the suspect, who had been arrested on a burglary charge.

As we took turns with the bottle, the captain asked me if I had covered the murders. I showed him the clips, and he ended up telling me about the suspect. It became clear that the suspect, who had lived in the Ypsilanti area, had only a superficial knowledge of the murders. He knew a little bit of what had been in the papers, but much of what he claimed to know was wrong.

I had a break on the story, but it did me no good. Back then, only radio had a twenty-four-hour news cycle. This was decades before the internet. Because The News was an afternoon paper, my first deadline for the bulldog edition wasn't until midnight. By that time, everyone had the story of the false confession.

It turned out that the burglar cooked up his story so that the authorities would take him back to Michigan. Once there, he figured they would have to let him go when they realized he wasn't the killer and that he would be too small a fish for Nashville to extradite back to Tennessee. It didn't work out that way.

The Nashville episode is like much of newspapering: Something promising that turns out to be a big nothing burger. I never bothered to restock the booze in on my desk.

Chapter 20 Kicking A Hornet's Nest

I had intended to write a fluff feature story on a magnificent construction project but accidentally provoked one of the state's most influential businessmen into trying to get me fired.

The Detroit News editors had given me three merit raises plus a step raise during my first year at the paper, but it takes years on the job to accumulate enough time off for a decent vacation. I was the favored son of the moment, so they suggested I take my wife and travel around Michigan for a week or ten days on their dime and return with a story or two. I came back with six.

Consumers Power Company (now Consumers Energy), with Detroit Edison as its junior partner, was hollowing out the top of a sand dune 100 feet above Lake Michigan. When they were done, the bowl would be two-and-a-half miles long, one mile wide, and hold twenty-seven billion gallons of water. At lake level, they were pouring concrete for penstocks that would hold six massive, sixteen-feet wide pump-generators brought in by freighter from Japan.

Late at night, when power usage was minimal across the state, the excess electricity would be used to pump water up into the elevated pond. At times of peak electrical demand, the water would flow back down, turning the pumps into generators. The $315-million Ludington Pumped Storage Power Plant had so much peak-load capacity that the utilities signed a ten-year contract to supply the excess power to Commonwealth Edison of Chicago.

At the time of my story, Consumers had a rate-hike request pending before the Michigan Public Service Commission. The utility had publicly and repeatedly warned that state residents would face blackouts and brownouts if the rate increase wasn't granted. I tossed a paragraph high up in the story that the threat was false, a scare tactic. Blackouts and brownouts are caused by a lack of peak-load capacity, and Consumers had more than enough coming on line with the Ludington project .

Consumers' executive vice president traveled from Jackson to Detroit, and complained to Editor Martin Hayden that I was threatening to unfairly destroy their rate hike request. He demanded that I be fired. Hayden called me to account. I brought him a copy of Consumers' own announcement of the Commonwealth Edison contract, plus other information on peak load versus base load. Hayden was seriously pissed and offered me the opportunity to go head-hunting. I demurred, adding that, if the man happened to seriously screw up at some point in the future, I would be there. I was.

Hayden's style of management was to work through the editors who reported to him. You almost never saw him in the city room. There were only a couple of senior reporters he talked to. Probably because I'd pulled his bacon out of the fire on the "crime in the streets" episode and the Consumers matter, I became one of them. It was a mixed blessing.

Hayden had the a reputation for having a ferocious temper. There were a number of subjects the city desk considered "Martin's sacred cows," which no one wanted to touch. One was the Detroit-owned Herman Kiefer Hospital, founded in 1911 to combat rampant tuberculosis, diphtheria, scarlet fever, mumps, measles, and other infectious diseases. The head of the hospital was a childhood friend of Hayden's. In the early 1970s, the hospital was under fire for involuntarily confining poor TB patients while treating the more privileged, including then-United Auto Workers President Walter Reuther, as outpatients. Hayden was also protective of Henry Ford Hospital, which was being sued by a female ophthalmologist who had been fired for allegedly being disagreeable. Her one one-sentence letter of reference read: "She fulfilled the duties assigned to her." That signaled to anyone in human resources that she was toxic, making her unemployable.

In both instances, I wrote modest stories after researching and finding answers to every possible question Hayden might throw at me. Without telling the city desk, I took the stories directly to Hayden, who cross-examined me in detail and then said, "Fine." I turned in the stories, assuring the desk they were fireproof. They never asked if Hayden had seen them, and I never volunteered.

There was one instance, however, where I couldn't save Hayden from himself. Detroit Recorder's Court Judge George Crockett had earned the enmity of the city's conservative Whites, including Hayden, by releasing virtually any defendant who had been beaten by the police. Moreover, he imposed lighter sentences on nonviolent criminals than most of the court's other judges. Then, in 1969, the Republic of New Africa, a supposed radical group, was meeting in the New Bethel Baptist Church, pastored by C.L Franklin, Aretha's father. A sniper shot and killed a White Detroit Police officer in the vicinity of the church. The police descended on the church and took 140 Black men into custody, intending to test each for gunpowder residue even though it was unclear where the sniper's shot had come from. Judge Crockett, on his own initiative, went down to police headquarters and ordered the release of all the men against whom the police did not have probable cause. Only a handful remained.

In the early 1970s, Judge Crockett called me into his chambers. He said he had been asking the Detroit Police Narcotics Squad to focus its enforcement on major dealers, but all they brought him was an endless parade of users and small-time street dealers. He told me he was getting ready to dismiss every minor drug case on his docket until the police started going after the bigger dealers. I told the judge that Martin Hayden was going to blow a gasket. "That's what I'm counting on," he said. In exasperation, I asked him whether he understood that I had to inform Hayden of the judge's strategy. Judge Crockett said that's why he was telling me but that it wouldn't make any difference to Hayden.

I told Hayden that the judge had explicitly said that his intent was to provoke him into an overreaction. I wrote the story when Judge Crockett started dismissing the drug cases. The Detroit News editorial page thundered against Judge Crockett, who used the over-the-top criticism to generate enough public support to force a change in the police drug enforcement priorities. I never underestimated George Crockett.

One of the marvelous things about reporting is that you never know when you are going to be blindsided by something arcing out of left field. A consortium of U.S. utilities wanted to build an environmentally problematic pipeline to carry natural gas and liquid petroleum products from the Prudhoe oil field in Alaska across the Yukon to join up with the Trans-Canada pipeline. If built, it would supply ten percent of Michigan's future natural gas needs.

On my way to the Yukon, I stopped in Ottawa to interview the Canadian national energy minister about the project. He questioned me, seeking to determine whether I was a shill for the utilities. Satisfied that I wasn't, he reached into his files for a letter he had written to Consumers' executive vice president a decade before. Consumers Power had been getting ready to build a liquid gas conversion plant that would be totally dependent on feedstock from the Trans-Canada pipeline. The letter warned that the feedstock would be available only as long as it wasn't needed by Canadian industry. It also contained an uncannily accurate year-by-year estimate of the decreasing amounts of feedstock that would be available.

Consumers Power went ahead with the plant, which was never able to operate at full capacity because of the lack of feedstock. It was operating at only twenty-five percent when I got the letter, costing Michigan ratepayers tens of millions of dollars. The lead paragraph of my story attributed the loss to the executive vice president by name.

Three days later, I got an off-the-record call from Consumers' vice president for public affairs, a man with whom I had been friendly for years. He said he didn't dispute any of the facts in the story but wanted to know why I had so harshly singled out his boss, who was retiring the following week. I asked him if he remembered the flap over the stored power facility in Ludington. "Oh shit, I warned him not to do that!" he said.

I retold this story a few times, and it got around. I worked to cultivate a reputation as someone not to be trifled with.

Chapter 21 Tear Gas, Pepper Spray, Billy Clubs, Bricks

ANN ARBOR — My eyes were burning from tear gas, and I barely saw the chunk of brick pass into the cone of illumination from the streetlight and arc straight for my head. I jerked back. It cracked into my left shin.

I headed for the Huron Valley Ambulance parked at the corner of South University and East University avenues, a stone's throw, so to speak, from both the Engineering Arch entrance to the University of Michigan central campus and my old high school. The attendant slapped on some antiseptic and fabricated a pair of butterfly bandages to pull together the two inches of flesh that had split away from the bone. It stopped the bleeding. I went back to work.

For The Detroit News, I had covered all the anti-Vietnam War demonstrations in downtown Detroit, spent time on the streets of the inner city, and would be shot at once. I had to come home to get bloodied on June 17, 1969, the second night of what was called "The Battle for Ann Arbor." Some referred to it as the "Street People's Riot." Others called it a police riot. It was all of those.

It started with a crowd of onlookers frustrating an Ann Arbor patrolman's effort to ticket a motorcyclist. Their victory celebration that first night included a pair of stoned young people fucking in the street at the corner of South U and East U. That drew a crowd of university students and hippies, which the Ann Arbor Police dispersed amid some relatively mild skirmishes and rock throwing.

The second night brought more students, more counterculture types, and a flood of young people from all over southern Michigan. Some came to watch the uproar, others to be a part of it. There might have been 2,000 or 5,000. It was impossible to make even a reliable estimate since they surged back and forth along South U and three cross streets.

The crowd attracted Washtenaw County Sheriff Douglas J. Harvey, who, while personally amiable and forgiving, cultivated the southern sheriff mystique of a Buford "Walking Tall" Pusser. Harvey's men took their cues from his approach to law enforcement, which included giving any longhair in their custody a Marine haircut, for sanitary reasons, of course. Five other police agencies brought in manpower under a mutual aid pact. Almost all of the out-of-town officers I saw wore their badges out of sight.

My first injury was more or less my own fault. A skirmish line of six Ann Arbor policemen, equipped with shields and gas masks, fired tear gas canister after canister to drive the crowd on South University back past U-M President Robben Fleming's house and on toward State Street. I didn't want to miss anything, so I was trailing a dozen feet behind the skirmish line, walking through the tear gas. My eyes cleared pretty quickly after I left the scene to get bandaged.

A bit later, I was walking east on South U as Harvey's deputies were using their billy clubs to urge the crowd toward Washtenaw Avenue. One deputy said, "There's that fucking Cain," and jabbed me twice in the left kidney, just hard enough to pain me, not hard enough to injure. Detroit News photographer James Hubbard told me he got billy clubbed repeatedly on the back of his legs. They teach law enforcement officers to avoid hitting someone on the head. Split scalps bleed like crazy and photograph dramatically. The preferred blow is to the top of the calf—it renders the leg unusable and doesn't leave marks.

Law enforcement officers even used their billy clubs to rough up Dr. Edward Pierce, physician, former Ann Arbor city councilman, and candidate for mayor. Then they dragged him off to a bus that was serving as a paddy wagon. He had allegedly crossed a police line, and officers said he was being arrested on felony riot charges. Pierce was released several hours later for lack of evidence.

I broke off from my encounter with the billy clubs and headed south on Forest Avenue, where out-of-town deputies were pushing back another part of the crowd. A helmeted young man, returning from studying, had parked his motorbike behind a home on Forest that had been converted into student housing. He walked around toward the front porch. "There's one!" shouted a deputy, thinking the helmet marked him as a rioter. Several deputies rushed to the porch. The young man turned out to be Scott MacKay, the younger brother of a high school classmate. He fumbled with his key. Unable to get the door open, he jumped the porch railing.

The deputies ran him down. He fell in the street, pressed against the curb, and put his hands over the back of his neck as they pummeled him with billy clubs. I was running after them, my notebook out. A deputy with a pepper fog machine, which looks like a flame thrower with its backpack and wand, turned and sprayed me directly in the face from a dozen feet away. I managed to grope my way to the U-M Undergraduate Library bathroom and spent the next two hours flushing my eyes. Scott turned out to have been bruised but not severely injured.

The final incident of the night took place on the steps of the president's mansion. Robben Fleming had come out to talk with the Rainbow People, John Sinclair's renamed White Panther Party. They had been trying to quell the violence with about as much success as the Black preachers who tried to intervene in Detroit's 1967 riots.

Ann Arbor Police Deputy Chief Harold Olson and I stood to one side, listening as a crowd gathered around Fleming. Sheriff Harvey and a couple of his deputies snuck through the Engineering Arch, slipped alongside the president's house from the rear, and lobbed a tear gas grenade at our feet. Fleming ducked back inside, ungassed. Olson and I got minor doses. Olson stomped back to the staging area at the corner of South U and East U. He confronted Harvey with language that never appears in a family newspaper. The sheriff insisted he didn't know Olson was there. I hadn't thought to ask Harvey if there was a law enforcement reason for the gas attack.

The rioters had pretty much exhausted themselves, and the third night ended, as T.S. Eliot would say, not with a bang but a whimper. I wrote up a story each night but included no mention of my own incidents. There was an an unwritten rule among big-city newspapers at the time: Nothing happens to reporters, photographers, or newsboys, and the reporters are never a part of their stories. That has changed, not always for the better.

I turned in a routine expense account, including the cost of a new pair of chinos and a pair of socks. The pencil pushers rejected it. Managing Editor John O'Brien was livid, but I said I would take care of it. I resubmitted my expense report in red ink and stapled it to my bloody pants and socks. They paid. For the next year, I filled out all my expense accounts in red ink. I never had another expense account questioned during my entire time at The News.

Chapter 22 Blood Disappoints One, Enriches Another

The confused and haunted thirty-four-year-old man may or may not have been the answer to the first kidnapping that the FBI's famed Flying Squad failed to solve after several dozen consecutive post-Lindbergh triumphs.

To Detroit News Assistant Managing Editor Boyd Simmons, who had been one of the best gumshoe reporters in an earlier era, Cordon Davison seemed to represent the resolution of a case that had bedeviled him for most of his career. Simmons had done five-year, ten-year, and twenty-year anniversary stories about the unsolved Browe Baby kidnapping.

In the strange and unexpected paths that big-city newspapering can take, my part of the Davison investigation resulted in a first-of-its-kind forensic test and the development of a world-satisfying supply of a blood antigen that was significant in transplant medicine, blood transfusions, and genetics research. It also led to an extraordinary windfall for an inner-city single father and an entry in the Guinness Book of World Records.

First, some history. Earl J. Connelley, J. Edgar Hoover's favorite G-man, had led the takedown of John Dillinger and later Alvin "Old Creepy" Karpis. He had orchestrated the Karpis arrest so that Hoover, photographed with a Thomson submachine gun, could claim credit. Hoover rewarded Connelley by putting him in charge of the anti-kidnapping Flying Squad after Congress passed the Lindbergh Law, making kidnapping a federal crime in 1932.

During the next four years, Connelley solved every kidnapping he chose to investigate until the September 5, 1936, snatching of the chubby nineteen-month-old Harry "Buddy" Browe from a pram in southwest Detroit's Clark Park. The person who kidnapped the Browe baby was a dowdy, somewhat overweight, early-middle middle-aged woman. There was never a ransom note. Editor Simmons figured the kidnapper had either lost her own baby or couldn't have one, and that the case would not be solved until an adult, Harry Browe, went looking for his birth certificate.

When Cordon Davison walked into The Detroit News office and asked if he might be Buddy Browe, Simmons called me in. We checked every hospital in Detroit as well as Windsor, where Davison's mother was from, and found no record of Cordon Davison's birth. We interviewed every living relative. Some said they remembered a baby Cordon, others not.

We were finally able to establish that Ann and Orwell Davison did have a son, Cordon, born at home in an apartment on West Palmer on July 25, 1935. That didn't rule out the possibility that the baby Cordon had died, and Harry Browe was stolen as a substitute.

That might have seen been far-fetched except for one other fact: Harry Browe had undergone a double mastoidectomy. The Davison family insisted Cordon had never had such an operation, and no scars were visible to the naked eye. Simmons took Davison to Harper Hospital, where tests revealed that he had, indeed, undergone a double mastoid operation. Simmons wrote the article that presented the evidence pro and con.

And there it rested until I got a call from Dr. Frank R. Ellis, a pathologist and director of the Red Cross Southeast Michigan Blood Bank, the largest in the country. Harry Browe had ten brothers and sisters living in the Detroit area. This was long before DNA sequencing, which would have made establishing paternity a snap. However, Ellis said we could use the children to reconstruct the blood types of the parents and then test to see whether or not Cordon Davison could be their long-lost brother. People generally know that everyone is blood type A, B, AB, or O, but it turns out that there are dozens of additional protein systems, all of which follow the laws of genetic inheritance.

Davison and nine of the ten Browe sibs drove to Ellis's private lab in Dearborn to give blood samples. Ellis tested twenty-one separate protein systems. Three more tests were done by Dr. Henry Gershowitz of the University of Michigan Department of Human Genetics. Three of the tests yielded positive results. The first two put the odds at a thousand-to-one that Davison was not Harry Browe. The third pushed the odds to one-hundred-thousand-to-one against. That wasn't the answer Davison or the Browes had been hoping for. This testing was unique. I wrote an article for the Journal of Forensic Medicine under Ellis' name, getting credit as co-author.

Several weeks later, I got a hesitant call from Ellis. He wanted my help but also asked that, if a story developed, I not savage him too badly. I promised. Because of the huge number of donors, his blood bank had one of the nation's largest pools of rare-blood donors. These were people whose blood had unusual proteins or the proteins in unusual concentrations. Their plasma was important in tracking down bad transfusion reactions, in establishing tissue compatibility for transplants, and human genetics research. It was also worth money.

Ellis had been trading rare blood plasma with other Red Cross blood labs across the country and also with several university research programs. He had sold some to support his own blood bank. Most of the donors were aware that they had rare blood, but Ellis had not told them of its commercial value. Ellis' confession to me was prompted by his discovery that someone had broken into his records room and copied the names of the rare blood donors. Or, it might have been an employee. What the pathologist did know was that he suddenly started getting calls from his donors saying they had been approached by a Miami-based biologics firm offering to buy their blood.

The thieves, however, missed the grand prize. Some years before, Ellis had performed a paternity test on a Detroiter named Joe Thomas, who turned out to have an unprecedented concentration of a rare blood protein called Anti-Lewis B. The pathologist had bled him several times, paid him modestly, and kept his records separate from the others. Then Thomas dropped out of sight. Ellis said he had information that a private detective, armed only with Thomas' name, was searching for him.

Ellis had several addresses and phone numbers for Thomas, but none were current. He also had been told that Thomas had once worked at Chrysler. That was some help, but Chrysler listed more than two dozen current and former employees named Joe Thomas. Ellis had one old address for Joe Thomas that the phone book listed in the name of a woman. Thinking it might be Thomas' sister, I paid her a visit. She didn't know if I was a bill collector, process server, or something else. The rare blood story seemed hard to credit. She wouldn't acknowledge she was related to Joe Thomas but said she would ask around. I gave her my number and said I would meet Joe anywhere, anytime.

Joe Thomas called me the next day, and specified a mid-day meeting in a dive bar on a bombed-out section of Gratiot Avenue. I was the only White guy there. When I walked in, it was so quiet you could have heard a mouse fart. I ordered a drink, and sat at a table. Fifteen minutes later, a guy detached himself from the bar, came over, and sat down. Joe was skeptical, but how could something so improbable not be true?

I sent him to Dr. Gershowitz at the U-M, who assayed his blood and drafted a notarized affidavit affirming the protein's potency. Prior to Thomas, the serum of the most potent Anti-Lewis B donor in the world had to be used undiluted and gave a positive reaction only about half the time. With Thomas, you could dilute his plasma by a factor of a hundred, use a smaller sample, and get a positive reaction every time. Using plasmapheresis, which is separating the blood, keeping the plasma, and returning the red blood cells, Thomas could supply the needs of the entire world.

Charles Burleigh, a senior attorney and later partner at one of Detroit's largest law firms, agreed to represent Thomas pro bono. Burleigh and I had been close friends since high school. I stood up at his wedding; he was the best man at mine. Burleigh sent the Gershowitz statement to every major biologics house in the nation, soliciting bids. The only bid that came back was from the same Miami firm that had gone after Ellis' rare-blood donors.

It took Burleigh six months to get the contract hammered out. The company would fly Thomas to Miami, separate out his plasma, give him back his red cells, and pay for him to relax on the beach for a week. Then, the company would repeat the procedure and fly him back to Detroit. They would do this twice a year, earning Thomas about $12,000 annually.

The story of the man with the golden blood got Thomas articles in Ebony and Jet, an appearance on the TV program What's My Line, and an entry in the Guinness Book of World Records. The Cains, the Burleighs, Thomas, and his girlfriend shared a fancy dinner to celebrate the man with golden blood. The News picked up the tab.

Chapter 23 Sesame Street And A "Disloyal" Doctor

Remembrance of things past: Watching an episode on CBS Sunday Morning on the fiftieth anniversary of "Sesame Street" took me back to a hotel room in Philadelphia in 1969. I'd turned on the television while I was getting dressed to attend a morning session of the American Public Health Association's annual meeting.

What came on the tube was a panoply of brilliantly colorful talking puppets, haunting music, letters, and numbers, and children's dialogue that was somehow adult at the same time. I'd never seen anything like it. Of course, no one else had either. I'm not sure whether they were test marketing "Sesame Street" or had decided to open in Philadelphia before going national.

I was in my second year at The Detroit News, which had hired me to do science and medical writing as well as general assignment reporting. I had always been more interested in the delivery of health care and how people maintained their health or didn't, rather than in the breathless breakthrough world of the latest wet-lab miracle.

An older me might have chucked the APHA and gone off to do a story on this magical thing I was watching. But I sat on the edge of the unmade bed until "Sesame Street" was over and then went off to the meeting. I missed the first session but was in time to hear Captain Howard Levy.

The year before, Captain Levy, an MD dermatologist, had been ordered to teach Special Forces soldiers how to treat the kinds of skin conditions common among South Vietnamese villagers. The motive was simple: The soldiers would cure some highly visible and easy-to-treat conditions, using that success as the basis for bringing in a pacification team. Levy viewed this as the military use of medicine, a violation of his Hippocratic Oath, and refused to aid and abet a war he hated. He was court-martialed, convicted of disobeying an order and promoting disloyalty, and sentenced to 26 months in Leavenworth Prison.

Released on appeal, he was invited to speak at the convention. I took notes on his talk and the question and answer session that followed, and then had a one-on-one interview with him. The News was a hyper-conservative paper and a strong supporter of the war, but it ran my story in full.

The featured speaker on the last day of the convention was Spiro Agnew, Nixon's reprehensible vice president. Before writing up a piece on his talk, I went to dinner at Bookbinder's, one of the nation's finest seafood restaurants. My dinner companion was Dr. Larry Altman, who had been an ace medical detective with the Centers for Disease Control before joining The New York Times as a medical writer.

I ordered cherrystone clams as an appetizer. Larry warned me against it, saying there had been a Hepatitis A outbreak associated with Chesapeake Bay clams. I rather smugly said that I had come down with hepatitis A as a kid in Brazil and had a lifetime immunity. Following dinner, I went back to my hotel to write my Agnew story and was hit with food poisoning, explosive from both ends. I did get the piece written, but it took me more than three hours of going back and forth from the typewriter to the bathroom. Agnew and food poisoning: What sin was I being punished for?

My more progressive friends would ask me how I could work for on a paper "like that." I answered that the editorial page's virulent wrong-headedness didn't intrude on my ability to write things the way I saw them, such as the Levy piece. That proved less true with time.

Chapter 24 Apollo 11's Unreported Brush With Death

While Apollo 11 was on the way to the moon, I shared a drink with a smarter and handsomer version of who I wanted to be when I grew up.

When I took a deep dive into the computer calculations that kept Apollo aimed at where the moon was going to be, NASA trotted out a pretty blond mathematician from the University of Texas but kept the "Hidden Figures" hidden.

I scored a lunch with Werhner von Braun and the rocket scientists he brought with him from Peenemunde, but every time the conversation got interesting, the creator of the magnificent Saturn 5 rocket switched to German. I flunked German in college.

And finally, from researching the navigation system for the lunar module's descent to the moon's surface, I realized the the astronauts had damned near crashed and died. NASA wouldn't admit the closeness of the brush with death for decades.

Nevertheless, it was an experience of a lifetime to be so close to and get to write about one of the grandest events of human history.

I was nursing a Jack Daniels Black Label at the bar of the Escape Velocity Press Club on the top floor of the Holiday Inn just outside the gates of the Manned Spacecraft Center. Houston was dry except for private clubs, so the reporters got together to establish the club. We even commissioned North American Rockwell to fly its corporate jet to Dallas and bring back several hundred cases of Coors Beer, which wasn't available locally. Seated next to me at the bar was Harrison Schmitt, astronaut and Ph.D. geologist.

These were the days when Apollo 11 was hurtling through space, its rockets occasionally firing to adjust its trajectory as the spacecraft approached lunar orbit and mankind's first moon landing. I was the third and youngest member of the three-person Detroit News team, and my experiences were both personal and profound.

I was the only child of a scientist father and a former English professor mother. They avoided having to hire babysitters by dragging me along to lectures,, and conferences, meetings, and sometimes even cocktail parties.

There is this thing about adults: Most of them don't know how to speak with children. The standard line I would get was, "What do you want to be when you grow up, Stevie?"

I hated the diminutive and didn't think much of the question. At age eight, I was both a rock hound and an emerging smart ass. I finally came up with an answer that appealed to me: "I want to be the second man on the moon." That, of course, raised the question: "Why not the first?" I would put on an air of great seriousness and explain: "The first man the government sends up will be an adventurer who may or may not get back. Once they figure out how to get a man there and back safely, there will be nothing to do on the moon except geology. As a lunar geologist, I will be the second man on the moon. There will still be plenty of glory, and I will have the opportunity to do serious science."

I was about twelve when I dropped the second-man-on-the the-moon bit. But it wasn't until after my freshman year in college that I realized I liked people better than rocks, dropped geology, and stumbled into newspapering. I had one more drink before I told Schmitt my childhood story. Schmitt laughed and said he got his doctorate in geology, joined the astronaut corps, and trained as a test pilot so he could go to the moon. But he acknowledged, sadly, that he had not yet been assigned a mission. When NASA cancelled the Apollo 18 and 19 moon shots, it looked as if Schmidt was going to miss out.

My other weird experience was dinner at a biergarten with the Associated Press' aerospace writer, plus von Braun, and a couple of the German rocket scientists who had come with the great man to the Redstone Arsenal and then on to Houston. A few quotes from him would elevate any story I might write. My only consolation for not being able to quote von Braun was that the AP guy came away quotelesss because he didn't understand German either.

I've had ambivalent feelings about von Braun ever since I saw "I Aim for the Stars," J. Lee Thompson's masterful 1960 movie of the rocketeer's life starring Curt Jurgens. Or, as comedian Mort Sahl is reputed to have said, "I aim at the stars, but sometimes I hit London." Before he was the principal architect of the U.S. space program, von Braun created the V-2 rocket that devastated London during World War II. He was a member of the Nazi Party and the SS, and paid many visits to the slave-labor V-2 factory, where more than 20,000 slave workers died. He insisted he joined the Nazis and SS out of political necessity so he could continue his research, claimed he was totally unaware of the torture and deadly abuse at the plant, and was only "interested in rockets for space travel, not killing."

After Neil Armstrong touched down on the moon and completed his walk, NASA held a massive press conference. There were 1,700 newspaper and TV reporters in the auditorium as Chris Craft and a dozen others took turns saying what the moon landing meant to them. Von Braun echoed his "I aim at the stars" apologetics. Once man was truly in space, humanity would survive even if we destroyed the Earth, he said. He was applauded. I was horrified. He could destroy London because he was aiming at space. Once we got to space, he was saying we could destroy the Earth because humanity would endure. That brought up the question of whether mankind would deserve saving. I couldn't write that, not in The Detroit News.

As the third person on the News team, I had the freedom to poke around wherever I wished. I was curious about how NASA would calculate the midcourse corrections, the rocket burns that would keep Apollo 11 on the proper trajectory to encounter the moon, not where it was but where it was going to be. NASA had developed the best computers in the world, but they weren't equal to the task, in part because there were more unknowns than equations to solve them. By making a first best guess of what the unknowns should be, the computer could do a much faster job of approximating what the course correction should be. At least, that's how NASA public relations folks explained it to me.

They set me up to interview a recent University of Texas graduate with a master's degree in mathematics. She was part of NASA contractor TRW's orbit calculation group, which was comprised of twenty-seven Ph.D.s. She had the unique ability to make a better first guess than any of her more educated colleagues. She also had beach-blond California good looks and was quickly taken over by the networks.

I had no clue that it was the "Hidden Figures" Black women who had actually done the pioneering work on orbit calculation. I'm delighted they finally got the recognition they deserved. America wouldn't have gone to the moon without them, but I remain profoundly irritated at NASA for its racism and for making me part of the deception.

I figured the astronauts had three main opportunities to die: Lift-off from Earth, the moon landing, and re-entering Earth's atmosphere. I couldn't do anything special about the beginning or the end, but I could take ownership of the middle. I searched out the engineer who designed the descent orbit that covered the time from when the Eagle separated from the command module and fired its retro rockets over the Sea of Fertility to its landing in the Sea of Tranquility. He wrote a paper titled "Eleven Minutes from Fertility to Tranquility." And people say engineers are humorless.

The principal difficulty, he explained, was that Armstrong would be flying retrograde (ass forward) and would be pretty much blind to where he was going. He had to depend on five sources of telemetry that, when combined, were supposed to locate the Eagle precisely: A transponder that pinpointed the Eagle in relation to the command module; forward forward-looking radar; downward-looking radar; a platform of gyroscopes and accelerometers designed by Charles Stark Draper's Lincoln Labs at the Massachusetts Institute of Technology that told you where you were by remembering all the moves you made to get there; and a gravity detector that measured the subtle differences in subsurface lunar density. Those density concentrations or mascons had been mapped during Apollo 10's lunar orbits, which I had also covered.

The Eagle's on-board computer had less computing power than the average smart phone of today and was unable to reconcile all the different sources of telemetry when they didn't agree perfectly. An alarm would sound when the computer's program froze, and the astronauts would switch the computer over to a second program, and then a third, a fourth, and so on.

I had a lunar map that showed both every surface feature from Fertility to Tranquility and each point at which it was anticipated they would be switching over from one program to the next. But the program alarms and switchovers came too quickly. It meant that Armstrong and co-pilot Buzz Aldrin couldn't know precisely where they were. They should have aborted, but Armstrong flew by the seat of his pants. He couldn't see directly below the lander, but he could see at an angle. He spotted an area free of boulders, moved the lander toward it, and touched down with twenty seconds of fuel left.

Aldrin would later note that "the alarms sounded when the computer couldn't keep up with the data flow … nothing serious. It was a distraction." That was a fable. I had the information but not the authority. I thought I knew what it meant, but I had no one to back me up, to say, "Yes, they had a close encounter with death." The significance of my great story was lost. The closeness of their brush with death would not be acknowledged for several decades. What was nuts is that, if NASA had been candid, it would have made Armstrong's piloting even more heroic.

NASA did get one thing right. Schmitt's fellow geologists mounted a pressure campaign, and the space agency assigned Schmitt to Apollo 17. In December, 1972, he became the twelfth, last man, and only scientist, to walk on the moon.

Chapter 25 A Dead-End Metaphor

How do you write, in a family newspaper, the humor surrounding a significant and compelling story that depends on the word "fuck." It eluded me, so the account became part of my oral tradition.

The significance was a ruling more than five decades ago by U.S. District Judge Thomas Patrick "Thunder" Thornton in Detroit. He held that a quasi-judicial government agency could not take significant action injuring an individual without giving that person the basic right to due process. It meant, for example, that a school district couldn't kick out a student without giving them a reason for the expulsion and the right to appeal. Those same rights would apply to a client whose benefits were chopped by social services, or a motorist whose driver's license was yanked. Today, we have rights that allow us to challenge most arbitrary and capricious actions by government bureaucracies. It was less true then.

The 1970 ruling came up during a dinner table conversation with Dr. Donald J. Holmes and his wife at our home in Lodi Township, south of Ann Arbor. Holmes, a brilliant and eccentric associate professor of psychology at the University of Michigan, told us about having been a plaintiff's witness in the case in front of Thornton the week before.

The issue began with the fear of Bellville High School's administrators that some of its students were getting high. During class, they launched a locker inspection of the entire school. It uncovered no marijuana or any other illicit substances. However, in the locker of a junior, they found a copy of The Ann Arbor Sun, the underground paper published by the White Panther/Rainbow Peoples Party. The student was summarily expelled. The school was unaware that the student's father was a lawyer who'd done work with the American Civil Liberties Union. The ACLU filed a federal suit on behalf of the student.

The ACLU lawyer demanded to know the basis for the expulsion. The school's attorney hemmed and hawed and finally acknowledged that the sole reason for the expulsion was the word "fuck" in one article on music. That article, by John Sinclair, was the reason the clarinet-playing student had the paper in the first place. The ACLU attorney maneuvered the situation so that the school's red-faced lawyer had to be the first one to mention the word "fuck" in open court, Holmes recalled.

The case was basically dead when the plaintiff's attorney introduced evidence that the school library included copies of J.D. Salinger's "The Catcher in the Rye." The book, which contained the word "fuck" in several places, was required reading in eleventh eleventh-grade English.

The frosting on the cake came when a U-M linguistics professor testified that the word "fuck," in most usages, is a dead-end metaphor. In other words, if someone says, "My fucking shoes are too tight," it means the shoes are uncomfortable, not that his feet are having sexual congress with his shoes.

Holmes then testified that the word "fuck" is part of the every day vocabulary to which adolescents are exposed and that neither hearing nor reading the word would damage them. Judge Thornton, who had earned the nickname "Tiger" when he was the University of Detroit's all-time greatest running back and later became "Thunder" for his no-nonsense judicial demeanor, leaned down from the bench and asked: "Dr. Holmes, does your opinion of the word's impact change if it is preceded by 'mother?'" The courtroom erupted with laughter.

I wish I'd been there it to witness it, but I still wouldn't have been able to convey the full flavor of the story. I also wish I had thought to do a profile of the eccentric Holmes, but my reporting in those days was much more focused on investigative work.

At the time, Holmes' wife owned two rundown Victorian houses on Ann Arbor's Hill Street that were rented by the Rainbow Peoples Party members and friends. Sinclair's brother, Dave, complained to me once that the houses were in such need of repair that "I had to shit, shower, and shave in three different bathrooms." It was through the house connection that Holmes became the go-to counselor for a number of counterculture types. The balance of his practice was with adolescents and women (mostly faculty wives) with sexual concerns.

In 1972, Little, Brown published his 1,077-page textbook with the overwhelming title of "Psychotherapy: Experience, Behavior, Mentation, Culture, Sexuality and Clinical Practice." He was particularly proud of having commissioned a series of explicit black and -and-white photos of a man and woman having intercourse in a wide variety of positions. They escaped pornography laws because they were part of a medical textbook.

I bought a copy. The pictures were explicit, informative, and boring. I gave the book away.

Holmes, bored with Michigan, resigned his faculty appointment and moved to Carefree, Arizona, because he liked the name, and became resident shrink to The New Dick Van Dyke Show.

Chapter 26 Six Armed Men, One Turned And Fired

The only time I was ever shot at, a uniformed officer with a carbine was on my left side, a uniformed officer with a twelve-gauge shotgun on my right. There were six men with long guns gathered around a Cadillac just down the street. One turned and shot at us, so we chased them. But I'm getting ahead of myself.

As part of The Detroit News' "Crime: The Search for Solutions" series of stories, I was riding with various officers in the high-crime Tenth (Livernois) Precinct.

Veteran White officers wanted nothing to do with me. But I had the backing of then Chief John Nichols, so they had no choice. One afternoon, I was with two White veterans. We rode in silence. It was raining. They got a call to take a burglary report. One of the officers addressed the elderly Black homeowner as "Auntie." They tromped into her living room with wet shoes. Her carefully blank expression betrayed nothing of what she was feeling. The human side of me wanted to apologize for to them. The professional side maintained the blank expression of a passive observer.

The next day, I chose to ride with two young White officers who were delighted to get off their exposed scooters and have a solid police cruiser around them. We spent a couple of hours driving around without any citizen interaction. It was sweltering, so we stopped for refreshments. I bought three Cokes, unaware that one of the officers had also bought three soft drinks. One of the officers said we should give our extra drinks to some kids, but they couldn't find any young people they felt comfortable approaching.

The Black officers I met didn't face the same silent hostility. I ended up riding with two of the best: A former high school biology teacher and a former foreman at Detroit Diesel, both of whom had left good-paying jobs to don the blue.

We were driving outbound on Michigan Avenue late one afternoon when the driver made a sudden U-turn. We pulled over a car with a driver and three passengers, all Black men who looked to be in their mid to late thirties. They ordered the guy riding shotgun to open his pants. He refused. They insisted. Eventually, he caved. His genitals were covered with white powder, heroin. The two men in the back seat were scrunched as far away from the middle of the seat as they could go. In the center of the seat was a small wooden box. At the officers' insistence, they opened the box, which contained about an ounce of marijuana.

The officers questioned the men extensively and then staged a mock debate on whether to take them in. One of the officers offered to flip a coin for it. The men thought it was a great idea but lost the flip. Then they lost two out of three. Finally, the "good cop" prevailed, ground the pot into the gutter, and sent the four on their way. The officers' notebooks were full of information on four men they could turn to in the future as potential informants.

I asked how they knew to pull the car over. The officer who was driving explained that, when the driver of the oncoming car spotted the police cruiser, he grabbed an empty pop bottle and pretended to take a drink. That told the officers that something was going on in the car. As they pulled the car over, they saw the man riding shotgun hunching his shoulders. When they saw a crumpled Kleenex on the floorboard, they concluded he had been snorting dope and had gotten rid of the powder down the front of his pants. It wasn't an unconstitutional "stop and frisk" because the experienced officers had observed a series of "furtive gestures" that gave them reasonable cause to pull the car over.

Another night, a landlord called the Livernois Precinct to report five men with long guns outside his modest apartment building. The dispatcher radioed us to meet the landlord around the corner from his place. The landlord hung in the shadows while the two officers and I marched three abreast down the middle of the street toward his building.

There were six men with rifles and shotguns, not five. The officer on my right racked his shotgun and yelled, "Halt, police!" One of the men swung around with his rifle, fired, missed. The officers held their fire. There were too many innocent people in the street. The armed men scattered in all directions.

In cop parlance, we gave chase. I suppose I should have been worried about getting shot, but my only fear that night was being left behind by two officers who were fast runners. The one gunman we singled out to follow disappeared down an alley several blocks away. As we entered the alley, we stumbled on three men who were in the process of breaking into a basement apartment. The officers turned their guns on the trio.

Suddenly, five very scruffy-looking men with handguns drawn burst into the other end of the alley. There was a dead-silent standoff of pointed guns. Nobody fired. Several of the scruffy men were carrying five-cell flashlights. That marked them as under-cover cops. They had been raiding a nearby dope house when they got the call that officers had been fired on. Imagine the scene from "Reservoir Dogs" where everyone starts shooting each other. It didn't happen, but the adrenaline remained. All seven officers turned their intensity on the would-be burglars. Two peed in their pants. We marched them back to the site of the shooting. I was walking too close to the would-be burglars. One of the officers grabbed me by the back of my belt and yanked me out of the way.

The shooting scene was chaotic. The street was filled with on-lookers. Some forty to fifty cops, including a number of Tactical Mobile Unit officers, had streamed in from all over the city. No one wants to miss a "shots fired at officers" call. I noticed a man standing on a nearby porch, laughing at the scene. His jacket was open. He'd forgotten he had a handgun stuffed into the front of his pants. I had nightmare visions of a shoot-out on the street. I grabbed a TMU officer who had a twelve-gauge shotgun dangling casually at his side and asked him to come with me.

We walked up to the porch. The man with the gun in his belt said, "What do you want, man?" I yammered that I was a Detroit News reporter and needed to interview him about what had happened, and we kept walking closer. I kept up a line of chatter. When we got to the foot of the steps, the officer swung the barrel tip of his shotgun up under the man's chin, forcing him up on his tip toes. The officer said, "May I have your gun, please?" and deftly removed it from his belt. Such a sweet move.

We later learned he was one of the six men with long guns. He had simply ducked around the back of the house, dropped the long gun, and come out the front to watch. He ratted out his companions. All of them were eventually arrested.

The two officers and I came back the next afternoon, driving at a crawl up and down the street. The officers ticketed cars for being parked facing the wrong direction, being too close to a driveway, and being too far from the curb. A middle-aged Black man came boiling out of his house, screaming at the officers for ticketing his car. They patiently explained that we were the ones who were shot at the previous night, that we were driving up and down the street so everyone in the neighborhood would know we had not been scared away, that we were there, honest to God, "to serve and protect." The officers offered to rip up the ticket, but the man held on to it.

Back in the early 1970s in Detroit, virtually all illicit drugs were sold indoors. The dope houses were easy targets for robbers, so major dealers hired tough guys with reputations who would come after you if you hit one of the dealer's houses. That's who the gunmen were who shot at us.

The homeowner, still clutching his ticket, identified which unit in the small apartment building was the dope house. He went on to tell us about a fellow who drove a truck around neighborhoods selling fruits and vegetables door-to-door. In a riff on "Cotton Comes to Harlem," he said the dope being delivered was hidden inside a hollowed-out watermelon. The narcotics squad arrested the watermelon man several days later.

I have great admiration for good cops.

Chapter 27 A Lesson From A Colleague

Bob Pisor's year of reporting from Vietnam ended in 1967, shortly before the Tet Offensive and not long before I joined The Detroit News. Bob was one of the finest reporters I've ever known, a man of integrity and insight, and we were friends during our years together at the paper.

The persistent rumor was that The News had been unhappy with Bob's questioning of General William Westmoreland's body counts of enemy dead, the general's "proof" that we were winning the war. Bob never talked about the circumstances of his removal, but he did tell one marvelous story about having drinks at the Caravel Hotel in Saigon with a Green Beret colonel and the CIA's assistant station chief.

"I've had ten years experience in guerrilla warfare, and we're going to beat the 'Slopes,'" the colonel said. "No," answered the CIA man. "You've had one year's experience repeated ten times over." Tet proved the CIA man right.

I was the new kid at The News. My experience was at a weekly paper and two small dailies. I was in awe of the old-timers. Managing Editor John O'Brien, who began his newspapering at the end of Prohibition and the fading days of the Purple Gang. Assistant Managing Editor Boyd Simmons, who would become my principal mentor, was there for the United Auto Workers' transformative sit-down strike in Flint and was the paper's best investigative reporter in the 1950s and early 1960s. I learned an immense amount from the old timers and treasured their experience.

But Bob's simple yarn haunted me about the risk of getting stale, becoming jaded. I was too new to have done the same thing over and over again for years. Even in my attenuated academic experience, however, I'd encountered professors who had been teaching from the same class notes for decades. Big-city newspapers in those days were pretty staid institutions, long on doing the same thing over and over again, and short on innovation. Too many of my colleagues just seemed to be coasting along.

I vowed I would never allow myself to become like Bob's Green Beret colonel. My undercover assignments were all at my own initiative and a break from the conventional. I made a career of going after stories that no one else was doing.

Chapter 28 A Phony Medical Student Guesses Right

My cover story that I was an academically troubled first-year medical student at Wayne State University had one flaw: The third-year resident recognized an earlier version of himself in my supposed classroom struggles. He took me under his wing, too much.

We were walking down a hallway in old Detroit Receiving Hospital's emergency department. Gurneys, chairs, and the occasional bundle of dirty laundry were stored on the cracked, faded linoleum. He paused to look at the tag on an old guy sitting in a chair, head down, half asleep. The man had a several-day growth of beard and multiple scars on the top of his head. He was wearing a mask and hadn't bathed in a long time.

We ducked into a darkened side room. There was a frontal chest x-ray on the light box. He turned to me and said, "What do you see there?" There were light and dark splotchy areas in both lungs. I had no idea which were the lesions, which was the normal lung tissue. I figured it was an X-ray of the guy in the chair. I took both index fingers, pointed simultaneously to where the dark and light areas met on each lung, and exclaimed, "My God, he's bilateral!" I turned back to the resident and asked, "How long do you think his TB's been untreated?"

My guess wasn't totally out of the blue. The Detroit News had hired me in 1968 with the understanding that part of my time would be spent as a science and medical writer. I knew that alcoholism and tuberculosis were chronic problems in the Cass Corridor area south of Wayne State, a section the city since gentrified and renamed Midtown. The mask on the old guy was the give away. I got it right, and my cover was good for the time being.

Security was virtually nonexistent at Receiving Hospital. I had simply put a stethoscope in my back pocket, swiped a white coat from a closet, and started wandering around, chatting with people. I invoked the name of a professor well known for his concern for students. I said he had told me to spend several nights at Receiving, to see medicine in the trenches and decide whether or not I really wanted to be a doctor. "But for God's sake, don't touch anybody!" In those days, I didn't know what couldn't be done.

The third-year and the other residents took me in and talked candidly about what they were up against. There were too many sick and injured patients, too few operating rooms, too few recovery rooms, too few Intensive Care Unit beds, not enough supplies, antique equipment, and everyone — janitor, orderly, nurse and doctor — spread too thin.

Seeing it for myself seemed the best way to get at the truth, the reality of how people were cared for at the city-run hospital. Dr. Robert Coye, dean of Wayne State's med school, talked about the hospital's needs, but not too candidly. The university didn't want to overly badmouth the place it sent its students for training. And if the city admitted how bad things were, it would have had to pony up more money.

Receiving was more than just a name. It was where the Detroit Police dumped the derelict drunks and acute-phase schizophrenics that they swept off the streets. It was where people with no insurance and too poor to pay went for treatment. But the poor usually didn't show up until the problem had festered. It was where the City Physician's Office sent the saddest and sickest of the poverty-stricken. It was where the gleaming white private hospitals sometimes dumped patients when their insurance ran out. And it got most of the city's trauma. The people that Receiving treated didn't have much of a voice to demand better care. The Detroit News had given me a megaphone. I used it.

Detroit, in the late 1960s, had the highest murder rate in the nation, and Receiving was the hospital of choice for people who were stabbed or shot. The murder rate would have been even higher except for one fact: Receiving was equal to or better than any hospital in the country at saving patients with stab or gunshot wounds of the heart. The doctors would catch them at the ER loading dock, slap some yellow antiseptic on both arms, put a shunt in each arm, and begin pouring in fluids as fast as possible. It's vascular collapse that kills, and the key was to pump in fluid as fast as it was leaking out of the wound in the heart. That would buy them time.

The technique had its origins in the Mobile Army Surgical Hospitals (MASH units) in Korea. A doctor at Detroit's Hutzel Hospital refined it. The doctors at Receiving perfected it through lots of practice. A surgeon would crack the chest, cut through the sheathing around the heart, and reach in. With a gunshot, there would be two holes. A thumb would go in one hole a finger in the other. That would stop the gusher of blood as they began to stitch up the holes, being careful not to suture thumb or finger into the wound. "The whole thing takes less than five minutes from when the guy is wheeled in the door," said Dr. Ronald Krome, the head of the emergency department.

If there were any signs of life at the emergency room dock, a patient with a stab wound of the heart had an 85 percent chance of survival. With gunshot wounds of the heart, the survival rate the previous year was an extraordinary 37 percent. But if you weren't on death's doorstep, Receiving Hospital could be one of the worst places to end up because the city and WSU, who shared the responsibility for financing the hospital, never put up enough money to meet the needs.

The residents told me about an earlier incident in which an elderly man was brought in one night suffering a heart attack. A bit later, an old woman dressed only in a housecoat rushed into the ER. She was hysterical, and no one could make sense of what she was saying. They put her in restraints, only to discover hours later she was the heart attack victim's wife and spoke only Polish.

Krome could have been angry about my undercover sojourn in his ER but decided instead to use my expose in a successful effort to squeeze more support for the emergency department. A tacit partnership evolved. When Receiving was in crisis and at the point of turning away patients, he would call me. I would do stories, and Krome would get more resources. Reporters are generally supposed to be dispassionate observers. I wasn't dispassionate.

There was an incident in which Henry Ford Hospital, on the day her insurance coverage expired, loaded a cancer patient in an ambulance, added her boxed-up medical records, and deposited her unannounced on Receiving's emergency room dock. Krome called me. Patient dumping didn't end because of my subsequent story, but it happened less frequently, and patients were never dumped unannounced.

Another time, the Detroit Police brought in an Army veteran who was in the midst of an acute schizophrenic episode. He had been under treatment at the Battle Creek Veteran's Administration Hospital, but Battle Creek refused to come all the way across Michigan to pick him up. Krome's staff next called the VA in nearby Allen Park, which responded that it was not their problem. Krome called me at home on a Saturday night. I called the deputy director of the Allen Park VA. I told him I was disinclined to ruin my weekend, but if the man was still at Receiving when I went to work Monday morning, I would do a story. Monday morning found the patient back in Battle Creek.

What I got in return was free access to Receiving. Whatever was happening on the streets of Detroit, whether drugs, alcoholism, violence, police brutality, or the health consequences of poverty, was reflected in what came across the ER dock. It was my listening post.

When surgeons did their first kidney transplant, they invited me to put on a mask and gown and join them in the operating room. A man in his late teens had crashed into a tree at high speed. His brain was mush. His parents gave permission, and each of his kidneys saved the life of a young person. I remember the surgeon working with speed and fanatical concentration as he removed the diseased kidney from the prospective recipient. First, he attached the recipient's renal artery to the donor's kidney. Even as he was then sewing the renal veins together, the pale, whitish donor kidney began to pink up as the blood flowed in. The more it pinks up, the more of the kidney survives. A few moments later, the surgeon gently held the new kidney's ureter. 'Look," he said, "a drop of golden urine!" The new kidney was working, a life saved.

I would go up to the Intensive Care Unit at night, talking with the nurses and resident physicians as they wrestled with impossible choices. They would have only one open bed. Who would get it, the young heroin addict with bacterial endocarditis from a dirty needle or an eighty-year-old man with moderate cognitive impairment who had suffered a heart attack? That is what rationing of health care meant in Detroit.

What I didn't realize when I first met Dr. Krome was that the cigar-smoking, straight-talking doctor (he also had a magnificent mustache) had just completed his surgical residency in 1969 and been named to run the ER. His spectacular career took him at various times to the presidencies of the America College of Emergency Physicians, University Association of Emergency Medicine, and American Board of Emergency Medicine. Nationally, he was the driving force for the establishment of emergency surgery as a recognized specialty and was the inaugural editor of the Annals of Emergency Medicine. He always had time for me.

Dr. Krome died in 2013, which frees me to tell one final story. For the 1980 Republican National Convention in Detroit that nominated Ronald Reagan, I was assigned to assassination duty. Receiving had an ER-equipped trailer parked behind the Joe Louis Arena. I hung out in the trailer during the convention. If a shooting happened, the doctors in their white coats were set to rush into the arena. There was an extra white coat in the trailer. If I grabbed it and followed them in, they could plead ignorance. Reagan wasn't shot then.

Chapter 29 She Falsely Confessed To Infanticide

MIDLAND — Margaret Lynch's life was a miasma of despair. As an early teen, she had been repeatedly raped by her stepfather. When she finally got up the courage to tell her mother, her mother blamed Margaret for driving her man away.

Margaret's third child, a girl, was born with a cleft lip and palate and failed to thrive. Her mother blamed Margaret for not taking better care of the infant. Margaret's best friend thought her husband was the baby's actual father and spurred a police investigation after the baby died. Victimized again by both prosecutorial misconduct and an incompetent defense, Margaret was convicted of first-degree murder and sentenced to mandatory life in prison.

Only she was innocent.

Driven by my own demons, it took me eleven months to win her freedom. Had Pat's and my eldest son, Michael, not been born with a bilateral cleft lip and palate, Margaret Lynch probably would have spent the rest of her life in prison. Had I not sought to make amends for the most harmful story I had ever written when I was a beginning reporter, I would not have recognized the falseness of her confession. And had the late Detroit Recorder's Court Judge Joe Gillis not received an unexpected call during a confrontation interview with me, I would never have known Margaret Lynch existed.

The idea that justice could depend on such an improbable combination of circumstances is not what they teach in a high school civics class or even law school. Welcome to Cain's world.

I worked mostly as Assistant Managing Editor Boyd Simmons' troubleshooter. If he needed something, I was there. If something blew up in his face, he could turn to me. If I had the lead on a good story, I would do enough work under the radar to be reasonably sure I could land it and take the idea to Boyd. He would let the Monday editors' meeting know what I was working on and protect me from getting other assignments. The idea was to underpromise and overdeliver. Boyd would also get credit when I delivered.

In Detroit's halls of justice, Judge Gillis was famous for what he called his "white sales," a curious appellation since most of the people brought before him were Black. If the case against a defendant looked reasonably solid, Gillis would make an offer of a modest prison sentence if the defendant would plead guilty. But if he or she rejected the plea offer, Gillis would take them immediately to trial and, upon conviction, sentence them to at least twice as much prison time as they would have received had they pled.

It is standard in federal and state courts to give lighter sentences to defendants who plead guilty, particularly if they appear to express genuine remorse. But to punish a defendant for exercising their constitutional right to a trial is a blatant denial of that right. However, Gillis ran the court's most efficient docket, and his fellow judges never called him on the practice, which would have increased their case loads. I was conducting the obligatory confrontation interview with Gillis before publishing an expose of his "white sales" when he took a call from the Detroit House of Correction. We headed out together to the state's women's prison.

There was a young mother of five who kept getting arrested for shoplifting, A succession of judges took pity on her and kept her out of jail. But when she came before Gillis, he sentenced her to six years as an habitual criminal. His plan was to let her serve one year and then vacate the rest of her sentence if he felt she had learned her lesson. But Gillis forgot about her. After serving five years, she escaped in desperation but was quickly recaptured. Hence the phone call to the judge.

While we were waiting at DeHoCo, he told me about a Genesee County (Flint) lawyer who unseated an incumbent judge by running a get-tough-on-crime campaign. The entire Genesee bench immediately began handing out much more severe sentences. Gillis claimed he could look at the crime and sentence on a prisoner's card and discern whether the judge was from Genesee County or elsewhere in Michigan. Inspecting the cards together, he got four straight correct until he hit Margaret Lynch of Midland, who had been convicted of first-degree murder and sentenced to mandatory life in prison for starving her baby to death.

The matrons at the women's prison said they felt sorry for Margaret. I sought her out, finding a somewhat overweight, homely, befuddled woman in her mid-thirties who seemed to have only a vague understanding of what had befallen her.

I was thunderstruck. In the late 1960s, infanticide was generally prosecuted as manslaughter, a recognition that it typically stemmed from a mother's postpartum depression.

Moreover, I knew from our first-born son that infants with cleft lips can't get suction to nurse. We fed Mike with a turkey baster fitted with a soft rubber tube until the lip was repaired. Margaret had been trying to feed her baby conventionally, but the cleft lip meant her infant could get, at best, minimal suction. The girl's missing palate meant that phlegm dripped directly into her stomach, causing her to spit up much of the little nourishment she was receiving. Margaret's 80 IQ made her borderline retarded, and I would later learn that she had never been given adequate instruction on how to feed her baby. She had confessed after a seven-hour marathon interrogation. That was another red flag.

Years before, when I was covering western Wayne County for the Ypsilanti Press, I wrote a piece about Road Patrol detectives opening a homicide investigation of parents whose infant child they believed had been smothered in its crib. I printed the names of the parents. The autopsy report came back several days later, showing the baby had died of SIDS, sudden infant death syndrome or crib death. The parents were blameless. Not only had they lost a child, they had been victimized first by the authorities investigating them for murder and then by me.

I researched crib death and wrote a mea culpa story about how their tragedy had been compounded by both the police and the press. I learned that crib death mothers often are overwhelmed with feelings of guilt. I found several instances in the medical literature where mothers had even confessed to killing their children.

I had a lot of credibility built up with Simmons. He turned me loose. I headed for Midland, and pored over the police file and trial transcript. In getting Margaret's confession, the sheriff's detective had played on her guilt feelings. In the end, she said, "My baby wouldn't have died unless I took her bottle away. Yes, I did it." It seemed really thin, but the court held a so-called Walker Hearing and ruled that Margaret's confession was both voluntary and sufficient.

I didn't know how I was going to get Margaret out of prison, but I knew I had to. It was clear from the interrogation that the detective went into it believing to a moral certainty that Margaret had intentionally starved her daughter. But the record gave no hint of what made him so sure. I bought two six-packs of beer and went over to the detective's house. We retired to his finished basement, consuming all the beers. At the end of a long evening, he revealed that Margaret's best friend had told him that Margaret had starved the family dog to death as a dry run for the baby. That was why he knew she was a murderer.

I called the Humane Society. They had a record of the dog. It had died of throat cancer. It turned out that the best friend believed Margaret had been having an affair with her husband. In the trailer park, there had been "joking" that the baby had black hair, just like the best friend's husband.

Then there was the matter of prosecutorial misconduct. I discovered that Margaret had taken her daughter with her to the Midland County Department of Social Services the day before the baby died. Margaret was giving the baby a bottle in the presence of two social workers even as she was making arrangements to have a surgeon in Bay City correct the cleft.

The social work supervisor went to the prosecutor. He asked if the social workers had actually seen formula going into the baby. It was an absurd question since it was not something one could directly see. He then said they should forget it, that Margaret was trying to use the social workers as an alibi. Margaret never thought to tell her attorney she had been to Social Services.

I went to see Ty Gillespie, Margaret's court-appointed trial attorney. He was a Dow family attorney (as in Dow Chemical Co.), president of the Midland County Bar Association, and had virtually no criminal trial experience. Moreover, he was the attorney for the Mid-Michigan Medical Center, where the baby had been transported by ambulance. The infant had been taken directly to the morgue without being seen by a physician. She was later declared dead by a physician in the morgue.

Gillespie was unaware of what I had uncovered and was devastated to learn how badly he had blown the case. I asked the him what he was going to do about it. Gillespie agreed that his firm would hire a first-class criminal trial attorney with experience in appellate law. In my subsequent story, I didn't whitewash Gillespie, but I didn't go out of my way to savage him either. I felt that was appropriate after he agreed to do all in his power to make amends.

I wrote the factual narrative for the appeal while the new attorney wrote the law. We won in the Court of Appeals. The prosecutor appealed the ruling, but the Michigan Supreme Court voted 7-0 to vacate the conviction. The prosecutor threatened to retry Margaret for first first-degree murder unless she pleaded guilty to involuntary manslaughter with the sentence to be time served. I would have preferred that she hold out for full exoneration and punish the authorities for the wrongfulness of their prosecution. But she did the sensible thing and accepted his deal.

I wrote the story of her road to freedom, carefully omitting any reference to my role because reporters in those days were supposed to be invisible. The News ran the story on Pg. 3. That was extraordinary, and not in a good sense. There were, at the time, 1,748 daily newspapers in the country. While a paper would occasionally campaign on behalf of a prisoner they felt was falsely convicted, and I can't recall hearing of a reporter actually digging up the evidence to free a convicted murderer.

Freeing Margaret Lynch was a singular accomplishment, but, as always, I was on to the next story.

Chapter 30 An Inspired And Shameless Con Job

VANCOUVER, B.C. — The cruise ship Oronsay had been docked and under quarantine for two weeks after an outbreak of typhoid fever and an avalanche of publicity about conditions on board.

I was late to the story. The only remaining mystery was where the fifty confirmed cases of on-board typhoid had come from. I was desperate for something that would distinguish my Sunday story from all the others. I was utterly shameless and freakishly lucky.

It was close to midnight on Friday when I wandered over to the British Columbia Provincial Health Department laboratory. The building was unlocked. There was one light on. The name stenciled on the door was Dr. Ernest J. Bowmer, the lab chief. The name was vaguely familiar. Then I placed it. I recalled a footnote in an article I'd read in the Journal of the American Public Health Association the year before. It referenced an article by an E.J. Bowmer, who had traced a case of typhoid to a woman whose septic tank drained directly into a river somewhere in British Columbia.

I knocked on the door and identified myself as a Detroit News reporter. He said only the provincial epidemiologist was authorized to speak. "That's okay," I said. "I just came by to shake your hand. You have been one of my heroes." He looked befuddled. I told him that I had grown up with "Eleven Blue Men," a dozen stories of extraordinary medical detective work published in 1953. That much was true. I told him I had been at the Dorobos fishery in Grand Haven, Michigan, in 1963 when "Sullivan" from the Center for Disease Control tracked down the source of the deadly Type E botulism outbreak. That was an inspired invention. I had been at The Grand Haven Daily Tribune but the year before the outbreak. I'd forgotten the name of the CDC detective, Larry Altman, who later became a New York Times medical writer and was to be my dinner companion when I got food poisoning in Philadelphia. "Sullivan" was actually the name of The Times' science writer. No matter. I was on a roll.

Then I told Dr. Bowmer I had read about his masterful work in tracking down a typhoid carrier and said how fortunate it was that the Oronsay had come to a city so well prepared to deal with the outbreak. I had no idea whether Bowmer's detective work was inspired, but Vancouver was, in fact, well prepared. He invited me in.

It was January, 1970. I had been flying out of the Niagara Air Force Base in New York with the Miami-based hurricane hunters, who were doing cloud seeding experiments over Lake Erie. Then I went on to Boulder, Colorado, to talk with scientists at the National Center for Atmospheric Research who were working on weather modification. An editor at The News who couldn't read a map called me and told me to hop on up to Vancouver and give him a Sunday story about the typhoid ship. It was a 1,080-mile hop.

Dr. Bowmer was caught between professional modesty and pride, but the chance to lay it all out to an admiring hero worshipper won. He told me his technicians tested the entire six hundred-person crew and most of the passengers with an uncomfortable purge technique that empties the bladder. They also conducted blood tests looking for three types of antigens the body produces to fight the typhoid bacteria.

The lab chief and his staff identified the strain of typhoid as native to the Indian subcontinent. They focused their attention on forty Goanese crewmen who had boarded the ship in England. A special serum was flown in from England and was used in the only test known to medicine that can pinpoint someone who has been hosting the typhoid bacteria for a long period of time, a carrier.

They succeeded in identifying the carrier as one of the Goanese crewmen and removed him from the ship. It was his fecal material, introduced into one section of the crew's potable water system, that had caused the outbreak. Bowmer said they hadn't yet told the man he was the carrier but were probably going to do it the coming weekend. Their solicitousness for a man who had contaminated a cruise ship's water supply, causing massive illness and millions of dollars in damages, was, well, Canadian. "We wouldn't think of identifying the carrier," the lab chief said. "It would make him an outcast, an untouchable, a pariah. The glare of publicity can be very demoralizing."

The Oronsay, one of ten British-based Peninsula & Orient cruise ships, had been on a round-the-world tour. From London, it had stopped in Cherbourg, Portuguese Madeira, Bermuda, Port Everglades, Nassau,

Cristobal, and Balboa in Panama, Acapulco, the Los Angeles port of San Pedro, and San Francisco before Vancouver.

The first passenger to get sick had gotten off in Florida, but the illness wasn't diagnosed as typhoid fever for two more weeks. As the ship entered the Canal Zone, several crew and passengers came down with what the Oronsay's two young doctors thought was flu. Typhoid is known as the "great pretender," but by the time the Oronsay approached San Francisco, the doctors suspected typhoid. A specialist consultant was brought on board, but San Francisco health authorities declined to hold the ship over night to await the lab test results that would confirm typhoid and make it their responsibility. In public, Canadian authorities were painfully proper in exonerating their American colleagues for passing the typhoid ship on to them. In private, they seethed.

There had been way too much going on for one person to cover. I hooked up with a Vancouver Sun reporter, trading him my Bowmer interview for his information on what the passengers had been doing to combat boredom. The Oronsay had been put on a very tight quarantine enforced by the Royal Canadian Mounted Police. The Sun reporter and I took turns trying to con or bluff our way past the Mountie guarding the gang plank. We failed to break the quarantine but still ended up with excellent Sunday stories.

Chapter 31 "Super Breeze" Borrows A .40, Hunts Me

Frankie "Super Breeze" Meyer borrowed a .40 caliber revolver from his uncle and told everybody who would listen that he was going to "kill that mother-fucker Cain." He made one visit outside the old Detroit Receiving Hospital, where he thought I might be hanging around.

I wasn't particularly frightened but thought it prudent to avoid my usual haunts. Frankie's pride had been wounded by an article naming him that I had written in The Detroit News after my under cover stint driving an ambulance in the inner city. I knew he was primarily showboating for friends.

But after two weeks of looking over my shoulder, I was sufficiently annoyed to set him up for arrest. Unfortunately, the Detroit Police grabbed the wrong Black man.

There is this reality about working undercover: Things never unfold the way you expect.

Several weeks before, I had been taking a smoking break while working as a phony medical student in Detroit Receiving Hospital's overcrowded and MASH-like emergency room. The Detroit Police, who operated what amounted to a non-medical snatch and transport ambulance service, had arrived at the ER dock with a drunk on a rubberized stretcher (rubberized to make it easier to hose off blood and vomit). I watched the officers on either end of the stretcher do the old heave heave-ho, bouncing the drunk off a brick wall and onto a hospital gurney parked there. I decided ambulances would be my next undercover assignment.

There was no time to establish a false identity, so I got a chauffeur's license and Red Cross first aid certificate in my own name. I figured only parents and politicians read bylines and that the risk would be minimal.

I was hired immediately by the misnamed Safeway Ambulance Co. and assigned to No. 19, an aging red Cadillac with soft springs, an empty oxygen bottle (which didn't matter because there was no regulator), and an inflatable splint for a child's femur. For my partner, I drew Frankie, a heroin addict who had served time for armed robbery and was in violation of his parole from Southern Michigan Prison in Jackson. "Mother, Jugs, and Speed" we were not.

We did no trauma work, instead subsisting on nursing home transfers and taking deathly sick poor people to Receiving Hospital on orders from the City Physician's Office. Frankie had me on edge from the beginning. He stole from patients, although few had much of of value. When we dropped off a patient at Receiving, he would come out with something under his tunic he had found lying around. And when we stopped for gas, he had me pump so he could loot the service bay.

One of our first calls was to a third-floor walk-up to transport an elderly man named Walter Sain, who was in his seventies and dying of pneumonia. His girlfriend, who was half Sain's age, met us at the door. She couldn't wait to tell us that he was the "famous Walter Sain, blind bank robber." I checked later. It was true. Several years earlier, she had walked him into a bank branch. He handed the teller a bag to fill with money and a note that said he had a gun. They didn't get far. She led us into his darkened bedroom. The lights had all burned out. The stench was overpowering, and roaches crunched under foot as we walked to the bed to load him on our stretcher. We got him to the hospital alive.

It was a twenty-four-hour job, but we were paid minimum wage for eight hours and had to sleep in a room next to the ambulances in a warehouse at Brush and Beaubien, one of the worst parts of the city. All night, there was the sound of crunching in the walls. It was probably mice, but I had convinced myself they were rats. I hate rats.

Sunday morning, my third day undercover, I got a nasty surprise. I picked up a copy of The Detroit News. The eight-column headline across the top of the front page read: "Dope pushers dash a landlord's hope" by Stephen Cain, News Staff Writer. I'd written the piece several weeks earlier. I hadn't thought to make sure my editors held it while I was undercover. A more sensible person would have bailed on the undercover assignment.

The article told of Maltese immigrant Charles Costa's efforts to stay afloat when the only tenants who regularly paid were each building's heroin dealers. I had visited four of Costa's inner-city apartment buildings, written about and listed the addresses of each, and included photos of each building's exterior.

One of his buildings, 35 Charlotte, had been the locale of the murder of an unarmed prostitute, Cynthia Scott, by a Detroit police officer in July, 1963. The slaying sparked a series of angry Black protests that prefigured the 1967 riots. Most of the many newspaper stories on the killing and the protests had mentioned the address, often with a photo.

The notoriety of the building attracted a "Murphy gang." The name comes from a Boston-Irish con of more than a century ago in which a make-believe pimp would tell a "John" looking for a prostitute, "I got a lady name of Mrs. Murphy who would like to give it to you." He would collect the fee and send the the John to an address where no one was waiting.

In the Detroit variation, the make-believe pimp would wait outside 35 Charlotte, directing Johns to an apartment on an upper floor. Once inside, the the John would be mugged and stripped of all his clothes. Costa thought to foil the gang by putting a case-hardened steel chain on the back door to cut off any escape. The gang called the fire marshal, who made Costa take it off. I interviewed the building manager, an elderly widow who said she had already given away all her late husband's clothes. "Mr. Cain," she said, "I'm tired of naked White Johns knocking on my door at all hours of the night!"

I was gambling that Frankie didn't read newspapers, and that, if he did see the headline, he wouldn't associate it with me. That Sunday evening, "Super Breeze" had me drive the ambulance to his dope house. The address plate over the door read "83 Edmund." It was the worst of the Costa buildings that I had featured in my article. "This place is full of bullet holes, and I've personally seen two bodies carried out," Costa had said. "I'm afraid to go in there alone, even with a gun."

Frankie and I were met at the door to an apartment by a person who was black as ink, stood at least 6-foot-4, weighed north of three hundred pounds, was naked to the waist, and wore a skin-tight black leotard. The voice was androgynous. The breasts could have been male or female, and what showed of the crotch was ambiguous. I introduced myself as "Steve" (no last name). The half-naked giant turned out to be pleasant, and fed me a fried pork chop and okra while Frankie bartered his stolen goods for a deck of heroin and shot up in the other room.

Once my pulse dropped closer to normal, I was able to taste the food. I was reminded of my favorite panel from "Up Front," Bill Malden's World War II book of his "Stars and Stripes" cartoons. It showed dogfaces Willie and Joe hunkered behind a ruined stone fence somewhere in France. The farm field was full of artillery craters, and machine-gun bullets buzzed overhead. Willie turned to Joe and said, "I feel like a fugitive from the law of averages."

Feeling more comfortable in my undercover role, I befriended two Black co-workers. They were both married and in their early thirties. They hated Safeway, Safeway owner Clyde Marshbank, and didn't have much use for Frankie. They saw Safeway as exploiting poor Blacks. But we were in the midst of a national recession (a depression in inner-city Detroit), and they had wives and children to feed.

I had written a story months earlier about Teamster-sponsored research showing that low-frequency vibrations, mainly tire noise, took a toll on the health of long-haul truckers. The president of a Teamsters local had insisted he owned me a favor. I gave him a call. He promised my two guys union jobs at a Kroger Supermarket loading dock at twice their current pay, plus benefits. I broke my cover, and told them about the jobs but said I needed them to keep tabs on Marshbank and Frankie for a couple of weeks. They were enthusiastic.

The day after my expose appeared, Frankie called Marshbank and asked if he could do a hit on me. Marshbank turned him down. Frankie offered to do it for $100. Marshbank turned him down again. One of my guys was with Frankie when he made the call. The other happened to be in Marshbank's Pontiac office.

I was sure Frankie wouldn't find his way to my home in a rural subdivision south of Ann Arbor. But I took the precaution of asking the couple that lived across the street to keep an eye out for an older car with at least two young Black men inside (I was profiling), and gave them the number of the U.S. marshal for the Eastern District of Michigan, a friend who happened live around the corner.

After a few days, I decided it was time to get Frankie off the streets and out of my life. I had my guys tell Frankie in front of witnesses that I probably would be covering a press conference with Detroit Police Chief

John Nichols at 1300 Beaubien. If Frankie wasn't bullshitting, they said, he should wait for Cain outside of police headquarters. They would all come along to watch. Frankie couldn't stand the idea of losing face after all his bragging.

Plainclothes officers from the 1st Precinct, which was housed at Police Headquarters, had Frankie's mugshot. Frankie showed up with a bunch of friends, but the cops grabbed the wrong Black man. They did catch up with Frankie later in the week, and he was shipped back to Jackson Prison.

I thanked the neighbors, and told them the danger was over. Pat, who had been nine months pregnant and approaching her due date while I was undercover, gave birth. Several weeks later, the neighbors across the street hosted a lawn party for all the families in the neighborhood. The woman told Pat, "You must be so glad that man is no longer trying to kill your husband." I hadn't told my wife.

Chapter 32 Peter Posey and Henry the Cigarette Eater

Things go bump in the night.

The heavy steel door was locked from the outside. The light switches were controlled by keys only the orderlies had. It was a cloudy night and pitch black in the dorm room I shared with fifteen other mental patients in a locked ward at Michigan's Northville State Hospital.

I awoke out of a deep sleep when a pair of hands grabbed my shirtfront, shaking me vigorously. A barely understandable voice demanded, "Cigarette, cigarette!" I broke his grip and rolled under the bed, a simple cot with a flat steel screen topped by a three-inch-thick mattress. The man I came to know as "Henry The Cigarette Eater" shuffled off to shake another patient. I climbed back into bed. Twice more, other patients woke me looking for cigarettes. The fourth time I was awakened that night was by an orderly wanting to know the color of my eyes so he could complete some paperwork.

The Detroit News published my undercover series in June, 1971, with the overheated title "Deadlier Than a Snake Pit." That was a misnomer. Northville wasn't Nellie Bly's 1887 "Ten Days in a Mad-House" or Ken Kesey's 1962 "One Flew Over the Cuckoo's Nest." Nevertheless, it destroyed patients, not with violence but through the combination of a patient care bureaucracy organized for the convenience of the bureaucrats and patients being unable to cope with the consequences of living too long in a psychotic culture. Medical science was just beginning to catch up with what I experienced firsthand.

The doc who prepared me for my role said I wouldn't be able to understand the consequences of living in a mental hospital unless I experienced its effects. He ruled out my going in as a psychotic depressive because the drug of choice would have tended to wipe out my near-term memory. Schizophrenia was out because even the worst diagnostician would pick up on someone trying to fake disassociative rambling. Also, giving a sane person Thorazine, the drug favored for treating schizophrenia,, could produce psychotic symptoms. That would call for more Thorazine until the patient was effectively a zombie.

We settled on reactive depression with psychomotor retardation. That meant I couldn't cope with the self-induced failures in my life and was spiraling downhill toward suicide. My surrogate wife (fellow reporter Barbara Hoover) set the stage with a series of increasingly frantic calls to the Wayne County Suicide Prevention Bureau. She said her husband was talking about killing himself but refused to go to the hospital. Finally, she called the bureau to say that her cousin was taking her husband (me) to Detroit Receiving Hospital. She asked the bureau to call and tell the hospital I was coming. The fact that another bureaucracy knew an incoming patient was suicidal was insurance guaranteeing Receiving wouldn't let me fall between the cracks.

I was diagnosed "correctly" in Receiving's ER and ordered to Northville. I had to wait in a chair next to a man in an acute schizophrenic episode who had been strapped to his gurney. As I sat with my head bowed, a professor at Wayne State University Medical School, with half a dozen students in tow, paused in front of the schizophrenic. "Seen any pythons?" he asked. I came half-way out of my chair before sitting down again so as not to break cover. It was seventeen hours before the ambulance showed up to take me to Northville.

It was Safeway Ambulance, the target of my earlier undercover expose. The driver and attendant were two of the hostile men I'd worked with. But in preparing for this undercover assignment at Northville, I'd gone ten days without a shower. I had a seven-day growth of beard, no mustache, no glasses, dirty, longish hair, and I kept my head down. They didn't recognize me but still wanted to put both me and an elderly older woman they were transporting in restraints. I had this paranoid thought that they would recognize me mid-trip, kick a helpless me out the back door of the moving ambulance, and claim I had gone berserk and jumped. They were furious when the hospital's ambulance supervisor ordered them not to put us in restraints. I could have kissed her.

The entrance into K Ward was through a steel door with solenoid bolts that clicked loudly into place behind me. It was the sound of finality. Leaning against the hallway wall was a tall, slender, deathly pale man with one blue eye and one brown eye who was staring at me. "Don't look at me!" he shouted as an orderly led me past.

Life on the ward was deadly boredom. The midnight shift would roust us ninety minutes before breakfast and lock both the dorm rooms and the day room behind us, Isolating us in the hall. That made it easier for the orderlies to conduct the morning census and hand out medications. There were no chairs, so you learned to sit with your back against the wall, your legs splayed in front of you. You had to ask an attendant for your toothbrush and toothpaste. Most men didn't. Bad teeth were pulled, not filled, because it was easier. Meals were ten minutes long and not memorable. I was lucky to find a six-month-old magazine to read in the day room. There were ratty incomplete decks of playing cards and an overhead television, but only the staff could change channels.

About half the patients were chronics, including back-ward neurosyphilis patients whose brains had been eaten out by spirochetes (think Capone at the end), and one-time acutes who had been ground down by staying so long and had become lifers. The schizophrenics, bipolar, and depressive patients, brought in during the acute phases of their conditions, were supposed to be released once they had been stabilized on drugs. Sometimes that happens.

The ward was a cigarette culture. The heavily drugged and slow-moving Henry, who had no money for cigarettes, would shuffle after elderly patients, pinning them in a chair or against the end of a sofa, extracting their smokes. Once lit, he would puff energetically, chewing the tobacco on one end and flicking the ash off the other end with a finger until the burning end flicked off. Other patients would follow Henry around to pick up the remnants of his cigarettes. Another patient fished cigarette butts out of the urinal to dry and smoke. He always peed on the bathroom floor, which made perverse sense.

Shower day was the best illustration of what it meant to your humanity and sanity to live on the ward. All thirty-three of us were locked in a day room and made to strip, putting pants in one pile, shirts in another, underwear and socks in a third. Then we sat naked, pressed against the wall, for more than an hour while the staff showered the most helpless patients.

There was one patient named Peter Posey, the man who had shouted at me when I first came on to the ward. He would move from patient to patient, shaking his genitals in our faces, and yelling, "Hee, hee, hee, hee."

The attendants usually weren't there to restrain him. But if you got up and slugged him, you would to get a shot of tranquilizer and be put in a padded cell. You learned to survive all the daily insults by disconnecting yourself from your environment, letting your eyes and mind glaze over, effectively turning yourself from an acute into a chronic. I was there less than a week, and I and could feel myself withdrawing.

The ward was run by a charge nurse. I was initially wary of her, thinking of Ken Kesey's "Big Nurse," but she seemed mostly involved in managing her staff. I never saw her interact with any of the patients. The only problem I had with the staff was with a well-meaning psychiatric social worker, a man of about my age, who seemed to see elements of himself in my troubles. He singled me out for friendly conversations, and I quickly reached the limits of my carefully prepared cover story. I didn't dare try to ad-lib, so I feigned anger and said, "I don't want you inside my head." He backed off.

My cover name was Michael Hoover, Michael because it was our eldest son's first name and easy to remember, and Hoover because it was my surrogate wife's last name. I had needed to use fellow reporter Barbara Hoover's address so I would be to sent to Northville rather than Ypsilanti State Hospital.

One patient came up to me and said, "You're not a patient. You're here to spy on us." Gulp. I asked why he would say that, fearing my cover was broken. "Your name is Hoover," he said. "You're here from the FBI." I protested that J. Edgar Hoover was in his seventies and didn't have any children. "I know," he said, walking away laughing.

I was worried about taking notes. I had taught myself mirror image writing as a kid after learning that was that was how Leonardo DaVinci protected his lab notes from the Inquisition. After a few pages, I realized that nobody cared and reverted to regular writing. I recorded several versions of this conversation with the attendants:

Q. "What are you doing, Mr. Hoover?"

A. "Writing a letter to my wife."

Q. "What are you writing about, Mr. Hoover?"

A. "This place."

Q. "What are you saying about it, Mr. Hoover?"

A. "That I don't like it."

Q. "That's nice, Mr. Hoover."

That's the principle from Edgar Allen Poe's "The Purloined letter." You hide something secret in plain view where no one would think to look. Then there was attendant Frank Winchester, a nineteen-year-old Black man who had yet to be socialized into the ways of the ward. "You should take it to the newspaper," he said of my letters. "Okay," I said. "No, I mean it," he insisted. "Okay," I said.

I faced the problem of how to get out without breaking the cover. I could just see myself confiding to a staffer that I was really a reporter. "That's nice, Mr. Hoover." After a day on the ward, I had switched from depressive to hyper. It was the only way I could interact with patients and staff on my own terms, but it scared the hell out of the staff. When a suicidal patient suddenly becomes asymptomatic, even manic, it usually means they have decided with finality to end their life and are only waiting for the right opportunity when they can do it without interruption.

The ward psychiatrist called me in on the fourth day and probed for the reason my depression had suddenly vanished. I told him I didn't like this place, that I saw all those people who were really sick, and realized I had been magnifying my problems. He didn't quite believe me, so he set a trap. He said how delighted he was at my recovery. He said he would release me that afternoon so I could go home, have a nice dinner with my wife, and begin repairing that relationship. Then he said I would come back in the morning. We would talk, and he would then give me a full release. If I had been genuinely suicidal, I would have jumped at the opportunity. I refused. Suppose things went really well at home, and I had to face the depressing prospect of returning. I told him I would wait until he was ready to release me, which he did the next day. I slept okay my first night home, had a full-blown nightmare the second night. Then I was fine.

I wrote the stories of my five days on the ward. Before they were printed, I made an appointment as Stephen Cain to see Northville Hospital Superintendent Dr. Richard Budd. I told him I had been in his hospital. "You didn't need to sneak in. I would have given you a tour," he said. I explained I had come in as a patient under cover. His face became a frozen mask. I handed him a copy of the stories, something journalists supposedly never do, and offered him the opportunity to alert me to any factual errors. I had inferred certain policies and estimated staffing levels, for example. I told him I would correct factual errors but that he shouldn't try to talk me out of what I had seen. I told Dr. Budd that there would be one more story, his. He could either get into a pissing contest with me, which he would lose, or he could acknowledge the problems the hospital faced and talk candidly about what he would need to correct them. He took the second option.

When I came back to the ward after the stories were printed, I reintroduced myself to Frank Winchester. He remembered the conversation with Mr. Hoover. He, laughed so hard I thought he would get sick. I had been worried that the acute patients I had befriended would feel betrayed. Some celebrated my return to sanity. Others understood I had done it for them.

I wanted to think that my stories helped the hospital clean up its act, but I found no evidence of meaningful, lasting change. However, my psychiatric social worker, too far down the chain of authority to confront bureaucratic stupidity directly, told me he used to say at staff meetings, "My God, what if Cain found out?" He used that as a wedge to counter idiocies.

The hospital would discharge patients into the care of the chronically under-funded community mental health system. For years, I would get calls from parents who felt I was sympathetic and were desperate to get help for their mentally ill adult children. Sometimes, I could help, mostly not.

The Michigan Department of Mental Health billed The Detroit News for my stay. The News paid.

The hospital limped along until it was closed for good in 2003.

Chapter 33 Manipulating justice to save a junkie

The car raced down Reid in southwest Detroit, braking to a screeching stop in the middle of the street. Freddy and Effie Pruitt, working in their front yard a few feet away, watched as two men, hunched over with objects hidden under their coats, jumped out and ran into the apartment building across the street. Then the car sped off around the corner.

Effie Pruitt turned to a neighbor standing nearby. "I wonder what they've stolen now," she recalled telling him. "I thought it was a TV or something." Under their coats were money bags taken from Brinks guard Stanley P. Kaniuk, whom they had murdered only minutes before in the stairway of the General Motors Fisher Body (Ternstedt) Plant six blocks away.

The Pruitts flagged down a Detroit Police car running full code: Lights and sirens. They told the officers what they had seen. More patrol cars flooded to the location. Uniformed officers, guns drawn, ran into the apartment building as many of the building's residents poured into the street. "There's the driver," said one of the Pruitts, pointing out Glenn Ford, 20, who had just exited the apartment building's front door. Ford was arrested on the spot. It was an unprompted, spontaneous identification.

Inside the building, officers found Dwight D. Hunt, twenty, in an apartment with the two Brinks money bags. William Teasley, twenty-six, was found in the basement hiding behind the building's furnace. He had Kaniuk's gun, which Hunt had used to put two bullets into the back of the guard's head. It was the kind of case that prosecutors dream of, the kind that guarantees slam-dunk convictions. The problem was that the Pruitts had made an honest mistake. The actual getaway driver was Ford's half-brother, Tony Heard, twenty-four, who had fled unnoticed out the apartment building's back door.

I had been doing a series of in-depth stories on the criminal justice system for The Detroit News. It was the fall of 1971. The city in those years had posted either the highest or close to the highest homicide rate in the nation. I had cut a deal with Detroit Police Chief John Nichols to spend time with homicide detectives as they worked on cases in real- time. I would be present at everything they did without restriction, but I would only write about closed cases of the same detectives. That way I wouldn't taint their cases with pre-trial publicity. I had made an absolute and unconditional pledge to Nichols.

I was with Detective Sergeants Robert Smith and John Roffey as they assembled the evidence against the three Ternstedt killers. Roffey took me aside and laid out the reasons he believed they had the wrong half half-brother. I agreed with his assessment. But he said he couldn't buck Smith, who was the senior officer. He wanted me to win Ford's release, something he felt he couldn't do. In those days, things were looser in the world of big-city journalism. Even at that, I shudder to think of all the lines I crossed. My editors never questioned me on what I was doing, so I simply plunged ahead.

Heard, the guilty half half-brother, was a smalltime heroin dealer. The Detroit Police Narcotics Bureau told me who Heard worked for and supplied me with the addresses of five dope houses the boss dealer ran. This was several years before most dope dealing moved from inside to street corners.

The boss dealer had a case coming up in Detroit Recorder's Court. His lawyer, a former homicide detective who had gone nights to the Detroit College of Law, agreed that the three of us could meet in the courthouse. I outlined what I knew of the man's heroin operation, including the addresses of his dope houses. I asked that he set up a meeting between Heard and me at a time and place of his choosing. I said I had no interest in him or his business and wouldn't hold him responsible for whatever Heard decided to do, as long as Heard agreed to meet with me. He turned to his lawyer, who said I could be trusted.

Three months following his half half-brother's arrest, Heard met me in his aunt's apartment. He said he didn't know how he could help his brother without putting himself in prison for the rest of his life. I took him to meet the disbarred former partner of Ford's lawyer, Samuel Gardner. Gardner, a friend, eventually would become Detroit Recorder's Court's chief judge.

The disbarred attorney, a man with street credibility, met privately with Heard. Afterward, I took Heard to meet with the detectives. He admitted to driving the getaway car to the plant, but said he left it there and walked back to the apartment building. He fingered the two killers and insisted his brother had nothing to do with the crime.

Sgt. Smith came around to the belief that Ford was probably innocent but insisted that Ford stand trial. The sergeant's position was straightforward: The criminal justice system should run its course without regard to a policeman's belief in a defendant's guilt or innocence.

I explained the situation to Michael Connor, chief of the Wayne County Prosecutor's Recorders Court Division and also a friend. He met with the attorneys for Hunt and Teasley. The deal was struck that would allow Hunt and Teasley to plead guilty to second second-degree murder and be sentenced to life in prison. Unlike felony murder, which is life without the possibility of parole, the lesser plea meant that Hunt and Teasley might, in theory, be free someday. It also freed them to testify that Ford was not the getaway driver.

The trial, in front of Judge William J. Giovan, was a morass of conflicting testimony. Ford testified he was in the apartment when Hunt and Teasley were planning the robbery but was high on heroin and only vaguely aware of what was going on. He said he didn't leave the apartment until the pair returned. The case was hanging in the balance.

"I can't testify," Heard told me. "They'll get me for murder." But he agreed to meet one more time with the disbarred attorney, who told him that, if he testified to driving the car to the plant but took the Fifth Amendment against self-incrimination on whether he drove the killers back to the apartment, he might escape prosecution.

That's what Heard testified to under oath, but the court adjourned for the day before the assistant prosecutor could complete his cross-examination. Heard was a no-show the next morning. The judge delayed the trial for an hour. If the assistant prosecutor couldn't complete his cross-examination, he could ask that Heard's entire testimony be stricken.

There was a young man in the visitor's gallery who seemed out of place amid the usual court watchers. I took a guess, and asked him if he could find Heard. Sergeant Smith gave him a dime for the pay phone. Twenty minutes later, with the assistant prosecutor half way through his closing argument, Heard called the court. Judge Giovan, who was aware of the backstory, recessed the court until Heard arrived. The assistant prosecutor concluded his cross-examination. The jury took only thirty minutes to return a not-guilty verdict. Ford walked out of the courtroom arm-and-arm with his mother, a free man for the first time in six months. No charges were brought against Heard.

I wrote a story published under the headline "How an innocent man won freedom." This was the second time I had freed someone on first-degree murder charges, but I omitted any reference to my role. The journalistic ethic in those days was that a reporter was never a part of his story. Moreover, my actions in bending the system of justice to achieve the right outcome couldn't stand the light of day. Everything I had done depended on trust. Both of the detectives, Connor, Giovan, Gardner, his disbarred former partner, Heard, his dope boss, and even the boss' lawyer all depended on my being good to my word. Telling everything would have compromised them.

Giovan, who remains a friend to this day, told me later that he had thought for years about writing a book about the case but never got around to it. I went on to other stories.

The News had been illustrating stories on street drug use with an absurd picture of a hypodermic needle. In the name of authenticity, I had a patrolman friend shake down a junkie for a deck of heroin wrapped in tinfoil, a used cooking spoon with the handle doubled over, a nylon stocking to tie off the arm, and a needle taped to the end of an eyedropper. After the photographers took their pictures, I stored "the works" in my desk.

Ford would come by my office at The News about once a year with a tale such as needing bus fare so he could get to a drug treatment program in Flint. I would offer Ford the choice of the works, which was what he really wanted, or $20. He knew if he chose the works, he could never come back. He accepted the money. Five years later, he joined the Seventh Seventh-Day Adventists and turned his life around.

Chapter 34 He Watched The Waters Take His Mother

RAPID CITY, South Dakota -- I was driving up Dark Canyon Road toward where the Canyon Lake Dam used to be. A slender, middle-aged man was sitting with his feet dangling off the side of the road, facing Rapid Creek, his elbows on his knees, his face cupped in his hands.

I parked the car, walked over, and sat down next to him, saying nothing. He started talking. His name was Don Taylor, a building contractor. He had constructed fourteen homes on a shelf of flood-plain land just a few feet above the creek. He'd built his own house on the opposite side of the road on high land overlooking the creek.

When the power went out, he ran down toward where he was building a house for his mother, Flora Taylor, eighty. The earthen dam had already burst. The water was too high, rushing too fast. He had installed her in a mobile home during construction. She had lit a candle. He could see the candle light moving back and forth in her window, but he couldn't get to her.

"Stan Bice and I were up on the road," he said. "Then Stan's house cut loose from its foundation. We saw his house ram right through my mother's trailer. Then it was gone in the darkness." The water took four more of the houses he had built, mostly sold to people he knew.

The final tally for the sixth worst river flood in the nation's history was 238 dead, 3,057 injured, 1,335 houses destroyed, and more than five thousand cars demolished. A Chicago Tribune reporter and I were the last journalists in town before they temporarily shut down the airport and access roads. It was a short respite from the breathless television hoards that descent on even minor tragedies.

I had been riding with two Detroit Police patrolmen in the high-crime Tenth (Livernois) Precinct on mid-day Saturday, June 10, 1972, when the call came over the radio to take their passenger to 615 W. Lafayette, Code Three (lights and siren). I was met at the front steps of my Detroit News office by Assistant Managing Editor Boyd Simmons, a portable typewriter in one hand, $500 cash in the other. He said I had barely enough time to catch a flight from Detroit Metro to St. Louis, connecting to Rapid City.

Details of the killer flood were just coming in. I was supposed to be at a party that night. I told Simmons to call my wife. He forgot.

The memories that move me even to this day are not so much the scenes of destruction but of the people who exceeded the limits of their jobs, some who worked quietly to make a difference, the few who failed their moment of truth, the personal tragedies, and one monumental irony. Those were the stories I wrote.

Alex Koscielski, a meteorologist with the South Dakota School of Mines, watched the storm build up on his radar and called Derry Newby of the U.S. Weather Bureau at the Rapid City Airport. Newby had only a radar repeater, so he called the nearby Ellsworth Air Force base. Their radar was down. An amateur weatherman in the Black Hills called in a rain estimate from his backyard gauge.

Newby was supposed to feed his information to the river forecast office in Sioux Falls, which was to relay it to Kansas City before any flood warning was issued. He realized there was no time. He issued the flash-flood warning on his own. It turned out that thirteen inches of rain had fallen within a short period of time on a fifty square mile section of the rocky Black Hills west of town. Without that warning, many more would have died.

Henry Baker, a former mayor and retired banker, had been named Civil Defense operations chief. He heard the warning siren while at a Shriners meeting. He thought it was an exaggeration, went home, and slept through the disaster even though his residence was only two blocks from the high-water mark.

City patrolman Sam Roach pulled two men from a floating car and drove them to the Mountain View Rest Home and adjoining Bennett-Clarkston Community Hospital. The trio evacuated seventy-three senior citizens to safety only to have one of the residents, ninety-year-old Ena Ellison, slip back into the rest home just as a flood-weakened west wall collapsed onto her.

Dan Simpson left his younger brother and his wife of three months, Claudia, on the roof of their small home as he went off to help in the rescue effort. He turned around to see his house collapse and the roof supporting his wife and brother float off. The boy grabbed a tree and lived. Claudia's body was found three days later.

Ron Stevenson, fifty-three, the owner of a piano company, rescued a Native American family from a floating trailer and then made his way to the Pennington County Courthouse, which was designated to serve as the staging area for formal rescue operations. But no one was in charge.

The county's CD director was stranded in the Black Hills. The county commission chairman was trapped up a tree. The deputy CD director, a pleasant and unassuming woman of advancing years, had developed laryngitis. Someone asked Stevenson a question. He answered. Someone else asked him another question. He answered. Within a few minutes, he became the de- facto disaster coordinator. A master sergeant from the air force base, who happened to be in town when the waters hit, organized many of the rescue efforts. What struck me was that, when the bureaucracy broke down, competent people simply stepped in, and others followed their lead.

If someone was handing out medals, one should go to Ron Koenig, associate director of Wayne State University's Center for the Psychological Study of Death, Dying, and Lethal Behavior. In town to speak at a conference on death and dying, he organized a cadre of doctors, nurses, social workers, ministers, and Red Cross volunteers to staff Rapid City's three funeral homes. There were close to two hundred bodies and more coming in all the time. They were laid out like cord wood in the funeral home garages and covered with sheets. Bodies caught in flooding are bloated, pasty white, battered, and often stripped of their clothes. I tried to imagine the horror of going from body to body to body looking for a missing loved one. What Koenig's team did was to inventory every body by sex, approximate age, height, and weight, noting any clothes and identifying characteristics. It meant fewer bodies for loved ones to look at. Team members served as guides and grief counselors in the process. In two days, they had half the bodies identified, Koenig said. I spent little time in the garages.

I've always had mixed feelings about the Red Cross. They do a lot of good work, and they came to town with almost their entire national disaster staff of fifty full-time workers. The very first thing I saw them do was stretch a massive Red Cross banner across the front of a school being set up as an emergency shelter. They advertise their presence and never miss an opportunity for a national fund-raising campaign.

I was more impressed by the blond kid in bib overalls with a wooden tool box who was rebuilding a woman's ruined porch. He wouldn't give an interview, but he told me I could help. I did for a couple of hours. What I learned was that he was part of the Mennonite Relief Corps, and he would stay until the job was done.

The irony, or perhaps you should call it karma, was that the city fathers had used the federal Urban Renewal Program to evict members of the Oglala Sioux Nation, who lived in slum conditions along the banks of Rapid Creek as it snaked through the center of town. The displaced Native Americans were moved to public housing, which was built on high ground safely outside the city limits. That opened the way for the car dealerships and other business enterprises that the flood swept away.

Chapter 35 I Savage A Rival Reporter

The cloak of self-righteousness doesn't sit well on the shoulders of reporters, including mine.

The Detroit Free Press was running a series of sensational front-page stories in the early 1970s about the Internal Revenue Service's war against Belleville tax preparer Mary McKee. The war took the form of a series of punishing assessments, liens, and garnishments against her clients, all recounted in agonizing detail by the Free Press.

My editors at The Detroit News, embarrassed by the Free Press' exclusives, ordered me to follow up so we could have our own stories. Chasing somebody else's scoop is about the most hated assignment a reporter can draw. The follow-up story almost always comes off as a pathetic imitation of the original.

I would have preferred to do a quick-and-dirty and be done with it. But a lawyer-friend of my parents, a man I had known for years growing up and who had sold me my first car, had a story to tell. He said a client of his had sent extensive business records to McKee, but she had failed to file his tax returns. Moreover, she refused to give back his records unless he paid her for work she claimed to have done. Months had gone by. Interest and penalties from the IRS were piling up and would only continue to grow. The client finally paid McKee what the lawyer characterized as her extortion, extortion since she had, in fact, done no work.

That motivated me to start seriously digging into McKee. It turned out she had been fabricating deductions and exemptions for her clients. For a local barber, she had claimed more chairs in his shop than he actually had. For another client, she invented an employee so she could deduct his phantom pay from the client's taxable income. Her clients were delighted with the money she was saving them.

When the IRS started challenging the returns, she convinced her clients to stay home, to let her deal with the government. And when the IRS started imposing liens on her clients, she claimed this was simply part of the government's campaign against her.

It was possible that the Free Press reporter, a Pulitzer Prize winner, had simply been sloppy. It seemed more likely to me that he had chosen to turn a blind eye to what McKee was doing. In my stories, I called out The Free Press and the reporter by name. Getting personal wasn't necessary to correct the record, but I was angry at the assignment and angry at the other reporter. There was animosity between the papers. It was one of the two most intense newspaper rivalries in the country. The other was The Chicago Tribune versus The Chicago Sun-Times. My editors were happy to take a shot at The Free Press, and they didn't tone down my story in the slightest. The Free Press dropped the McKee story after mine appeared.

The feds ended up indicting McKee on twenty eight counts of fraudulent tax preparation. She was convicted on fifteen counts and sentenced to three years in prison. The convictions were upheld on appeal.

I had a chance to take a second bite out of the same reporter but declined. His Free Press story had severely criticized Washtenaw Circuit Court Judge James R. Breakey Jr. for improperly holding open an estate for almost two decades despite a demand from one of the heirs that the remaining assets be liquidated and the estate closed. Breakey, appointed to the bench in 1945, had gone on to become one of the most respected jurists in the state and the dominant political influence in the county. I had a personal issue with Judge Breakey and was perfectly happy to see him taken down a peg. But I never could leave things alone.

My personal issue with the judge started with Washtenaw County Clerk Luella Smith's method of jury panel selection. She divided all the registered voters into separate envelopes for Ann Arbor, Ypsilanti, four small towns, and twenty townships. To assemble a jury panel, she would draw one name from each envelope. That meant that, at the beginning of the year, each jury panel would be overwhelmingly from rural townships. The panels would become increasingly urban as the year went on and the supply of voters from the lightly populated township voters was exhausted.

Earlier in the year, defense attorney Arthur Carpenter had an African-American client from Ypsilanti who faced the prospect of an overwhelmingly rural, White jury, hardly a jury of his peers. Carpenter challenged the jury selection process and was certain to win on the facts. Breakey was willing to give Carpenter's client a more representative jury but was pressuring the attorney not to upset the judicial apple cart. If newspaper stories on Carpenter's suit forced the judge to throw out Smith's jury selection process on constitutional grounds, it could unravel previous convictions.

Judge Breakey refused to talk to me, so I went to Judge John Conlin. He walked me into Breakey's office and asked my questions for me. Breakey answered his fellow judge and then told me I would "seriously regret it" if I printed his answers. I caved. My failure to write the full story potentially cost a number of defendants the basis for challenging their constitutionally flawed convictions. I hated myself for giving in, and vowed to never again allow myself to be bullied.

I was tempted to let stand the Free Press story savaging Judge Breakey. It was entirely factual as far as it went. But I knew there was more. I swallowed my anger and wrote the rest of the story.

The bulk of the estate had consisted of German World War I bonds that were virtually worthless at the time of the death. But Breakey, who treated the estate as a hobby, held the estate open while he negotiated for years with the West German government. He made at least one trip to West Germany and ended up collecting most of the bonds' face value. The interim distribution to the heirs was several times the estate's initial value. Moreover, Breakey had not billed the estate for any of his services. He continued to hold the estate open to get the best price for the last piece of property.

Breakey had violated the legal requirement that an estate be closed within ten years, but he did so to the immense benefit of the heirs. The Free Press reporter's main source was the husband of one of the heirs, who wanted the last property in the estate immediately sold so his wife would get the final distribution. The other heirs were quite happy with the money Breakey won for the estate.

My story took a balanced look at the good and bad the judge had done, took a bite out of the greedy husband, and ignored the Free Press entirely.

Chapter 36 Old Crow Survives A Pipeline

INUVIK — It was the 11 p.m. closing time at the Mackenzie Inn. On the floor were several pools of blood and vomit. There were thirty Inuit and Metis (mixed-race) men and women in the barroom, most asleep or passed out. A young Inuit woman approached me and my companion, Aris Foster, a Canadian jobs program officer. If we had a bottle, she said she would go to our room with us. We turned her down.

It was mid-summer in this Northwest Territories city, which meant there was a thin layer of slick mud over the permafrost street. When the drunks from the Mackenzie Inn stepped off the boardwalk, some did the Arctic Circle version of slipping on a banana peel. It was not funny.

Drunkenness and epidemic VD were what oil and gas brought to the native peoples of the far north. Inuvik was what Old Crow hoped to avoid becoming. This was why I was heading the next morning to Old Crow, the only Yukon settlement inside the Arctic Circle. A Canadian government panel would be holding a hearing on whether to recommend a pipeline that would forever change this village of two hundred First Nation Vuntut Gwich'in and three Whites: A Mountie, an Anglican priest, and a shopkeeper married to a native woman.

American Natural Resources, the parent company of Michigan Consolidated Gas Company, had put together a consortium of seventeen companies that wanted to build a pipeline to carry natural gas from Prudhoe Bay in Alaska to the Trans-Canada Pipeline. If built, it would supply about 10 percent of Michigan's natural gas needs.

It was late June, 1977, and my first stop was Ottawa to interview the senior member of the pro-development Canadian National Energy Board and the national energy minister, both of whom favored the pipeline.

Then it was on to Yellow Knife for a sit-down with Northwest Territories Commissioner Stuart Hodgson. Hodgson, who proudly said the native people called him the Inuit phrase for "Old Walrus," insisted that people from down south shouldn't be trying to save a culture that was already dead. "You've crossed the Red Sea, and the waters have closed behind you," he said. "You can't go back." Foster, whose heritage was a mixture of Inuit (Eskimo), Dene (First Nation), Black, Irish, and English, said no one had told Hodgson that, to the Inuit, Old Walrus was a term of derision.

Sam Raddi, the blind Inuit who headed the influential Committee on Original Peoples Entitlement (COPE), insisted that the native cultures would survive just fine if they could win their land claims and put a harness on oil and gas development. Besides, they had Canadian Prime Minister Pierre Elliott Trudeau (Justin's father) on their side as long as no one disrupted the fragile political balance.

Raddi told me a marvelous story of how Leonard Peltier, out on bond for the murder of two FBI agents at the Pine Ridge Reservation in South Dakota, had gotten permission from the federal court to take a "fishing trip" to northern Canada along with Russell Means, a fellow member of the American Indian Movement (AIM).

Their real intent was to organize their "brown brothers" up north. Raddi said the Inuit, Metis, and Dene were already well organized, and he feared that Peltier's visit would be used by conservative Whites such as Hodgson to undermine Trudeau's support. Raddi had his people meet Peltier and Means at the airport, loaded them into a float plane, and dropped them off at a remote fishing camp, where they remained incommunicado until it was time to return to the states.

After my stopover in Inuvik, I hitched a ride on a Trans-North Air charter to Old Crow. The five young First Nation men, who had chartered the plane to return home, said I could come along if I paid half the tab. They congratulated themselves about hustling the White guy, but they actually saved me having to pay full price for my own charter.

We were met by two Mounties, who checked our luggage for alcohol. In addition, I was greeted by thirty seven mosquitoes between disembarking the plane and slipping inside the Mounties' hut. I counted the bites. Because of the billions of tiny puddles left by melting permafrost during the Arctic's brief summer, the bloodsuckers are so thick they actually exsanguinate some caribou calves born on the north slope of the Richardson Mountains. Deet worked for me. The Old Crow residents were largely unbothered by the bloodsuckers.

John Joe Kay, the village's elected chief and its best traditional fiddler, didn't know The Detroit News from Adam. But he said the village would like to host a dinner for me and hold a jigging contest in my honor. The roasted caribou was stringy. I thoroughly enjoyed the music even though I knew the "contest" was actually the rehearsal for their planned concert for the government commission the next day.

Kay and the others played English, Scottish, and Irish jigs that musicologists say were largely unchanged from the tunes brought up the Arctic Red River by Appalachian trappers beginning in 1836.

"My grandfather's name means 'Man Who Raises Family Out of This Land,'" Kay told the commission the next day. "His son, Joe Kay, raised a family out of this land. I have raised my family out of this land. I now have grandchildren that I am teaching."

Very few aboriginal cultures have been able to survive the onslaught of Western technology, goods, money, booze, disease, religion, and music. Old Crow has preserved much of the old ways.

Most of the native villages of the far north were either Anglican or Roman Catholic, depending upon which missionary had arrived first. There was a tacit understanding between the branches of Christianity that life was fragile in the far north, and you didn't poach on the other's village.

Old Crow was Anglican, but in the 1950s, the Catholic Oblate provincial, whose district included the Yukon, ordered one of his priests to Old Crow. Not willing to rip the village apart by competing for souls, the Catholic priest built a meeting hall rather than a formal church, and donated it to the band. It was where they staged my jigging contest. The old priest had said Mass there every Sunday. Everyone was welcome, but he didn't proselytize and very few had attended.

The Anglican priest also told me his Oblate counterpart had never skied in his life but got the idea that cross-country skiing might give the young people a purpose. He begged for and got equipment. The young people took to it with such intensity that five of them made a Canadian Olympic team in the early 1960s.

The Vuntut Gwich'in have been in Old Crow, located at the confluence of the Porcupine and Crow rivers, for at least a thousand years. Archeological digs on either side of the village indicate that it may have been occupied since shortly after the end of the last ice age some twenty thousand years ago.

What sustained the people of Old Crow and their ancestors was the 125,000-head Porcupine caribou herd that winters in Alaska. A major branch of the herd's migration crosses the Porcupine River shallows just west of the village. The villagers shoot enough animals to meet their annual needs, quarter the carcasses, suspend them several feet into the permafrost, and cover the pits with boards and dirt. That keeps the frozen meat fresh until the next migration.

The villagers told the commission that, in addition to their fear of Inuvik-like changes, they worried a pipeline would alter the migration pattern of the caribou.

In the years since I left Old Crow, the young people have built a sophisticated and extensive web site that they use both to preserve and promote Vuntut Gwich'in culture and to lobby the outer world on behalf of the village. The band finally succeeded in expanding the local education through high school, heavily involving the village elders in teaching about the culture and language.

And they haven't had to deal with consequences of a pipeline. The pipeline commission, chaired by the chief justice of the British Columbia Supreme Court, drafted the most persuasive environmental and social impact statement I've ever read and voted to kill the project. And it looks like Old Crow will continue to be spared. Fracking, the process of extracting gas from shale that is so hated by many progressives and environmentalists, has lowered gas prices sufficiently to make an Arctic gas pipeline to the Mackenzie uneconomical for the foreseeable future.

Chapter 37 Gallows Humor Keeps Us Sane

Judge Crater is missing., So is Amelia Earhart. D.B. Cooper, the only successful hijacker in the history of aviation, has never been found. Teamster-mobster Jimmy Hoffa disappeared without a trace. Each spawned a mini-industry devoted to speculating how they met their fate.

Among the reporters at The Detroit News, "Whatever became of Jimmy?" was an informal parlor game with an overlay of gallows humor.

Hoffa was installed as president of the Teamsters Union in 1957 with the help of the Mafia. He rewarded the Mob bosses by allowing them to use the Teamsters Central States Pension Fund as their personal piggy bank during his fourteen years at the helm of the union. He was a business partner of the Mob, not a subservient tool.

Hoffa was convicted of jury tampering and sent to federal prison in 1971. But President Richard Nixon, who had strong political support from the Teamsters, pardoned Hoffa with the proviso that he stay out of union affairs. Hoffa had been replaced on an interim basis by Frank Fitzsimmons, who was widely seen as a Mob patsy.

On July 30, 1975, Hoffa, amid reports that he was planning to move against Fitzsimmons, agreed to a lunch date with a New Jersey Mafia boss and the Detroit Mob's chief enforcer. They were to meet at the Machus Red Fox Restaurant in Bloomfield Township north of Detroit, but neither mobster showed up. Hoffa was last seen at the restaurant. No one has ever doubted that it was a Mafia hit.

At The News, the two most popular theories were that Jimmy was encased in cement being poured for the Walter P. Reuther Freeway (the two powerful labor leaders hated each other) or in the footings of the Renaissance Center, which was then under construction.

Another theory that was at least superficially plausible was that Hoffa was either double buried or cremated by the Grosse Pointe Park funeral home that served the Mob.

The Quaserone brothers, low level mobsters, had reportedly won a small soap factory in a poker game. The theory there was that Hoffa was run through the rending vats. I suggested that the soap could be marketed under the slogan "Come clean with Jimmy."

My semi-serious entry in the parlor game was that Hoffa was shoved into the restaurant's dumpster, which was serviced by Tri-County Sanitation, a Mob outfit, and subsequently fed into the St, Jean Incinerator, another Mafia-connected enterprise. That way, the body would always be hidden from view, and no "citizen" would be involved in any part of the permanent disposal. Actually, I thought that was plausible. I subsequently learned that the FBI had checked it out.

Mike Wendland and Joe Wolf, who were covering the Hoffa affair for The News, traveled east to investigate the New Jersey connection. They got a bottle of whiskey and spent a couple hours staking out the Moscone Brothers Dump in East Orange on the theory that Hoffa had been stuffed into a fifty-five-gallon drum and trucked there for disposal. They came up empty.

Two different self-proclaimed Mafia hit man, one of whom said he was the trigger man, offered unverified accounts. The former Giants Stadium field was searched with ground-penetrating radar, and the FBI dug up a field in Oakland County, all without result.

The FBI, according to a leaked forty-page memo, claimed to know the identities of the men involved in the murder. All have since died of natural or unnatural causes. But the Feds never learned what happened to Hoffa's body.

Newspapers are fond of anniversary stories. When they do the 50th in 2025, I expect the location of Hoffa's body will still be a mystery.

Chapter 38 I Play At Being Lt. Colombo

Far too many of Dean Lee Bollinger's University of Michigan law students were aping the worst of legal writing: Long, run-on passive-voice sentences with dependent clauses that multiplied like tribbles.

I had dropped out of Amherst once and the U-M twice, but Bollinger, who had come from a newspaper family, cared more about whether I could shake at least a handful of his students out of their turgid writing habits.

Lee would go on to become provost at Dartmouth College, return to Michigan as its president, and then move on to the presidency of Colombia University. He was someone I had known since his associate professor days and watched as he became one of the nation's leading First Amendment scholars and freedom of speech advocates. I was an unabashed fan. He also had beautiful legs that coeds would line up outside the Law Quad to admire as he returned from his noon runs.

Lee teamed me with Jim Krier, a professor of property, and had Jim pay me $2,000 a term out of his discretionary account. We called our course the "Michigan Writers Seminar: Legal Writing for a Lay Audience." We limited the course to a dozen students who would write no more than a three-page paper every week or sometimes every other week, on some legal issue. They were to assume their readers were literate non-lawyers. There would be no textbook, no lectures. Every student would read every paper and be prepared to discuss what worked, what didn't work, and what would be a better way of expressing what the writer was trying to say. Krier and I would critique them as well.

The first papers came in on some Fourteenth Amendment issue, and I was utterly flummoxed. I picked one of the papers, read it once, read it again, and went through it a third time. I didn't understand his argument and started to doubt my own intelligence. I grew up with my father's graduate students. My IQ rated me as "borderline gifted," but perhaps that wasn't good enough. The U-M Law School was then ranked fifth in the nation, and the seminar students were mostly seniors in the top quarter of their class academically.

In pure self-defense, I adopted the approach of Peter Falk's Lieutenant Colombo from the great 1970s television police drama. Colombo was the distracted, seemingly not-too-bright detective who pecked at the edges of the suspect's story, complaining he didn't understand, and always asking, "Just one more thing." I picked one of the papers I didn't understand. What I said was, "You guys are all brighter than I am. You are going to have to translate, so I get it."

The most amazing thing happened. The student, reading aloud and then restating what he had written, got about halfway through his paper when a look of abject horror came over his face. His argument didn't hold water. His convoluted prose had hidden the flaws in his argument from himself. Having to tell it in straightforward prose exposed the illogic. Suddenly, I was a genius.

The great thing about the students was that, even if they didn't have ears for the elegant flow of language, they were smart. They rarely made the same mistake twice, learned what worked and what to avoid, and ended up being reasonably competent writers. Implicit in the course was this proposition: If you can't explain it clearly, perhaps you don't understand it all that well.

The course turned out to be a major boon for my own writing. I couldn't say, "That just doesn't sound right to my ear." I might have been able to get away with that in editing a green reporter. With the U-M law students,. I had to be able to articulate why one thing worked better than another.

Chapter 39 I Violate A Journalistic Standard

The 1973 Detroit mayoral election pitted State Senator Coleman A. Young, a long-time African-American civil rights activist, against fired conservative White Police Chief John Nichols, whose department had deployed a squad whose primary function was the execution of Black street criminals.

I put my thumb on the scales for Young. I justified it to myself as countering an act of Detroit News censorship aimed at electing Nichols. But as a newspaperman, I had no right to do it. This is the first time I've told the story.

STRESS, an acronym for Stop The Robberies, Enjoy Safe Streets, was a police decoy unit whose members would typically pose as stumbling drunks, hippies, priests, and even women. In poor Black, high-crime neighborhoods, they would set themselves up to be robbed and then shoot the robbers if they disobeyed the order to halt and tried to flee. In two-and-a-half years, the decoy unit shot and killed twenty-two men, twenty-one of them Black. It was the central issue in a bitter, racially-tinged campaign.

I was The Detroit News' Detroit-Wayne County Bureau chief. On my own initiative, I had been poking around on Nichols' conduct as chief. Mayor Roman Gribbs, former Wayne County sheriff and pretty much a law-and-order guy, had fired Nichols when the chief filed to run for mayor. Gibbs had replaced him with Philip "Jerry" Tannian, a straight-arrow former FBI agent whom Young would initially keep on as police chief.

I solicited background information on Nichols from Tannian, then pursued his tips to dig up the evidence against Nichols on my own. It took me several weeks, but I was able to document three instances of petty corruption:

— Nichols personally owned an aging horse that was not suitable for the Detroit Police Mounted Division. Nonetheless, he had the horse kept in the Mounted Division stables at the city's expense.

— The chief owned a wood-hulled power boat he berthed on the Detroit River. Officers under his command stripped and refinished the hull.

— The Narcotics Squad had confiscated an elegant black limousine from a dope dealer. Nichols used it, but only for taking out-of-town trips where he was unlikely to be witnessed. The limo was also used a number of times, with a police officer driver, to take his wife shopping. The limousine disappeared after I started asking about it. I finally located it at the department's Chene Garage, inside a secure screened area and hidden behind other vehicles.

I took the information to my editors, but they refused to print the story. Their explanation: Because The News had endorsed Nichols, my stories, published only two weeks before the election, would be given too much weight.

Had the story been given the green light, my final step prior to publication would have been a confrontation interview with Nichols to get his explanation. Unknown to my editors, I made an appointment to meet Nichols and his senior staff at his campaign headquarters in the old Pick Fort Shelby Hotel. I took along Bob Pisor, who was in charge of covering the campaign for The News, but it was my play.

I told Nichols that my editors had decided against running a story on the three items, which was true. But then I lied, saying that the non-publication was dependent on the balance of the campaign being run honorably, no eleventh-hour false accusations. Then I asked for and got his explanations of the three items.

Nichols promised to pay for the boarding of his horse. He did. The former chief claimed that his men worked on the boat out of respect and affection for him on their own time. Even if true, it would not have passed an ethics sniff test. And his insistence that his use of the limo was entirely proper was bull. Pisor and I were two of the paper's most prominent reporters. I was gambling that Nichols would think my approach was authorized by my editors and that he would lie low. If Nichols had checked with my editors, they would have been justified in firing me. Nichols was strangely muted during the remaining two weeks of the campaign and lost to Young in a close vote.

I covered Young during his first year in office. He abolished STRESS, set about making the police department more racially balanced, and instituted a successful community policing program with large numbers of citizen volunteers. Young vowed to make his administration fifty-fifty Black and White. It included a White police chief and the city's two top moneymen whose job was to tell the mayor exactly how much money he had to spend. He successfully courted Detroit's business community. Young developed a strong partnership with Republican Governor William Milliken, who helped out the city financially, and Young became President Jimmy Carter's favorite big city mayor.

Young was both bigger than life and a great storyteller. I followed him around a couple of times on Sundays when he made the rounds of Black churches, his core constituency, even though he was not religious personally. He would entertain the congregations with anecdotes about how this minister or that one would engineer important collections to ensure maximum donations.

He was also a master at "playing the dozens," an inner-city game of trading insults while never quite uttering fighting words. The mayor would roll you over if you didn't stand up to him, but it was politic to let him get the last word.

One day, we were heading toward a meeting in the Renaissance Center. But Young got turned around, and we ended up in a lobby area with some two dozen Dearborn Rotarians. It was hardly a friendly crowd, but he joked with them, romanced them, and had them eating out of his hand. As we headed off to the meeting, he looked over at me with raised eyebrows as if to say, "See how good I am?"

Young was well-read but usually kept that side of himself hidden. At a staff meeting, he once compared someone to Dostoevsky's Raskolnikov. Bob Pisor, who had resigned from The News to become Young's press secretary, went off to check the mayor against his copy of Crime and Punishment. Young had it right.

With the election of Ronald Reagan, a man he referred to as "Old Prune Face," Young lost his pipeline to Washington. He turned more inward to his Detroit constituency, spent less effort romancing outsiders, and, I think, became a less effective mayor.

White flight and a shrinking tax base bedeviled Detroit during Young's twenty-year reign as mayor, and he was blamed for much of the malaise.

At Young's death, Carter called him "one of the greatest mayors our country has ever known." I agree.

Chapter 40 A Manipulation Had Unintended Consequences

Upon his inauguration, Mayor Coleman Young kept his pledge and disbanded the Detroit Police STRESS decoy unit, which had proved proficient at killing nearly two dozen young Black criminals during its two-and-a-half years of existence. But one massive irritant remained: Stop-and-frisk, the practice, mostly by White officers, of subjecting Black motorists to shake-down searches. Blacks complained bitterly, but a large portion of the White community countered with, "If they have nothing to hide, why are they complaining?"

I had been wondering whether there were ways of essentially tricking White people into feeling a modicum of empathy for Blacks who had been profiled. That would be a good outcome, but I put off the question of whether I had any right to try.

I had succeeded Clark Hallas as The News' Detroit-Wayne County bureau chief. I assigned a young and still green reporter I'd been mentoring to do a feature story on the City Physicians Office. He described as "angels of mercy" the six medical doctors and osteopathic physicians who would often make night-time home visits to the sickest of the poor in the worst areas of the inner city. From my earlier undercover time as an ambulance driver in the inner city, I knew what else he would find.

One middle-aged Black osteopath mentioned, as an aside, that he faced two irritations as he made his rounds: He had to have a bodyguard-driver because junkies would eye his black medical bag as a source of drugs, and White cops would see a Black man in a fancy car at night in the wrong area and pull him over, thinking they had bagged a big-time dope dealer. One called him "Boy."

In editing the story, I deliberately slipped that information in sideways so that the readers wouldn't see it coming and be able to discount it in advance. There was an outpouring of angry calls and letters to the editor from folks who suddenly empathized with the Black doctor.

I was proud of my sneaky success but also realized I'd opened a can of worms. You can cast a story in different ways to produce different reactions in your readers. When you come to a greater understanding of how readers react, aren't you at least partly responsible for their reaction? It's a serious question without easy answers. I can avoid being deliberately inflammatory or pandering to people's prejudices, but I don't always know where to draw the line.

I recall covering an anti-Vietnam War demonstration that drew about five thousand peaceful protesters to Detroit's Kennedy Square. Some two hundred young people broke away from the protest and headed up Woodward toward the Wayne State University campus. They threw rocks at police cars and broke several windows. An elderly woman flattened herself against a doorway, looking terrified even though the rock throwers were ignoring her. I could have led the story with a portrait of the terrorized woman but chose instead to focus on what brought people to the protest. It won one of the state's top news writing awards, I think in part because the judges were surprised by the soft tone of the Detroit News coverage. Today's Fox News would have handled it differently.

There was one unfortunate consequence of the city physician story. I had been giving the young reporter good assignments and working closely with him to make his stories sing. The main office took notice.

At that time, the managing editor was Burt Stoddard, the weakest to occupy that post during my years at the paper. His wife was on one of Detroit's regional boards of education, and Stoddard had been pressuring education reporter Harry (Mike) Salsinger to expose what he believed were the misbehaviors of the central board. Mike wrote about the board president's drinking on the airplane flight to an educational conference. It turned out that Salsinger had encouraged her to drink, may actually have bought her the drink. Stoddard yanked him off the education beat and reassigned him to my bureau. Without consulting me, he took the green kid and made him an education reporter. The kid crashed and burned, partly because he didn't have an editor working closely with him, partly because he was unable to deal with Stoddard's efforts to shape his stories.

I called the bureau staffers together, and we made a deal. Salsinger would work only half days doing all the crappy little stories we hated. Then, we would cover for him while he sought another job. That worked happily for several months. Then Salsinger was hired as public relations chief for the Wayne County Road Commission at twice his newspaper salary.

Chapter 41 The Malpractice Crisis And Rescuing A Friend

One of the best things I did during my years at The Detroit News was to help resurrect the career of Clark Hallas, one of the finest reporters I've ever worked with. I had been assigned to the paper's Detroit-Wayne County Bureau, then headed by Clark. After a year, he was unceremoniously yanked back to the main office and given mostly crappy assignments. I was made bureau chief. While I enjoyed covering Coleman Young's first year as mayor, it was a job I did not want. It took me a year of lobbying to convince the editors to bring me back to the main office as a general assignment reporter, focusing mainly on projects of my own devising.

I turned my attention to the rapidly worsening medical malpractice crisis in Michigan. Lawyers were soliciting cases, some involving actual negligence, but many simply bad treatment outcomes where nobody was at fault. Hospitals or their insurance carriers increasingly settled cases where there was no negligence rather than risk a large jury award. Some hospitals, feeling they were under siege, covered up their mistakes and bad results rather than working to make the injured patients whole. Doctors were practicing defensive medicine, including the ordering of unneeded medical tests, to try to protect themselves from suits. Lawyers were pocketing excessive amounts of the settlements, and malpractice insurance premiums were skyrocketing.

I never learned why Hallas was in the doghouse. I had to press hard for the editors to release him to me. It was a great partnership, and together, we were able to document nearly everything that was tearing apart the healthcare system, with one exception.

During a period of several months, the lawyer-son of one of Detroit's major Mafia figures had filed more than a dozen medical malpractice cases against Henry Ford Hospital. It seemed obvious to us that someone with access to hospital treatment records had been feeding the lawyer information on patients who had experienced bad treatment outcomes. The last names of the patients signed up by the lawyer were all from the same third of the alphabet. From the list of the plaintiffs, we tracked down their telephone numbers and planned a coordinated phone blitz to see if we could tease out how the solicitations took place. Our script was to identify ourselves as Detroit News reporters, talk about how hard it was to find a good lawyer to go up against something as influential as Ford Hospital, and ask them how they found their attorney.

We were three calls in without uncovering anything meaningful when my phone rang. It was the attorney. I motioned Hallas to pick up the extension. We spent forty-five minutes trying to pin him down, but he kept dancing us around. I don't remember which of us first realized we were being played. We broke off the interview. We resumed our calls to plaintiffs, only to learn that, while the attorney held us on the phone, his associates had telephoned all their clients and told them not to talk with us. He outsmarted us fair and square, and we were never able to document our suspicions.

We finished up our series. The News copyrighted our stories and ran them on the front page each day with great fanfare. The stories gave a boost to state legislation that provided arbitration as an alternative to many malpractice lawsuits. The state also imposed limits on the percentage of awards and verdicts the lawyers could pocket.

Our series won top awards from both the Associated Press and the Detroit Press Club Foundation. Armed with those awards on his resume, Hallas got a reporting job at The Arizona Daily Star, where he shared the 1981 Pulitzer for an expose of financial wrongdoing in the University of Arizona athletic department. Six years later, he was the Pulitzer runner-up for stories on mismanagement at Hughes Aircraft.

Chapter 42 Four Outlaw Bikers Framed For Murder

ST. CLOUD, Minnesota -- Judy Weyer had put on a few pounds, and her under-wire bra had left a pair of angry red half-moon welts on her pasty white flesh. She offered to show them to me. I took her word for it.

At the murder trial of five outlaw motorcyclists in Albuquerque, New Mexico, the prosecution's doctor had testified that those welts were "scars from a heated knife." That was offered as dramatic confirmation of Weyer's carefully prepared testimony that the bikers had cut her with a knife that had been heated in the flames of the gas heater in the $6-a-night motel where she worked. She also testified they had forced her to watch the murder and emasculation of William B. Velten and then cut her breasts and sodomized her. Or maybe they sodomized her first and then cut her breasts. The sequence was not clear from her testimony.

But Weyer was unprepared for the doctor's revelation in court that the tip of a heated knife was also responsible for "long red scars" down the back of each leg. The marks were from the seams of her ill-fitting pants, but she didn't tell the court that until after I had tracked her down to a Saint Cloud trailer park.

Detroit News reporter Douglas Glazier and I, working under the direction of Assistant Managing Editor Boyd Simmons, would eventually spend fourteen months assembling evidence that the bikers had been framed and that the actual killer was a man named Kerry Rodney Lee.

We were never able to explain the ineptness of the four defense attorneys who failed to unravel a patently absurd prosecution case that put four innocent men on death row. It would have been five, but Weyer forgot to point out one of the defendants. At least Albuquerque's law-and-order politics could explain why the trial judge would deny a new trial even though the only witness had partially recanted and would later fully retract, explaining under oath that she had been bribed and blackmailed for her testimony.

Our involvement in the case started with a misunderstanding. Detroit News Sunday Magazine features editor Bill Lutz received a letter from a Detroit woman saying her "old man and his brothers" had been framed for murder. Lutz felt sorry for a woman whose father and uncles were on death row in Santa Fe. He forwarded the letter to Simmons, who knew instantly she was talking about outlaw motorcyclists.

We sent for the trial transcript. I flew to California to interview the gang's lawyer and the one biker who went free. Glazier flew to Albuquerque to talk with the defense lawyers and to look at police reports and witness statements. We came back uncertain of the bikers' guilt but convinced that the case had, at minimum, been sanitized if not constructed out of whole cloth.

The case was one absurdity built on another. Velten's partially clad body was found in an arroyo just east of Albuquerque by two crow hunters on February 13, 1974. He had been slashed repeatedly with a knife. His penis had been severed and placed in his mouth, and he had been shot five times in the head and neck with a .22.

A state pathologist told sheriff's detectives the autopsy showed that Velten had the "leathery ass" of a long-time homosexual and that his cuts had also been made with a heated knife. He would later recant all his statements. A local pathologist, who had been attending a conference in Dallas when Velten's body was discovered, told the detectives by phone they should look for a band of roving homosexuals. He recalled reading about two cases in Germany where such a gang added to their thrill by forcing a woman to watch mutilation and murder. Someone else suggested outlaw motorcyclists. The detectives had no suspects, no leads.

Then Bernalillo County Chief of Detectives Santos Baca recalled hearing a police radio transmission from Tucumcari, New Mexico, to be on the lookout for a van with five men who had robbed a pair of hippie hitchhikers. The five were later arrested outside of Oklahoma City. They turned out to be members of the Vagos motorcycle gang. They were on the run from Los Angeles to Detroit and may have passed through Albuquerque at about the time of the murder.

The detectives showed pictures of the bikers to employees of various dive bars and motels in Albuquerque. When they interviewed Weyer, they came away feeling she was nervous. She told detectives about a group that had registered as "Mr. and Miss Butt," who had stayed at the motel for several days, had several female visitors, were raucous, and left the room a mess.

During the course of multiple interviews, the Butt group became the bikers, and Weyer became the witness and victim who was sodomized and forced to watch the murder. The authorities had their case. Weyer was unshaken on the witness stand, thanks in part to the judge's decision to cut cross-examination short. She disappeared immediately after her testimony. The authorities refused to say where she went.

Weyer had said on the witness stand that she was born in St. Cloud. Simmons felt she was the key and dispatched me to St. Cloud to see if I could pick up her trail. Through court records, I traced her parents, John and Dorothy McCall, to a ramshackle house without indoor plumbing on the banks of the upper Mississippi. I bought a pint of peppermint schnapps and paid them a visit. I shared the pint with her father. They told me where I could find their daughter, who was back with her husband and four young children after abandoning them the year before.

During our interview the following day, Weyer continued to insist the bikers had killed Velten. But she only showed animosity toward the sheriff's detectives and the assistant district attorney assigned to prepare her testimony. Twice, she had tried to recant her accusation against the bikers, but she said she was threatened with five years in prison for perjury if she didn't stick to the story they wanted. Weyer said the chief of detectives had promised to pay her way through secretarial school if she testified against the bikers, but she was sent away with nothing after her testimony.

Working the Albuquerque end of the case, Glazier pretty well-shredded everything else on which the conviction was based. There was, for example, a credit card receipt that showed the bikers had purchased gas in Arizona after Velten had been murdered. That required District Attorney James Brandenburg's painful argument that the bikers had killed Velten, doubled back to Arizona, and then resumed their trip through Albuquerque and on to points east.

The district attorney also asserted that I had threatened and coached Judy Weyer during the multiple times I had turned off my tape recorder when her children had interrupted my interview. None of what we turned up was enough for Judge William Riordan to order a new trial.

Taken together, Simmons, Glazier, and I had more than sixty years of experience dealing with law enforcement under all kinds of circumstances. We knew that the authorities rarely frame someone out of whole cloth. Typically, what leads to a false conviction is that a detective comes across some piece of often secret information that convinces him he has the right person. He shades evidence when he doesn't have enough to build his case. But if the detective discovers that the person is actually innocent, he has the choice to push ahead for a conviction or to risk being prosecuted himself for subornation of perjury. Too many investigators and prosecutors subscribe to the "bad man theory of justice," a sophistry that holds that, even if they are innocent of the crime they are charged with, they must be guilty of something.

In reviewing one of the early police reports, Glazier found that singular piece of information that had convinced Bernalillo authorities of the biker's guilt. The bikers had, in fact, robbed the two hippies they'd picked up in Tucumcari. The hippies, according to the Bernalillo report, told the Tucumcari officers that the bikers had "threatened to cut us up like we did that guy back in Albuquerque." The "threatened to cut us" comment was allegedly made before Velten's body had been discovered. If true, it was a persuasive reason to believe the bikers were, in fact, the killers. I called Tucumcari and talked to the officer who took the report. He told me the hippies said no such thing, nor had he told that to the sheriff's detectives. That secret proof has been fabricated.

The whole case was a fraud. Simmons, Glazier, and I were convinced to a moral certainty that the bikers were innocent. There was no way we could leave them to face the gas chamber.

Chapter 43 L.D. Bickford Was The Wrong Killer

In the decades before he joined the ranks of the editors, Boyd Simmons had investigated the claims of several incarcerated men that they were innocent. All the claims proved false. "When I confronted them, most said, 'Well, it was worth a try,'" Simmons said. Under his direction, I had freed a woman serving a life sentence for murder that was actually an accidental death and a junkie facing certain conviction for felony murder. Simmons, who was approaching the end of an illustrious career, saw the bikers' case as his last chance and asked me to help him. He added veteran police reporter Doug Glazier to the team. There was money left in The News' travel budget because it had clamped down so hard earlier in the year. The paper was hungry for a Pulitzer after a drought of more than three decades. We were in it for the long haul, and the bosses were with us.

We had disproved every element of the state's case against the bikers, but it wasn't enough for the trial judge to order a new trial. Our investigation was stalled when Boyd got a jailhouse call from one of the bikers. They had heard via the prison grapevine that a jailhouse snitch was claiming that his lover had bragged, during sex, about "killing that guy" back in Albuquerque.

I hopped a plane to Albuquerque, rented a car, and drove to a rural county outside of Carlsbad, New Mexico, where the snitch was being held. I arrived at 2 a.m. and, by prior arrangement with the sheriff, sat down with the prisoner and taped an interview. The snitch, a mousy little guy who had survived prison by becoming some tough guy's lover, kept trying to put the make on me. My colleagues would later find the tape of that interview immensely entertaining.

Eventually, I got the snitch to identify his lover as L.D. Bickford, who was awaiting trial for murdering a Mexican-American acquaintance the year before. That victim had been shot in the head with a .22, his genitals cut off and stuffed in his mouth, a mirror of the Velten murder.

Following the Mexican-American's murder, Bickford and his girlfriend had driven north to Phoenix, passing through Albuquerque at around the time of the Velten murder. Leaving the rural jail, I retraced Bickford's route north, stopping at gas stations, diners, and fleabag motels, showing everyone I encountered Bickford's picture. I got a couple of tentative identifications but nothing I could rely on.

Along the way, I learned that Bickford had been arrested on a misdemeanor charge in a rural county outside of Albuquerque. The jail records showed he was behind bars at the time of the Velten murder. I thought I was out of business, but then it turned out that the sheriff was under investigation for a scam involving the early release of prisoners. The sheriff's wife had the contract to feed prisoners in the jail. Many minor miscreants were released on Fridays, but the county was billed for feeding them through the weekend. Bickford had an alibi, but it wasn't ironclad.

My last shot was his former girlfriend. Following Bickford's release from jail outside of Albuquerque, he joined up with her again, and they continued to Phoenix. They later split up, and he headed back to Carlsbad, where he was arrested for the earlier murder.

The Phoenix police had a record on the former girlfriend, who had been arrested for prostitution. They gave me her last known address, a one-room rental cabin on the wrong side of the tracks in Phoenix. I spent the night with my wife Pat's aunt and uncle, who lived on the right side of the tracks in Phoenix. Their son, John Gletne, was a freshman in criminal justice at Arizona State University in Tempe. I invited him to come along for the Sunday morning interview, giving him strict instructions to sit in the corner and say nothing.

Bickford's former traveling companion was a shade over thirty and a bit fleshy. Her bleached blond hair had an inch of exposed black roots long before that was fashionable, and her nose was covered with blackheads. She also had an astonishing bust. She sat at the head of the room's one bed in a too-tight and not very clean terrycloth robe. I sat at the foot of the bed. On the wall behind her was a nearly life-sized frontal nude photo of John Holmes. The late porn star was renowned for his equine endowment. As we talked, her robe kept falling open. She would pause a beat or two and then close it.

She didn't remember what day of the week Bickford had been arrested or the day of the week of his release. But she firmly asserted that she had been with him the entire time he had not been behind bars. I was certain she was being truthful. I had wanted Bickford to be Velton's killer, but I accepted that I had been on a long and convoluted wild goose chase. It was a tiring flight back to Detroit.

John Gletne had been admirably silent throughout the interview. But he was so embarrassed by the open robe that it was three days before he got up the nerve to tell his father.

Chapter 44 "Mr. And Miss Butt" Break A Conspiracy

There was a man in his late teens or early twenties named Hightower or Highhouse who may or may not have been part of the so-called Butt group. He may have come from Anaheim, California. He might be able to help us unravel the frame-up that left four outlaw motorcyclists languishing on death row in Santa Fe for more than a year. It was another tip from the Bikers via the prison grapevine and almost impossibly vague. But if "Mr. and Miss Butt" actually existed and we could find them, we might be back in business. Simmons dispatched me to Los Angeles, where I rented a car and headed for Anaheim.

I worked my way through several Hightowers and Highhouses in the phonebook. I knocked persistently on one Highhouse door. A man finally answered, flushed and wrapped in a towel. A woman stuck her head out of their bedroom, asking, "Who is it, honey?" They weren't the people I was seeking. I apologized for the interruption.

On my sixth or seventh try, I knocked on the trailer door of a person listed in the book as Charley Hightower. It was Charlene Hightower, a forty-something grandmother. She had a twenty-year-old son, Terry, who had been in Albuquerque at about the right time. She welcomed me to come in and wait for him to come home.

I've got no illusion I'm God's gift to women (or men), but Charley took a shine to me and asked me several times to stick around after I talked to her son. Terry eventually wandered in. He confirmed that he had, indeed, gone to Albuquerque with several friends and partied with prosecution witness Judy Weyer. He gave me a detailed taped statement and identified the two buddies and one girl he had been with. Terry said he had just been released from the Orange County Jail and knew only that his friends had a crash pad somewhere in Mission Viejo. I lied to Charley that I would try to make it back and left.

The police in Mission Viejo told me Terry and his friends were a loose-knit group of small-time marijuana dealers who also specialized in burglarizing vacation cabins. Between the police and the municipal court records, I found the latest address listed by two group members.

It was late afternoon when I arrived at the bungalow. There were half a dozen men there, most in their early twenties, drinking beer and hanging out. I told them the story of the bikers and my quest. I taped the statements of two who had been on the trip to Albuquerque. They said the young woman who had been with them was planning to stop by the bungalow in an hour or two. I was welcome to wait. The leader of the group, a big guy, showed up first. He was not happy with my presence but was stymied because the others were entertained by my stories and liked the idea they could play a role in freeing outlaw motorcyclists from death row. He sat down on the sofa next to me, put his arm around my shoulder and kissed my right ear. I let it ride. Then he went over to a fish bowl, ate a rotting goldfish that was floating belly up, and came back to kiss me again. I pushed him away.

Somebody rolled an impressively large joint and passed it around. I took a hit when it was my turn, but no one would take it from me. It was a test. I had to smoke the whole damned thing, and it left me seriously stoned. The young woman finally showed up, but I was in no condition to interview her. I made arrangements to reach her by phone without her parents' knowledge and left for LAX to catch a flight home.

It was raining. My rental car was a Dodge Charger. I found myself going either thirty or ninety. It was an act of will to keep the dial at the speed limit. When I reached the woman by phone two days later, she gave me details of what they ate, what they drank, what they smoked, and their interaction with the motel maid, Judy Weyer.

Part of the reason Weyer's testimony had seemed plausible during the Bikers' trial was the richness of her detail about the Butt group's stay at the motel, details she attributed to the bikers.

Armed with the new information, Boyd Simmons decided he wanted to be there when I reinterviewed Weyer. This time, her husband was also present. I told her I had found Mr. and Miss Butt, and they had told me everything. I said the authorities in Albuquerque were running for cover (that wasn't true) and asked who she thought they would blame. Her whole story poured out in a rush. She told of how the authorities had constructed her perjured testimony, including the bribery and blackmail.

Simmons arranged for the president of the Stearns County (St. Cloud) Bar Association to represent Weyer. The News flew the attorney, Weyer, and Weyer's husband to Albuquerque for the hearing on another petition for a new trial.

I was on the witness stand along with the formal tape I had made of Weyer's recantation. District Attorney James Brandenburg first accused me of getting her father drunk. I explained that it was only a pint of peppermint schnapps and that I was trying to be sociable. Then he accused me of bribing Weyer's children with presents. I said I had given them small coloring books and crayons to keep them from interrupting and handed the DA a receipt for $1.98 from Target.

Now thoroughly pissed, the DA again accused me of turning off the tape in order to coach and threaten Weyer. I said I hadn't, and "I can prove it." He demanded, "And how can you do that, Mr. Cain?" I said I anticipated he would make that accusation. I told the court I had a second tape recorder under my coat that had not been paused. "And where would that tape be, Mr. Cain?" Brandenburg stupidly asked. "Right here," I said, pulling it from the breast pocket of my sport coat. The spectators laughed.

Simmons followed me on the stand. Brandenburg spent the next ninety minutes savaging him, the closest thing to payback he could engineer for the humiliation he had experienced at my hands. Simmons was not happy with me.

Judge William Riorden again denied a motion for a new trial even though there was nothing left of the case.

I went on to other assignments while Doug Glazier continued to poke around with little result. Then, out of the blue, Kerry Rodney Lee, a drifter and former mental patient from Rome, Georgia, walked into the police station in North Charleston, South Carolina. He said he had found God and wished to confess to the murder of William B. Velten during a botched drug sale. The New Mexico authorities immediately branded the confession as false and refused to do anything. Lee was released.

Glazier and one of the bikers' original defense attorneys flew to Georgia to talk with Lee, who drew a detailed map of the murder scene. In quick order, Glazier was able to verify all the major elements of Lee's confession. Lee had, for example, stolen the murder weapon from his girlfriend's house. She confirmed it. Following the murder, Lee's car had gotten stuck in the sand near the Arroyo murder scene. An Albuquerque city policeman had happened by and called a tow truck for Lee. The patrolman had logged the encounter. Glazier also found the tow truck receipt.

After shooting Velten, Lee had accidentally left the murder weapon at the scene. He had rented a metal detector the next day in a failed effort to find it. Glazier came up with that receipt, too. It turned out that the sheriff's deputies had found the gun, and the assistant DA brought it to court each day of the trial in a paper bag. The assistant DA had denied it was the murder weapon. A new ballistics test confirmed it was. Lee came back voluntarily to testify but "took the Fifth" when asked if he had committed the murder. This time, the court had no choice. The convictions were vacated, and the four walked free after eighteen months on Death Row.

Brandenburg refused to charge Lee with Velten's murder, so Lee walked free as well. More than a year later, with Brandenberg out of office, the new district attorney finally got around to filing charges against Lee but made no effort to find him.

Several months later, Lee called me at The News. He said he wanted to turn himself in, but he was afraid he would be killed. I arranged for one of the bikers' attorneys to handle the surrender, which finally took place after several false starts. Lee's attorney was able to negotiate a guilty plea to second-degree murder.

Chapter 45 A Betrayal, My Pride, A New Murder

The fairy tales we read as children end with "and they lived happily ever after." Life is more complicated.

In early December 1976, when it was clear the bikers were about to be released from death row, Boyd Simmons, Doug Glazier, and I shook hands on a verbal agreement. Glazier and I would write long story memos detailing our roles in the investigation. Simmons, who was about to retire, would combine our memos with his own. He would be the principal author, and we would be co-authors. For Simmons, the book would be a fitting capstone to a long and distinguished career. Our role in freeing the four men from death row was unprecedented in the annals of American journalism.

Glazier flew to Santa Fe to greet the bikers on December 15 as they walked out of prison. I stayed in Detroit to shepherd the story into the paper and begin writing a Sunday Magazine piece: "The inside story of how The News freed four bikers from death row." Glazier took that opportunity to sign the bikers to a contract to co-author their book, freezing out Simmons and me.

Our stories won the Michigan Associated Press Sweepstakes award, the Detroit Press Club Foundation medallion, and the Michigan Bar Association Advancement of Justice award. But they missed a recommendation for a special Pulitzer Prize by one vote in committee. Detroit News Editor Martin Hayden came back from New York, seething that Washington Post Editor Ben Bradlee, also a member of the committee, had cost us the Pulitzer. Bradlee had noted that The News had earlier written a front page editorial blasting The Post and The New York Times for publishing the Pentagon Papers. That had made The News an anathema to most American journalists. To award The News a Pulitzer, even though the stories were deserving, would "send the wrong message," Bradlee had argued. The secretary to the Pulitzer committee told me privately, however, that Hayden himself was partly to blame for the loss. Hayden had been talking up the biker stories while praising the entries of the editors whom he was lobbying for support. Some on the committee thought he had been hinting at trading votes.

Later that year, Bradlee was the keynote at the Michigan Bar Association's annual meeting, where he presented the Advancement of Justice Award to Glazier and me amid lavish praise. Over drinks later, Bradlee invited me to come see him in Washington if I was interested in writing for The Post. The nation's most famous editor of what I believed to be the greatest newspaper in the land offered me a job. In my pride and resentment, I politely declined.

Glazier resigned from The News and began work on the book, mainly with freed biker Ron Keine, who had returned to the Detroit area. Glazier was a superb police reporter but not the great writer he imagined himself to be. Months went by as he struggled against writer's block. He planned a murder-suicide. Glazier shot and killed his live-in girlfriend, a Detroit Police sergeant, with her own handgun. But he chickened out when it came to taking his own life.

Glazier had friends on The News staff who visited him in prison. I was not among them. I didn't care about the book we were to write together, but Simmons was my mentor and friend. I found Glazier's betrayal unforgivable. Glazier died in prison.

Simmons retired to Walnut, Calif., planning to write a fictionalized account of the biker case. He died in 1983, his book unwritten.

Freedom was unkind to two of the four bikers. Richard Wayne Greer, known as "Doc," never adjusted after eighteen months on Death Row. He left New Mexico for Tennessee, where he had family, and ate a shotgun. Clarence Smith Jr., "Sandman," was the only one of the four outlaw bikers to return to the Vagos Motorcycle Club in Los Angeles. He became a falling-down alcoholic. Thomas Gladish, "Ten Speed," a provisional member of the Vagos at the time of their arrest, moved to Colorado and dropped out of sight. Ronald B. Keine, "Grub," started a painting and salt bagging businesses in his native Detroit and seemed to settle down to a normal life.

Keine and I would meet for drinks every year or two. He said if I ever had a problem, I could call on him to do anything. There was an emphasis on "anything." Keine told his story at several anti-death penalty conferences and hooked up with a retired former Detroit News colleague to ghostwrite his story. The colleague dropped Keine when he proved to be an unreliable narrator.

Chapter 46 They Ran Afoul Of Corrupt Feds

FORT LAUDERDALE, FLORIDA — George Haddad, a Syrian-American with lounge lizard good looks, had seen the movie "Shampoo." Forced to abandon his life in Detroit's criminal underworld, Haddad decided to emulate the movie's Warren Beatty character. He was in training, he told me, to become Southeast Florida's only heterosexual male hairdresser in the hope that he could then seduce an unlimited number of beautiful and well-to-do women. But first, he had to stay alive. That's why I sat across from him on the lanai in his walled Fort Lauderdale compound on a warm spring afternoon in 1977.

Haddad believed that two rogue federal Alcohol, Tobacco, and Firearms agents, his former partners in crime, were trying to save their skins by setting him up for an assassination. He figured that if he publicly spilled the beans to me, I would be his insurance against execution. I was okay with that. I was the bullet-proof reporter, the university professor's kid who didn't know what couldn't be done. I was hungry to land another hot story.

My route to Fort Lauderdale began with Doug Glazier's and my highly publicized Detroit News investigation that freed four outlaw motorcyclists from death row in New Mexico. A few months after they were released, I got a call from a lawyer representing Andrew Diminie, president of a Detroit-area motorcycle club. He had been falsely convicted in federal court of threatening to blow up the Federal Building in Detroit.

Diminie wasn't exactly John Q Citizen, but he wasn't a Hell's Angels either. Earlier, the feds had gone looking for him on some beef. The agents had leaned on his mother to reveal his whereabouts. When she complained to her son about her treatment, Diminie had some hostile words for the federal agents. When an anonymous threat, printed in all capital letters, was mailed to the ATF threatening to blow up the agency's headquarters, the agents went looking for the angry motorcyclist. Astonishingly, a handwriting expert testified that the block printing was Diminie's. That and his earlier threat produced the conviction.

Meanwhile, two corrupt ATF agents were busted for trying to buy a large supply of Mexican brown heroin from an undercover Michigan State Police lieutenant. Under intense questioning by the feds, the two agents confessed to an impressive variety of crimes, including writing the bomb threat. They said they wanted to see their fellow agents "running around like chickens with their heads cut off." An assistant U.S. attorney told Diminie's lawyer that he would have the conviction set aside. But when a couple of weeks passed without action, the lawyer called me. My story appeared in The News' early edition the next morning. By afternoon, Diminie was a free man.

Haddad was impressed. His lawyer set up the Florida meeting. I took a mid-day flight to Fort Lauderdale, grabbed my bag, went outside the terminal building, and waited. After forty-five minutes, Haddad pulled up. He said he wanted to make sure I wasn't followed, that he wasn't being set up for an assassination. We took a roundabout route to his compound. We settled around a poolside table. I pulled out my notebook and tape recorder.

Haddad was known in the Detroit underworld as a "five-percenter," an intermediary setting up transactions between Black and White mobsters for a cut of the deal. If a mob crew hijacked a truck of Cutty Sark Scotch, Haddad would get five percent for arranging the distribution to Black after-hours joints. He insisted that was a hypothetical example.

Haddad was under federal indictment along with the two ATF agents who had been his partner in crime. "They said if they couldn't be the world's best crime fighters, they'd be the world's best crooks," Haddad told me. But following their arrest, Haddad said they began portraying themselves as his pawns, seeking to minimize their criminality by laying things off on him. Haddad said that if he ever testified, their extensive lawbreaking would be publicly exposed, and the feds couldn't go easy on them.

Haddad said he had once been a trusted associate of a big-time heroin dealer named Felix Walls, then serving a term at the Federal Correctional Institution in Terre Haute, Indiana. He told me he had arranged for Walls' cousin to hold $50,000 in Walls' drug money for safekeeping, but the money had gone missing.

Haddad said the rogue agents had put out the word that he had stolen the money, expecting that Walls would arrange a hit on him. That seemed highly improbable. If the agents were, in fact, trying to get Haddad killed, it would have made more sense for them to leak that he was ratting out the mob. I had pretty much concluded that Haddad was a drama queen. But he was a man with major criminal ties. He was willing to talk. I was willing to listen. Still, I was somewhat on edge.

The deal Haddad offered me was that he would lay out all of the crimes involving the two AFT agents, but I would print only half. I would tape the other criminal acts that I would keep in a safe place. This was his insurance policy against something happening to him.

Items that I could print included the robbery of a Dearborn Police commander's extensive gun collection that the rogue AFT agents had set up. The agents also had bragged about setting up a body-disposal service. Haddad had been the lover of a Mexican-American woman who headed a family heroin smuggling operation. He also outlined his dealings with Walls.

I was already somewhat on edge when some asshole threw a string of Chinese firecrackers over the compound wall. We both dove under the table. I had been off a two-to-three-pack-a-day cigarette habit for less than a month and was still undergoing withdrawal. Haddad had been chain-smoking the entire time we talked. I grabbed one of his cigarettes.

Back in Detroit, I confirmed the Dearborn robbery, Haddad's relationships with both the Mexican-American woman and Walls, as well as several other items. He had given me a fairly detailed description of the disposal of the bodies of two murder victims, but I was unable to verify it.

I got one story out of the Florida sojourn. Haddad and both former AFT agents accepted guilty plea deals, so little beyond my story made it onto the public record. No one came after Haddad in prison, and I eventually threw away the tape.

After my story appeared, Walls filed a handwritten libel suit against me. It was the only time I'd been sued in a four-decade newspaper career. My co-defendants were everyone at The Detroit News and Detroit Free Press who had ever written a byline story mentioning his name. The suit died for lack of progress. I never had to file an answer.

The Diminie and Haddad stories were the kind of thing I could do half-asleep. The biker saga had left me emotionally drained. I needed something.

Chapter 47 Stan Swinton Knew Everyone

On an episode of "Jeopardy," all three contestants drew a blank on the name of the Viet Nam village where the Viet Minh had defeated the French in 1954. It reminded me of a great story.

In 1977, I was among twenty-four finalists competing for a dozen National Endowment for the Humanities Fellowships for Journalists at the University of Michigan (they are now the Knight-Wallace fellowships). We were gathered at the U-M's Inglis House for final interviews.

Stan Swinton, the Associated Press vice president and director of world services, was one of the judges who would select the twelve fellows. He was propped against a headboard in an upstairs bedroom with three or four of us, passing around a fifth of decent Scotch and telling stories.

"When I was with Ho Chi Minh just before Dien Bien Phu," he began. A television reporter with a stentorian voice and a model's good looks had just opened the bedroom door. He heard Swinton's claim, threw up his arms in disgust, said, "Oh my God!" and walked out.

Swinton, a notorious name-dropper, had, in fact, been with the head of the Viet Minh (later the Viet Cong) before the climactic battle that drove the French out of Indochina. His job was to set up foreign offices and negotiate access for AP correspondents. He knew every world leader, from Churchill to Marshal Tito to Chiang Kai-shek. I got the fellowship. Stentorian didn't.

The idea behind the fellowships was to take a group of promising early mid-career journalists and broaden their horizons with a year of liberal education. I was feeling rudderless from the biker saga and its aftermath. The prospect of the fellowship was irresistible. I knew I would be a shoo-in. Journalism Professor Ben Yablonky, a friend and head of the program, had recruited me to apply. Swinton and my father had served together on the National Geographic board. Even without the inside track, I had a stunning portfolio.

The Detroit News, however, refused to support my application and would not give me a leave of absence. They said they did not want to set a precedent for other reporters to seek leaves of absence, although there actually was a precedent. Shortly before I joined The News in 1968, reporter Joe Strickland was approved for a prestigious Neiman Fellowship at Harvard. Strickland, an African-American, had publicly opposed some of The News' racist practices. I think the paper viewed the fellowship as a polite way of getting rid of him.

Yablonky said the fellowship program would take me even without the paper's support. My editors said they didn't want to lose me, but if I resigned, they would rehire me after the fellowship and make me whole.

They did rehire me, but it wasn't until I took early retirement from The Ann Arbor News in 1998 that I learned that I had been screwed out of fourteen years worth of pension. During my Detroit years, you had to have ten continuous years with one employer to be vested in their pension. Everyone who had promised to make me whole had died by the time I discovered they hadn't.

Chapter 48 Cognitive Dissonance

I'd blown off three previous ventures in higher education. This time would be different. I had accepted the fellowship over the objections of The Detroit News and was looking forward to a year of classes and seminars at the University of Michigan without the worry of grades or credits. A decade-and-a-half of newspapering had given me a sobering look at how much I didn't know about the American experience.

One of my first encounters was with "The Making of an American Community," co-authored by Shaw Livermore, with whom I was taking courses. The author's study of Trempealeau, Wis., 1850-80 showed that when enough pioneers settled in an area, the first things they did were start a school and a weekly newspaper. It was what bound them together as a community. And that raised the question, then and now, about the role that the death of community newspapers plays in the unraveling of community.

The authors' review of newspaper clippings, letters, and diaries, together with Livermore's lectures, gave me clues to the origin of the independence and self-reliance so often portrayed as the centerpieces of the American character. The farmers in Trempealeau plowed the same ground. Their crops were subjected to the same weather. If you understood farming and worked hard, you prospered. If you failed to prosper, the failure was on you.

I had the sense that it was the descendants of people from places like Trempealeau who ended up in Muncie, Indiana, in the 1920s as subjects for Robert and Helen Lynd's great sociological work: "Middletown, A Study in American Culture." The Lynds returned fifteen years later for "Middletown in Transition: A Study in Cultural Conflicts." During the Great Depression, Muncie's glass works closed down, as did other manufacturers. Many workers, raised in a culture that taught them they were (or should be) masters of their own fates, internalized a sense of personal failure when they lost their jobs. There was an increase in spousal abuse as well as of men simply abandoning their families. Some struck out in a different direction, blaming others for their misery. Witness the resurrection of the Ku Klux Klan in Indiana.

Radio priest Father Charles Coughlin, pastor of the Detroit-area Church of the Little Flower and originally a Roosevelt supporter, turned fascist, telling hundreds of thousands of his radio listeners that they weren't failures, that the Jews were responsible for their misery. A surge in antisemitism followed. Caroline Bird's "The Invisible Scar- The Great Depression and What It Did To American Life" cataloged the social pathologies that resulted from the destabilized lives.

More recently, the forced isolation and massive unemployment from the great COVID-19 pandemic were also accompanied by an uptick in social pathologies.

Angus Campbell, a founder of the U-M's Institute for Social Research and senior author of "The American Voter," talked with me about the research he was gathering that would be published in 1981 under the title: "A Sense of Well-Being in America, Recent Patterns and Trends." What the data from a wide selection of studies showed was that a sense of well-being was less a matter of objective reality than a sense of where you saw yourself versus where you felt you deserved to be.

Slave owners knew that intuitively, which was why they worked so hard to keep the Blacks they owned ignorant, illiterate, and hopeless. Fast forward to a time when people began to see what their lives could be or should be but weren't. The name for it was "a crisis of rising expectations," and it was characterized by dissatisfaction.

Most of what I was doing during the fellowship year was trying to reconcile my Detroit experience with what I was learning from my professors and the books they assigned. A revolution in my thinking came from Leon Festinger's 1957 "A Theory of Cognitive Dissonance." In a nutshell, Festinger's theory says that information that challenges our attitudes (or prejudices) causes dissonance, which is emotionally uncomfortable. As a result, we either avoid it or discount it if we can't avoid it. Conversely, we seek out consonant information that supports our attitudes and prejudices and makes us feel good. When the book was first published, it was not highly regarded by academics, primarily because its examples couldn't be quantified, the gold standard of science. Dissonance theory has since come to be almost universally accepted because it is so useful, particularly in understanding how strongly held attitudes defy change, even in the face of objective reality.

Consider where we stand today: Dissonance theory goes a long way toward explaining Fox News and conservative talk radio's successes as an echo chamber for the disaffected, for people who feel they have been marginalized by an increasingly diverse America. It goes a long way toward explaining how Donald Trump can lie or mislead tens of thousands times and still be adored by a quarter to a third of the population. Similarly, progressives can find comfort in waking up to CNN and closing their evening with MSNBC.

The central ethos of newspapers is that you present your readers with a full slate of information so they can make informed choices. As the Internet emerged, I, along with many others, cheered what we saw as the democratization of information. It did that, but the internet also turned out to be the biggest echo chamber of all, congregating anti-vaxers, white supremacists, conspiracy theorists, Second Amendment absolutists, and insurrectionists into self-reinforcing pods. The left has its own cocoons.

I returned to The Detroit News refreshed, convinced I better understood the world around me.

I began digging into the history of the criminal justice system in Detroit, including the explosion in the crime rate in 1963 when veteran Detroit Times police reporter Ray Girardin took over as police commissioner. Girardin had been appointed by Mayor Jerome Cavanagh, a liberal reformer and civil rights advocate who had defeated racist incumbent Louis Miriani thanks to an overwhelming Black vote.

Actual crime didn't rise under Girardin, only reported crime. Black residents had not been reporting many of the burglaries, assaults, and robberies because they felt they wouldn't be heard, respected, or helped. It was an unfortunate irony that the deadly 1967 Detroit Riots (or Rebellion) occurred during the administration of the first mayor who actually tried to work on behalf of the Black community.

Here's a distressing thought: What if the riots were fueled by the fact that a progressive mayor and police chief had raised expectations but that people sensed their lives had not changed for the better? That was not the sort of question The Detroit News pursued.

The intellectual me, the heritage of my parents, crashed into the adrenaline junkie me, which often had its way. Sometimes, I wrote thoughtful stories. At other times, I was strictly gonzo.

Chapter 49 Putting Myself In Harm's Way

It was a geriatric lovers' triangle.

The woman, in her late sixties and mostly a sack of skin and bones, had been careening back and forth between rage and grief. Her lover lay on his back in the grimy basement hallway of the inner-city Detroit apartment building. The shotgun blast fired by her other lover had taken off the top of his head, beginning at the bridge of his nose. Blood, bits of bone, and gray matter were still dripping off the far wall.

I was in the crowded basement with a pair of veteran Detroit Police homicide detectives, part of a long-term project for The Detroit News. Detective Sergeant Henry Lahoose asked if anyone had seen the killer leave. No one had. Lahoose looked at the half-open apartment door, drew his sidearm, and plunged through. Gripping my notebook and pen, I went through the door on his right shoulder, half a step behind. The apartment was empty. No man with a shotgun was waiting. Lahoose gave me a quizzical look. I shrugged. There was nothing to say.

Risk-taking had been part of my persona since I went solo rock climbing in Colorado in high school and later scaled outside of college buildings at Amherst. I justified it in my reporting days by coming back with good stories. If there was some danger involved, I would work to minimize it and plunge ahead. If it was something other reporters would shy away from doing, so much the better. As I detailed in earlier chronicles, I had more or less put myself in harm's way by visiting a criminal in Florida who had reason to believe he was the target of a hit, by walking through tear gas to get my shin split open with a thrown brick in Ann Arbor, and by getting shot at while in the company of two Detroit Police officers. And then there were two of my undercover ventures: getting myself committed to a mental hospital under an assumed identity, driving an ambulance while living in an inner-city Detroit warehouse.

When my wife, Pat, learned that I had not told her about the felon who borrowed a gun from his uncle and was threatening to kill me, she made me vow to never again keep her in the dark. I had intended to keep my word.

There was a group of angry young men in Detroit who called themselves the Brown Berets and hoped to affiliate with the Black Panthers. They had emptied one of the predominately Black high schools and were exhorting the crowd with a bullhorn. The Detroit Police massed a block-and-a-half away. Behind the police lines were crews from all three local TV stations and a reporter and photographer from The Detroit Free Press.

I couldn't hear what was being said, so my photographer and I drove close to the crowd, parked, and headed toward the speaker. Half a dozen young men confronted us. The leader was carrying a seven-foot pole. Imagine Robin Hood's staff. He said we weren't welcome and ordered us to leave. I said we would.

Meanwhile, a short kid who couldn't have been more than thirteen or fourteen circled behind me and ground out a lit cigarette on the back of my neck. I told the leader to "get the little shit under control" so the police wouldn't have an excuse to come charging in. As we were being led back to our car, I had to keep myself between the photographer and the group, several of whom kept reaching for his cameras.

Returning to the office, I put some ointment and a small bandage on the burn, wrote my story, and forgot about the incident. When I got home, Pat was asleep. I didn't wake her. I got up and went back to work before she and the kids awoke. To my profound irritation, the Free Press staffer assigned to cover the protest, a man who had been hanging safely back behind police lines, included in his story that Detroit News reporter Stephen Cain had been burned intentionally with a cigarette. All morning, Pat fielded calls from friends asking if I was okay. I came home to an unhappy wife.

Then, there was Michigan treasure hunter Gene C. Ballenger's effort to bluff me into a softball interview. Ballinger ran a check-kiting scheme in Michigan's eastern lower peninsula between the Farmers and Merchants Bank of Hale and the Peoples State Bank of East Tawas twenty-two miles away. In the years before electronic transfers, he would write a bogus check on one bank and then, just before it cleared, write a check on the other bank to cover it, back and forth for several years. When winter storms closed the roads, he went by snowmobile. When the fraud was discovered, the Farmers and Merchants Bank was left holding the bag for the entire $753,923.24. Had the music stopped three days later, the entire liability would have fallen to the Peoples State Bank.

It would have been easy enough to write the story based on the indictment and a couple of phone calls, but I wanted to see Ballenger and get a sense of the man who had pulled off this colossal con. Ballenger was out on bond when my photographer and I met him in the basement office of his house in East Tawas. He sat on one side of a massive desk. I sat on the other. He pulled a .45 Colt from his belly drawer and plopped it down on the desk between us. I ignored it and conducted a normal interview, although I was polite. Unfortunately, the photographer was too nervous to take a picture of the gun between us.

I did a total of four undercover assignments while at The News. Three involved meticulous planning and resulted in sensational stories. I preferred to forget the fourth, which I'd launched with too little preparation and had resulted in my being robbed. To my chagrin, my editors ordered me to write up an account. They put it on page three, along with a telephoto picture of my assailants and me.

The largest nongovernmental methadone program in the country was operated out of a former convent house on Belmont Street, a stone's throw from the Archdiocese of Detroit's Blessed Sacrament Cathedral. The problem was that the program handed out the addictive heroin-substitute pills for some 1,500 addicts to take home. That resulted in the largest drug black market in the city. My plan was simple. I would make a buy posing as an out-of-towner desperate to get methadone for his strung-out addict girlfriend. News photographer Karl A. Payne would park down the street, capturing the buy with a 1,000-millimeter lens. But there were a lot of people milling around outside the former convent, and the two would-be sellers insisted, reasonably, that we move out of sight for our transaction. They led me between houses to a vacant garage. The one with a bulge in his pocket that looked like a gun put me up against the wall. They got my $25 and change and searched me twice for a hidden gun.

An older man joined the two, and the three had a nervous debate over whether or not I was an undercover STRESS cop. That was my "Oh shit!" moment. STRESS, an acronym for Stop The Robberies, Enjoy Safe Streets, was the Detroit Police decoy unit that had shot and killed twenty-two men during its two-and-a-half-year existence. Twenty-one were Black, including two teenage boys who were gunned down the year before on Belmont, less than a block from where we stood. This was what I had failed to research in advance. I was too embarrassed to put in an expense account item for the lost $25.

A Free Press reporter and I were the only journalists in the state doing undercover assignments. He'd do one, and I'd do one, back and forth. It was kind of an informal "Can you top this?" On his fourth, he disappeared for several days, surfacing with an elaborate story of his kidnapping. It turned out he'd had a mental breakdown. His story was a hoax.

Meanwhile, I laid plans for one more undercover assignment. I would become an inmate at the Southern Michigan Prison in Jackson, the world's largest walled prison.

A Detroit Recorder's Court judge and an assistant Wayne County prosecutor agreed to secretly assemble blank copies of arrest, plea, and sentencing documents, leaving them out where I could swipe them. I would do the forgeries. They would maintain deniability.

There were still a few details to work out when I took the plan to my editor, Boyd Simmons. He was furious with me. He said The News would be liable for anything that happened to me, even if I signed a waiver promising to hold the paper harmless. "Besides, you will be gang-raped the first time you shower in the general population," he said. I decided my undercover career was over. I learned the limit of how far I would go for a story.

Chapter 50 Harmonica Man Fades Away

CARO, MICHIGAN — The elderly man with a head of short gray stubble sat bent over, strapped into the heavy wooden chair. His beloved harmonica lay untouched on the attached wooden tray. No intelligible sounds came out of the man. His instrument was silent.

I had written the first draft of his sad, decades-long decline due to poorly treated epilepsy and the mind-and-body-crushing effects of institutionalization. I turned it over to Sydney Pat Freedberg, my partner in our investigation into the Caro Regional Mental Health Center. Sydney is the finest reporter I've ever met and an extraordinary writer. Her rewrite was so devastatingly powerful that reading it brought a tightness to my chest.

We had fallen into a pattern of good cop/bad cop in our interviews for the story. This Jewish Harvard cum laude graduate, who stood barely five feet tall, with bleached blond hair and crippling arthritis in her fingers, so terrorized Caro Superintendent Dr. Marlin Roll that he kept turning to me in hopes of a rescue that never came. We had made numerous visits to Caro, spending time among the aging epileptics and developmentally disabled, who were the facility's current focus.

This was 1981, ten years after my undercover assignment at Northville State Hospital. After my exposure of the state's treatment of the mentally ill, it seemed appropriate to take an in-depth look at what happened to the developmentally disabled men and women the state locked up in remote, gray institutions. What we found was stunning. It could have been the finest story of my career, but the project never made the paper.

The bureaucratic reality of the early 1980s was that Michigan's large institutions for the mentally ill and developmentally disabled were semi-independent fiefdoms. Most were located in small towns, with directors who cultivated local legislative support that insulated them from much oversight from Lansing. Understanding this, we approached Michigan Department of Mental Health Director Dr. Frank Ochberg. The Detroit News would pay for two independent facility evaluators with national reputations in the treatment of the developmentally disabled. They would have access to the patients, patient records, and staff at Caro, and their reports would go to Ochberg. This would give him leverage to institute reforms at Caro. A copy of the report would go to The News. We paid the evaluators' $10,000 fee plus expenses.

Nationally, the emerging ethic was that mentally ill and developmentally disabled patients should be kept in the least restrictive surroundings possible. This was based on extensive research that showed long-term institutionalization harmed the people it was supposed to help. Caro's Dr. Roll had built a couple of "cottages" on the Caro grounds, his superficial response to the deinstitutionalization trend that would let him keep control of the patients. The facilitators' report was a devastating portrayal of the deterioration of the human beings confined to Caro.

Through the Department of Mental Health, we had done a mass mailing to the guardians of Caro's patients seeking waivers of patient confidentiality. A waiver allowed Sydney and I to tell the story of Caro through the decline of the harmonica man. We had obtained copies of the medical records of an additional two dozen patients. who had died at Caro. Five of those deaths raised red flags for me. I took them to Dr. Ronald Krome, director of Detroit Receiving Hospital's emergency department and president of the American Academy of Emergency Physicians and Surgeons. He was willing to state on the record that each of the deaths was due at least in part to medical negligence. Five wrongful deaths from a very limited sample was astounding. One would have been too many.

I had visions of a story that might help break the back of a cruel, inhumane government bureaucracy that damaged generations of the vulnerable people it was supposed to help. But I had a second, less noble vision. For the biker's story five years earlier, I had lost the Pulitzer by one vote in committee. I thought this time would be different. But the harmonica man's family withdrew consent for the interview and the release of his medical records. I understood. They had essentially abandoned him to his fate and were being confronted with their own guilt. I took the issue to Lee Bollinger, a University of Michigan law professor and friend who would later become law dean and U-M president before moving on to head Columbia University. He said the family was within its legal rights and that the paper could become liable. The editors pulled the plug on the project rather than allowing us to approach it from a different direction. John O'Brien, Boyd Simmons, and Martin Hayden, the three senior editors who had been my mentors and advocates, were all retired. Sydney and I hadn't lined up an editor to oversee and advocate for the story.

Sydney, meanwhile, had teamed up with fellow News reporter David Ashenfelter in the investigation of the U.S. Navy's coverup of an area seaman's death. Their stories were awarded the 1982 Pulitzer for general reporting — one of three she eventually collected. Sydney rejoined The Miami Herald, where she worked for legendary editor Gene Miller, himself the winner of two Pulitzers. Gene supervised a trio of female investigative reporters, including Sydney, who were collectively known as "Here Comes Trouble!"

I was disappointed in the killing of the Caro story but accepted the right of editors to make news judgments.

However, there were other instances in which I felt stories of mine were killed for reasons that had nothing to do with whether they were newsworthy. I have written earlier about the worst: The editors' refusal to publish the evidence I dug up on former Police Chief John Nichols' wrongdoing.

The first story I lost at the hands of my editors occurred just after I joined the paper in 1968. "President Dave" Valler and a couple of fellow radicals had dynamited the Central Intelligence Agency office on South Main Street in Ann Arbor. I was curious about what the CIA was doing several blocks off campus. Working on that Saturday, I made a series of calls to U-M professors I knew. It turned out it was a recruiting office. The CIA had friends in some of the area studies departments who would screen and recommend promising graduate students for the spy agency to recruit.

Assistant City Editor Jack Crellin, who had been The News' long-time labor writer before being promoted to the desk, spiked the story on the grounds it would give "aid and comfort to the enemy." Crellin, who had chronicled Walter Reuther's battles to purge communists from the fledgling United Auto Workers, was adamant. I was new.

My next lost story was nearly a decade later. On my own initiative, I dug into the homicide rate in Detroit, which had tripled from the mid-1960s to the mid-1970s. However, aggravated assaults and homicides taken together had only doubled during that period. That meant serious attacks had gotten significantly deadlier. The conclusion from my data was that the majority of the increase in Detroit's murders could be attributed to the replacement of knives by guns. I thought that was significant for understanding how Detroit had come to be known as "Murder City." Moreover, that raised the question of whether more police resources should be aimed at trying to get illegal guns off the street, my research also could have become a marker in the debate over gun control. My editors decided they were not interested. The trend I documented so long ago has continued. Today, knives represent only a trivial portion of the nation's homicides.

Since statehood in 1837, Michigan has continued to outlaw capital punishment despite multiple attempts to change the law. I was curious about the lives of the men convicted of first-degree murder and sentenced to mandatory life in prison with no possibility of parole. These were people who would have been subject to execution had their crimes been committed in Texas or North Carolina.

In the late 1970s, I pulled the prison records of everyone in Michigan convicted of felony murder between 1965 and 1974. It turned out that they were written up for infractions at less than half the rate of the rest of the prison population. They were much more likely to be model prisoners than their fellow inmates, who could qualify for early release by good behavior. Some of the men, who would have been executed had they lived in a death-penalty state, had turned their lives around as much as the prison setting allowed. I thought that would be a valuable marker in the death penalty debate, which surfaces in the Michigan Legislature every few years. My editors thought not.

For years, my progressive friends would challenge me for working at the most conservative major newspaper in the country. My answer was that the editors didn't mess with the integrity of my stories and that I thought I was able to make a difference. That was beginning to ring hollow.

Chapter 51 The Detroit News Turns Cowardly

The surveillance photo I had arranged was the "money shot." Taken by a Detroit News photographer with a telephoto lens from a room on the second floor of a Lansing-area motel in late 1981, it showed three men, drinks in hand, holding a private poolside conversation. They were:

— Edward Brown III of Glendale, Illinois, the prime contractor for the Michigan Conference of Teamsters Joint Council 43's Health and Welfare Fund, the main conduit for looting the fund on behalf of the Chicago Mafia.

— Charles F. Collins, the fund's administrator, who recruited Brown and oversaw the payments.

— Robert Holmes Sr., head of the Michigan Conference of Teamsters, Teamsters international vice president, and the man who okayed the deal knowing who and what was involved. He was supposed to be the honest Teamster, the man the feds mistakenly hoped would clean up the chronically corrupt union.

Holmes was corrupt in the same way as the elder Chicago Mayor Richard J. Daley. There was no evidence that the Teamster lined his own pocket. Rather, Holmes, like the late Chicago mayor, allowed or actively facilitated the thievery of others in exchange for political power. Holmes also controlled the distribution of both The Detroit News and The Detroit Free Press, so I knew I was playing with fire from the inside as well as the outside. In the end, I got burned, not by the Teamsters but by my own people.

What brought me to the motel was a tip from the rebel Teamsters for a Democratic Union, which claimed union members were being scammed by the Health and Welfare Fund. They were attempting to use dissatisfaction with the fund as a wedge issue against the mainline Teamsters. I was deep into an investigation of the fund when Holmes ordered every Michigan Teamster local president and secretary-treasurer to the motel to whip up support for the fund.

I felt I had to try to attend the meeting openly rather than simply sneak around. The Teamsters blocked me at the door, so I retreated to the room, where the photographer and an armed FBI special agent awaited. I wasn't particularly worried, but the photographer was afraid of retribution from the Teamsters. He made me promise he would never be identified as the source of the pictures, which included close-up headshots of every Teamster official at the meeting.

For months, I had been tracking the wise guys and their agents from Michigan to Illinois, New Jersey, Pennsylvania, Florida, Arizona, Nevada, and California. The schemes were all variations of the same thing. The mob figures would arrange for certain dental or medical groups to provide services to union members in exchange for finders fees as high as 25 percent a year. This often was on top of management, consulting, and service contracts. Kickbacks would then be paid to the union bosses.

I filled twelve legal pads with notes, collected hundreds of pages of documents, and taped every on-the-record interview. I had dozens of confidential sources but was determined not to quote "unnamed sources" in anything I wrote. One reason was that I was trading information with federal and state investigators, some of whom were risking their jobs dealing with me. One of the main ways we worked was that an investigator would tell me where to find the information I sought. I would dig it out, and the information would be mine without having to quote anyone anonymously. I was trying to make my stories immune from challenge. When it came time for my confrontation interview with Holmes and the whole Michigan Conference board, I brought along Assistant City Editor Al Stark as my witness. It was their chance to explain and defend what I had dug up. It was tense, polite, but not very productive. I taped the meeting. So did the Teamsters.

As with much of my best work, the Teamster-Mob investigation began as an outgrowth of other things I was looking into. When Clark Hallas and I were doing the research for our prize-winning medical malpractice investigation, I was tipped off to rampant kickbacks in lab testing as well as fraud in medical billing for services covered by Medicaid, Medicare, and Blue Cross-Blue Shield. One of my sources was a crooked lab owner. He was also an informant for the FBI who made a practice of building his business by ratting out his rival crooks. He told me there was funny business in Teamster's contracts with small medical and dental groups.

The Teamsters-Mafia scams I was investigating had their origin with Paul "Red" Dorfman, a soldier for Al Capone during Prohibition. Dorfman became president of a Waste Handler's local union in Chicago and was an influential figure in Chicago Teamsters affairs. According to federal records, Dorfman paid New York Mafioso Johnny Dio to set up enough "paper" Teamsters locals (each with only a handful of members) to assure Jimmy Hoffa's victory over Dave Beck as the Teamsters international president. Hoffa rewarded Dorfman by naming his son Allan as a general insurance agent for the $4.5 billion Teamsters Central States Pension Fund, even though the younger Dorfman was then a high school physical education teacher only one year out of college.

Under Allan Dorfman's leadership, the Central States Pension Fund gave loans to Mafia figures, allowing them to take over most of Las Vegas' casinos. Dorfman even directed a loan to the Hillcrest Country Club in Macomb County — the Detroit mob's favorite watering hole — and $500,000 to the Home Juice Company, then owned by Detroit Mafia big men "Tony Jack" and "Billy Jack" Giacalone.

Jim Drinkhall, a reporter for Overdrive, an obscure trucker magazine, did an extraordinary series of investigative articles laying it all out. His stories, combined with a U.S. Senate investigation, resulted in the 1974 passage of ERISA, the Employee Retirement Income Security Act. Overnight, the mob was forced out of the union pension fund business. Dorfman and his colleagues then shifted their operations to the health and welfare funds of the Teamsters and other unions over which the mob had influence.

My entry into the story came by backtracking Edward Brown, who had the Michigan Teamsters medical contract, and dentists Charles R. Mitchell and Alan M. Stevens, also of Chicago, who had been hired to provide dental services to the Teamsters under a capitation contract. Under those contracts, the union pays a flat fee in advance for all covered services their members receive. I flew to Chicago. The Chicago-based American Dental Association, which at the time was dead-set against capitation programs, had publicly accused Mitchell and Stevens of Mafia ties. The dentists sued the ADA in federal court for conspiracy in restraint of trade and were poised to collect millions of dollars in triple damages.

The dental association hired Kirkland & Ellis, one of the largest and nastiest law firms in the country, and turned them loose on the mob. Their strategy was simple and brilliant: Prove the truth of the dentist-mob-union ties both in Chicago and around the country, and the mob would force the dentists to settle. It worked. I hired a cab and headed for the federal records repository on South Pulaski Highway in Chicago to look up the seven-page document settling the suit. Under terms of the settlement, the seven packing cases of damaging mob depositions taken by Kirkland & Ellis were to be put under permanent seal. But some clerk screwed up. The settlement document was sealed, but the seven packing cases remained available in open records. I wasn't allowed to make copies or bring in my tape recorder, but I did fill two legal pads with notes.

Those sworn depositions revealed that dentists Mitchell and Stevens were paying finder's fees to Dorfman associate Robert S. Greenfield. They were also paying 25 percent a year of the value of the contracts that Chicago mobster Angelo T. Commito set up with five Chicago union locals. At their high point, Mitchell and Stevens had dental contracts with some 200 union locals, contracts that brought them into relationships with convicted mobster Mike Rizzitello of Los Angeles, Frank "Frankie Flowers" D'Alfonzo and Harry Riccobene of Philadelphia's Bruno family, John Allu, who married into New York's Genovese family, Cleveland crime boss Jack "Jack White" Licavoli, and two associates of exiled New York Mafia chief Joseph Bonanno Sr., who had relocated in Tucson, Arizona.

Mitchell and Stevens also ended up connected to a one-time member of Murder Inc., the Albert Anastasia organization that carried out an estimated 400 to 1,000 contract killings for New York's Italian-American and Jewish mobs in the 1930s and '40s. He showed up as a union mob go-between in Los Angeles. That one nearly got me in trouble. I had called an assistant U.S. Attorney with the federal organized crime strike force in Los Angeles. He rebuffed my questions. Then he called the U.S. Attorney's Office in Detroit to say they should look into me because he thought some of my questions were based on secret grand jury information (they were). I got a call from a Detroit fed telling me to cool it.

I contacted a young female reporter for a suburban Chicago shopper who had written a story about Mitchell and Stevens. She introduced me to her source, an Internal Revenue Service criminal division agent who was working with the Organized Crime Strike Force in Chicago, which was investigating Dorfman and friends. I gave him information I had gleaned from the depositions. He reciprocated. I had also established a similar confidential working relationship with a U.S. Labor Department criminal investigator assigned to the Organized Crime Strike Force in Detroit who was looking at the Mafia connections to the Michigan Teamster fund.

As I tracked the wise guys and union health and welfare contracts around the country, I discovered that most were already under investigation by the IRS in one city, the Labor Department in another, and the FBI in a third. The New Jersey State Police had an active investigation of the mob's efforts to control the Atlantic City casino workers' health and welfare fund. Hardly any of the agencies were talking to each other. While being careful not to compromise a source or break a confidence, I traded information with investigators across the country. Reporters are supposed to be a check on law enforcement, not their handmaiden, but the information trade was the only way I could land the story. I never told my editors, and they never asked.

Bringing the story back to Detroit, I was able to establish that Edward Brown himself collected at least $2 million in fees from the Michigan Conference of Teamsters. I was not able to find out how much went to Dorfman and his associates, although Dorfman was also paid under a separate contract to provide eligibility lists and other computer services to the conference.

The stories I wrote were based 100% on taped interviews and documentation, with no anonymous sources. Weeks went past. Al Stark and I both pressed the senior editors but got no answers. The main story finally ran on Dec. 6, 1981. The second, which dealt only with Edward Brown's faked resume, ran on Jan 31, 1982. Virtually all of the damaging information on Robert Holmes had been edited out of the stories, and Holmes' picture was cropped out of the "money shot," leaving only Collins and Brown. No one would give me an explanation for the neutering of the stories. No one would even acknowledge who had done the editing. No one had challenged any of the facts in my stories. Their conduct told me they were ashamed of what they had done. All three senior editors I had been close to were retired. There was no one left to whom I could turn.

I don't think Holmes had necessarily threatened The News. The paper's executives knew an angry Holmes could shut down the paper. Moreover, I think gutting my story was Publisher Peter B. Clark's way of repaying a debt to the Teamster boss.

Clark, a prominent conservative, had lobbied hard to bring the 1980 GOP National Convention to Detroit and reportedly made a $1 million contribution to help underwrite the event. It was Clark's chance to showcase The Detroit News. But on the eve of the convention that nominated Ronald Reagan, five hundred Teamsters circulation workers walked off their jobs at The Detroit Free Press. Under the publishers' agreement, if one paper was struck, the other would voluntarily shut down. But Clark was unwilling. He did agree to let the Free Press staffers write a four-page insert on the convention that would appear in The News without advertising. Under normal circumstances, Holmes would have been expected to back the circulation workers and block the distribution of the combined paper. We held our breaths. The trucks ran.

I called Mike Maharry, my best friend in journalism. He had left The Detroit News a year earlier to become city editor at The Ann Arbor News. He offered me a general assignment reporting job at the top of the paper's pay scale. It was less than I was earning in Detroit, but I accepted on the spot. I wrote a letter of resignation to Detroit News Managing Editor Lionel Linder, spelling out my reason for leaving.

Rather than leave with guns blazing, I took my notes, documents, and tapes to Ann Arbor and continued to write extensively about the federal investigation for the next three years.

Brown, who was fired by the Michigan Conference, died before he could be indicted. Dorfman was indicted by the Federal Grand Jury in Detroit for his role in looting the Health and Welfare Fund but was murdered in Chicago before he could stand trial. Dorfman, who had made more money for the Mob than anyone, with the possible exception of the legendary Meyer Lansky, had been convicted, in a separate matter, of conspiracy to bribe former U.S. Senator Howard Cannon of Nevada. It made him an instant liability to the Mob. Dorfman was on his way to lunch on January 20, 1983, when two men pumped five .22 bullets into his head. The murder was never solved.

Collins was convicted of lying to the grand jury when he denied knowing of Dorfman's role in assuring the contract for Brown. Collins hadn't known that the feds, acting on a 1979 court order, had recorded conversations of Dorfman and his associates on more than 2,000 spools of fourteen and eighteen-inch tape. It was the largest interception of wire communications in the history of the nation. Fourteen of the conversations showed that Dorfman, Dorfman principal associate Sol Schwartz, Brown, and Collins had worked in concert to ensure the contract for Brown. Holmes, confronted with the evidence against him, resigned from his Teamster offices as the price of avoiding indictment. That was my personal vindication.

Chapter 52 A Father Of Integrity And Courage

My father was already two years deep into the mental decline of Alzheimer's when The Detroit News committed its outrageous act of censorship on my Teamsters-Mob investigation. He never would have known had I swallowed my integrity and remained in Detroit. But I know what he would have thought.

Stanley Cain was a world-renowned scientist. But one thing in particular struck me about him: Whether the matter was big or small, he simply did what he thought was right without Hamlet-like dithering. If I was to be my father's son. I had to leave Detroit.

Growing up, one of the first instances that gave me the measure of my father involved a lawyer for a U.S. Steel subsidiary who thought he'd found, in my father's expertise, the solution to his company's $100 million problem. But my father imposed a condition.

The situation was this: Back in 1895, the State of Minnesota had sold a lake in the Mesabi Range to the Oliver Iron Mining Company. Core drilling had revealed that, under the shallow waters of the lake, was $100 million worth of high-grade iron ore. That was $100 million in 1950s dollars.

Under Minnesota law, if the stream either into or out of a lake was navigable, the lake could not have been sold without special permission of the state legislature.

The streams were mere trickles in the early 1950s, but the state had come up with several old-timers who had worked for a logging company back in the late 1800s. They claimed to have snaked logs down the creek that flowed out of the lake. If true, that would have made the stream navigable and the state's sale of the lake illegal.

The state sued to invalidate the original sale with the intent of getting legislative permission to put the lake up for auction at full value.

My father had his Ph.D. in botany from the University of Chicago and had studied under a professor who had done pioneering research in pollen analysis. As chairman of the University of Michigan's Department of Conservation, he has done more research in the field. The U.S. Steel lawyer's visit to Ann Arbor amounted to a shot in the dark. Could the professor think of any way the company could prove its assertion that the sale had been legal? The professor could.

At the end of their meeting, my father drove the lawyer out to Willow Run Airport for dinner and to catch a flight back to Pittsburgh. I don't know why they invited a twelve-year-old to tag along. The lawyer said I could have anything I wanted from the airport restaurant. I checked the right side of the menu and ordered my first filet mignon.

My father's proposal was ingenious. There were extensive logging records of the number and species of trees that had been taken out of the Masabi Range year by year. That would let one chart the species that remained, year by year.

All trees give off pollen grains that initially float on water and can be identified under a microscope. The plan would be to select a sample of century-old trees at the water's edge and take core samples of the bark every inch going up the trunks. The last place up the trunk in which you found pollen grains would represent the high water in the creek. The mix of pollen grains would give you the approximate year of the high water.

My father asked the lawyer how confident he was that the stream had not been navigable in 1895. The lawyer said, "Very." Even though the proposed fee was quite large and would have supported a number of his graduate students during the actual data collection, my father said he would conduct the research only if he were allowed to publish the results, regardless of whether they helped or hurt the company.

The lawyer agreed, and the research proved to be compelling evidence that the stream had not been navigable. Looking back on it now, I'm amazed at the chance the lawyer took. If the evidence had favored the state, the lawyer surely would have been fired.

My dad was in Brazil on a UNESCO technical assistance mission in early 1955 when the lawsuit came to trial. The company flew him back to testify. Under cross-examination, the State of Minnesota's lawyer handed my father an 8 x 10-inch print of a large boulder at the creek's edge with a log balanced on top, several feet above the water. "And how do you suppose the log got there, Professor Cain?" my father recalled being asked. "For all I know, a Boy Scout put it there," he answered. The company won its case and gave my father a copy of the print in appreciation.

We originally had gone to Brazil in the early fall of 1954 for a joint research project my father was going to conduct with the Museu Nacional do Rio. But a month before we arrived, Dictator Getulio Vargas was deposed by the army and committed suicide. Vargas' sister was head of the national museum, and the new regime pulled the plug on all of her projects.

My dad hooked up with G.M. de Oliveria Castro, a naturalist with the Brazilian Malaria Service, and they embarked on a study of the structure of rainforests. Their research would produce a book — "Manual of Vegetation Analysis" — and put my father on a collision course with the House Un-American Activities Committee (HUAC).

The problem faced by the Brazilian Malaria Service was that bromeliads and other epiphytes grow on the branches of rainforest trees, sometimes hundreds of feet above the jungle floor. These parasitic plants cup rainwater and become millions of tiny breeding pools for the malaria-carrying anopheles mosquito. They couldn't be sprayed from the ground.

Their work on the rainforest structure allowed the Malaria Service to identify from the air where the epiphytes would be concentrated and how aerial spraying could be carried out without saturating the rainforest with DDT.

Back in the States, my father was approached by the National Science Foundation with an unsolicited offer of a too-generous grant to do a piece of genuinely interesting environmental research stemming from his Brazilian work. The stipulation was that he could not publish the results.

In the upper levels of plant ecology, everyone knows everyone else, and they talk. It turned out that a half-dozen scientists had received similar no-publish research offers. The pieces, taken together, would represent the basic knowledge needed to effectively deliver herbicides to destroy food crops on a wide scale in a variety of environments. Think of war by civilian starvation. They all agreed to turn down the research offers.

The word came back that their names had been forwarded to HUAC and subpoenas authorized. Weeks went by. I remember my father burning up the phone lines with his colleagues, waiting for the hammer to drop. Apparently, someone eventually concluded that prosecuting a bunch of scientists for refusing to facilitate starvation would not look good.

I don't think my father ever thought of himself as brave, and I never saw him have Hamlet-like doubts about anything.

During my father's tenure as Stewart Udall's Assistant Secretary of Interior during the Johnson Administration, someone ratted out Bruce Lee, a mid-level bureaucrat who worked for my dad and was homosexual. FBI Director J. Edgar Hoover called Udall, demanding that Lee be fired as a "security risk." This was during what became known as the "Lavender Scare," the widespread effort to drive gays out of government.

My father responded that Lee was a perfectly competent administrator, neither a star nor a drudge, and he wouldn't fire him. Udall backed my father's decision. Hoover let the matter drop.

When Lee retired in 1987, he gave my father an extraordinarily beautiful and valuable hand-colored silverplate print of Pleuronectes Maximum (a turbot) from Marcus Elieser Bloch's Histoire Naturelle des Poissons (1801). Bloch had done for fish what Audubon did for birds. My father was already in the throes of Alzheimer's and beyond understanding the meaning and historical significance of the gift.

He died of pneumonia in Santa Cruz on April 1, 1995. I finished up a story for The Ann Arbor News on the annual Hash Bash, wrote obits for The News and the Santa Cruz Sentinel, and then I grieved. He was ninety-two.

A few of my father's surviving colleagues and several former graduate students gathered for a remembrance at the Louise Cain Gatehouse to the Farm and Gardens at the University of California Santa Cruz. Lee showed up unannounced.

We all told Stan Cain stories. Lee, who was about eighty-five, hemmed and hawed, said my father had been really important to him but never said why. He was still in the closet. Most of the people there knew Lee's story, but none of us let on that we knew.

I was the last to speak. In going through his papers, I found a small snapshot of my father, in uniform with his left foot in a cast, walking down a street in the French resort town of Biarritz.

Following the end of World War II, the army hired my father, with the rank of lieutenant colonel, to head the natural sciences division of the American University in Biarritz. The officers were billeted in a chateau that had served as a whorehouse before the war. Although the Germans had evicted the women years before, drunken Frenchmen would occasionally rattle the gate late at night, demanding to be let in.

During a party one evening, my father stumbled into the deep end of the chateau's empty pool, breaking his ankle.

I grew up on Bill Mauldin's "Up Front," his great book of World War II Stars and Stripes cartoons featuring dogfaces Willie and Joe. While lieutenants and captains were frequently killed in combat, Mauldin had little use for the upper ranks, who kept themselves out of harm's way. He called them "garrison troopers" or "garritroopers."

I have this vision of Willie and Joe encountering my uniformed father in Biarritz, asking the lieutenant colonel how he was injured, and my father saying that was not something he talked about. As my father hobbled down the street, I see Willie turning to Joe, saying, "There goes one hell of a man."

Indeed.

Chapter 53 The Dairyman And The "Retards"

"Would you want a 'retard' with the mental age of a five-year-old bottling your milk?" asked western Washtenaw County dairyman John Bihlmeyer.

Bihlmeyer, who marketed through the Michigan Milk Producers Association (MMPA), was helping to lead a boycott campaign aimed at putting David Sweet of Kinship Dairy Farm Products out of the milk business.

Sweet, who ran five group homes and was providing job training and spending money for thirteen retarded men and women through Kinship, had committed two "sins" that angered Bihlmeyer and other area dairymen. He had refused to rejoin the MMPA and thus was able to wholesale his milk for seventeen cents less a gallon than the MMPA, undercutting the association's established price. And although the milking equipment installer — not Sweet himself — was at fault, a high bacteria count in one of Kinship's first milk deliveries had caused an entire tanker load of milk to be dumped. That included milk from Bihlmeyer.

I'd softened the Bihlmeyer quote. He'd actually said, "retards dripping snot into your milk," but the edited words didn't seem to diminish the impact of the May 23, 1982, front-page story in The Ann Arbor News. The story provoked a flood of phone calls and letters to the editor. That Sunday, the day the story appeared, a priest at St. Mary Student Chapel condemned the boycott during his homily.

I had just arrived at The Ann Arbor News after quitting The Detroit News in a protest over censorship. I brought with me a harder edge than Ann Arbor readers were used to. The News was in the process of reinventing itself and becoming what I would regard as the best medium-sized paper in Michigan, one of the better in the nation.

There were good reporters and good editors who were willing to experiment. They were willing to invest resources in what they thought was worth doing even if it somewhat squeezed the profits delivered to the parent Booth Newspapers. The scale was smaller than I was used to in Detroit but much more intimate.

My wife, Pat, was delighted with my move. We had seven children. She was the director of religious education at St. Andrew's Catholic Church in

Saline, and we had a big house in the country outside of Saline. I hadn't realized how much she had been underwriting my ventures in big-city journalism.

Folks in Saline used to gather on Saturday mornings at Walker's Bakery, which owner Benedetto Galimberti later renamed Benny's Bakery. Benny's wife, Claudia, taught in Pat's program. Galimberti was in high dudgeon when I happened to drop in.

Joyce Guenther, Benny's manager, had received a late-night call from one of the boycotters claiming that Kinship's milk, which the bakery carried, was "bad." This was followed by a morning visit, giving the bakery twenty-four hours to get Kinship's milk off the shelves or face a boycott.

"I hit four hundred degrees, hotter than my ovens," said Galimberti. "I talked to the inspectors. They said Kinship is fully licensed, and the product is A-number one. I told my help I would guarantee their salaries, no matter what. I yelled that the milk stays on the shelf, no matter what!"

Sometimes, a compelling story simply drops in your lap.

Stores in Saline, Bridgewater, Manchester, and Unadilla all dropped Kinship even though its whole milk tested higher in butterfat content, lower in bacteria, and was less expensive than milk from the MMPA. Some of the store owners called the threats "blackmail" but conceded they were afraid of losing the farm business. Others told me they were trying to avoid controversy in what had become a dirty little war dividing friends, relatives, and members of the same church.

One of the first to stock Kinship's milk had been George Wacker, who owned a farm fuel and convenience store at the corner of M-52 and Pleasant Lake Road in Manchester. But Wacker, who is a relative of Sweet's wife Sharon, said he was compelled to drop the milk because of the threat to his primary business.

The threats were effective. During the previous six weeks, Sweet told me he was forced to dump $300 worth of milk down the drain every day.

Only Walker's Bakery, Polly's Market in Chelsea, Barman's Store in Mooreville, five Big Boy restaurants in Washtenaw County, and 120 families on Kinship's home delivery route in Saline had stood up to the boycott.

"We're out to get him," said Bihlmeyer. "He's underselling us, and I'm not going to stand for it. We built up the milk market in this area, and he gets a free ride. We got him out of several stores, but Polly's in Chelsea decided we were crying wolf. Now, we have to get the message back to our shoppers. We will. We have our connections. Farmers may be few in number, but we have our bite."

Bihlmeyer, after reflecting on his harsh words for twenty four hours, called me to say that the boycott wasn't his idea and that he was merely trying to be a better salesman by explaining that he had a better product. That wasn't true, and I wasn't about to let the dairyman off the hook.

The MMPA's assistant manager, Paul Klofkorn, denied that the association itself was behind the boycott, saying it was the actions of individual members. But he added that the association originally had terminated Kinship not because of the initial bad batch of milk but for "ongoing quality problems that contributed to a shortened shelf life."

But the allegation of ongoing problems wasn't true either, according to the state inspectors who provided technical assistance in tearing down and re-assembling the milking equipment that had been improperly installed by the company Sweet had hired.

"There has never been a health problem with the milk since pasteurization kills every known pathogen, and there has never been anything wrong with Sweet's pasteurization," said Mason Smith, a supervising inspector with the Michigan Department of Agriculture's Dairy Division. "Sweet's a nice young fellow busting his butt to help these people (the group home residents). "I hope he succeeds."

I drove out to Manchester to interview Sweet and look over his operation, taking along my seventh-grade daughter, Susan, figuring she could spend time with the residents while Sweet and I did our business. To this day, Sue reminds me she wasn't happy being dumped in a strange situation, just as she was unhappy a couple of years earlier when I had picked her up from a dental appointment and deposited her on the steps of the University of Michigan graduate library while I circulated in the pot-smoking Hash Bash crowd.

At Kinship, Sweet had built up a nice operation on his leased farm. He had regular dairy employees doing all of the sensitive work, including operating the pasteurization equipment. But he said making work for his group-home residents increased his costs, even though the state compensated him for the training. Economically, he said, Kinship needed the extra revenue from selling directly rather than through the MMPA.

On the Friday before the story appeared, a Detroit distributor agreed to take all of Kinship's extra milk at full price beginning the following Monday. "So I guess I'm going to weather this thing," Sweet said. The boycott petered out.

In the long run, however, the economics of using group-home residents to help run a dairy farm didn't work out, and Sweet quit the milk business.

During my four decades in journalism, I'd done many harsh stories. I tried to follow two standards: Was it true, and could I look the target in the eye the next day and know in my heart that I had treated him fairly?

Sometimes, truth is elusive. But at other times, if you work hard enough and dig deep enough, you can get beyond the "he said/she said" false equivalency of quoting both sides of a story. While I quoted both Bihlmeyer and the MMPA, I went with the truth of the state's testing.

Several years after the Kinship story, I went along as a chaperone on a Halloween hayride Pat had organized for her religious education students. The man on the tractor pulling the hay wagon was John Bihlmeyer. Halfway through the ride, I realized saying nothing was the coward's way. I reintroduced myself as the guy who had written the "hard" story.

"I know," he said.

Chapter 54 A Lasting Impression

If you hang around long enough, you meet yourself coming around the bend.

I was fifteen in 1956 when I first encountered the crippled war hero who would become governor of Michigan, then a judge, then a convicted felon, and then an alcoholic before he finally found redemption. I was around to chronicle each of his transformations.

Rather than leaving me home alone, my parents dragged me along to the rural Superior Township Hall for a political rally featuring incumbent Michigan Governor G. Mennen Williams. The parking lot was a sea of loose gravel. I went to help a man on crutches who was having a particularly difficult time. He thanked me but said he would manage by himself.

I was mildly put off that my help was rebuffed, but my mother explained that the man was Lieutenant Governor John Swainson, thirty-two, both of whose legs had been blown off by a German land mine in Alsace-Lorraine in 1944. I was stunned by his grit. He succeeded Williams in 1961, served one uninspired term as governor, and lost his reelection bid to George Romney (Mitt's father).

Swainson was elected to the Wayne County Circuit Court bench in 1965 and went onto the Michigan Supreme Court in 1971. I joined The Detroit News in 1968 and covered him in a number of stories. He and a lady friend (not his wife) were fixtures at the Detroit Press Club bar, always surrounded by a coterie of journalistic drinking buddies. No one busted him for his infidelity. John and I were friendly. I had the occasional drink with him but spent more of my lunches supplementing my salary at backgammon.

On a Friday evening in the fall of 1975, one of my editors called me at home. The paper had cut a deal with Ralph Guy, Jr., the conservative U.S. attorney for the eastern district of Michigan. The editor told me that a grand jury indictment of Swainson for accepting a $20,000 bribe was going to be unsealed in time for the paper's Sunday deadline. That arrangement was designed to freeze out The Detroit Free Press.

The paper needed me to go out to the small town of Manchester some twenty-five miles away and get a comment from Swainson. Swainson's son played football for Manchester High School, and I was directed to ambush the elder Swainson while he was watching in the stands. I fully expected Swainson to bite my head off, but he was gracious.

Swainson was found not guilty of accepting a bribe but was convicted of perjury for lying about having accepted a color television as a gift. He served sixty days in a federal minimum security facility, lost his law license, and was forced off the court. He returned to Manchester as a gentleman farmer and dropped off the public radar.

In 1982, I quit The Detroit News in protest over censorship, settled in at The Ann Arbor News, and decided to check up on Swainson.

His had not been a trouble-free life. Following his brief prison stay, he had developed a serious problem with alcohol. He was busted once for drunk driving and another time for impaired driving (pot). His first time drying out was at the private Brighton Hospital. The second time, he elected to check into the Ann Arbor VA Hospital and joined an AA group. "Hello, my name is John, and I am an alcoholic." He never let the group know he was an ex-governor. If any of them figured it out, they never let him know.

He sobered up, straightened out, and looked around for how he could be of use. He became a regular at a gathering of old-timers for coffee most Saturday mornings in Manchester and joined the Manchester Historical Society, where he was of use.

After being higher than most and then lower, Swainson insisted he had ended up in a good place. I asked him how he kept his head straight. "Sometimes you eat the bear," he said. "Sometimes the bear eats you."
Some years later, Governor Jim Blanchard appointed Swainson to the Michigan Historical Commission, which he ended up heading.

Chapter 55 Choosing What's Right

One of the particular joys of newspapering is encountering someone who chooses to do right — particularly at a cost to themselves — and being able to write about them. Benny Galimberti was fresh in my mind when my wife Pat asked if I could help with a sudden problem at the religious education program she ran at St. Andrew's Catholic Church in Saline. The former priest who was scheduled to teach the high schoolers had just been diagnosed with cancer and would be unable to take the class.

When Pat and I were married more than five decades ago, I pledged to help raise our children as Catholic. I remain a nonbeliever but have supported Pat in every way I could. My challenge was to figure out how I could teach a religion class without being a hypocrite.

I had written a compelling story about Benny, whose wife taught for Pat and whose bakery had been threatened by a boycott for selling milk sourced from a group home in defiance of the Michigan Milk Producers Association. The question I posed to myself was, how does a person like Benny elect to make a moral choice rather than a practical one? Part of the answer, I think, is recognizing the existence of moral choices.

I titled the course: "Ethical Decision-Making." I offered the high schoolers the opportunity to judge adults. The standards they were to use included the Great Commandment ("Do unto others …"), the Sermon on the Mount (translated for their purposes as justice and mercy), and anything else they could find in the Bible.

Then, I brought in adults from the parish to present the kids with ethical dilemmas in their lives. The dilemma had to be genuine, and the answer couldn't be obvious. The adult would tell their story right up to the point of revealing what they did. The students would then debate and vote on what they considered to be the best choice. The adult would tell what they had actually done, and we'd talk about it.

The discussions were always spirited, always thoughtful. The adults were sometimes discomfited by the conclusions of the young people.

Unless they are compelled by their parents, kids tend to drop out of religious education as they get older. What was gratifying about the class was that the attendance actually increased during the year.

The best session of all was with Norma Smith, a supervisor at University Microfilms and Pat's best friend in the church. Norma was in charge of some two dozen women whose jobs were to inspect microfilm images to make sure they properly reproduced the underlying documents. One of the women, an African-American single mother of three young children, was nearing the end of her six-month probationary period. Norma had to decide whether to keep her on as a permanent employee or to let go.

The woman was pleasant and a diligent worker. But despite help, her level of productivity remained really low. The other women in the group said they would make up the difference and urged Norma to keep her.

The students went back and forth but finally came around to what turned out to have been Norma's decision, that the woman could not remain in the job. They reasoned that it was unfair and perhaps even unkind to keep someone in a job they simply couldn't do adequately. Letting her go, they reasoned, would open the job for someone equally in need who could do the work.

The decision could have properly gone the other way. My name is Cain, so I've always related to Cain's question to God in Genesis when God inquired about where Abel was. "Am I my brother's keeper?" Cain asks God. The answer, of course, is "Damned straight!" The problems are in defining who the brother is, deciding what being a keeper means, and actually doing the right thing. That's true in journalism as well as in life.

In Norma's dilemma, why couldn't the other women be allowed to sacrifice a little to make a big difference in the life of a friend, to be their sister's keeper?

In the end, Norma looked hard at the students and said, "Whenever you decide, don't do it casually!" I could have hugged her. I wasn't training ethical or religious scholars. I just wanted the kids to recognize the existence of moral choices, knowing that once they posed the question to themselves, it's harder to do wrong.

The final session was with the late William Delhey, Washtenaw County's long-time prosecuting attorney. When I asked Bill to do a presentation, he initially declined, saying, "I don't have ethical dilemmas in my work." I prevailed on him to present a case in which he gave one felon a break in order to get testimony against another.

His case involved two young men who had lured a vacationing gay German student away from Mickey Rat's pinball parlor in Ann Arbor with the promise of sex. They took him out to a rural area north of town and robbed him. One of them hit him in the head with a shovel. It proved fatal, although murder may not have been the intent. For months, the sheriff's detectives had no leads until one of the killers was arrested on some other matter and turned out to be in possession of the German student's watch.

The penalty for felony murder in Michigan is mandatory life in prison without the possibility of parole. One young man pled only to receiving and concealing stolen property in exchange for his testimony against his partner, the alleged shovel-swinger. Without the plea deal, there would have been no conviction for the murder.

Three-quarters of students couldn't come up with ethical or moral grounds to give the second murderer a pass on the killing. But by the same margin, they conceded they would have done the same thing as Delhey had.

At the end of that last session, one of the students went home excited to tell her mother that Mr. Cain brought a prostitute to class. A prostitute! The mother was horrified and reached for her phone to complain to the priest. But she knew Pat quite well and couldn't imagine her allowing her husband to do something so off the wall. So she questioned her daughter. "You know, Mr. Delhey, the prosecutor," the daughter said. Not a prostitute. Bill Delhey loved to tell the story on himself.

Judging the ethics and morality of what we do as reporters is not something most of us indulge in. I presented one ethical dilemma of my own to the class, a choice that could have gone either way. But in my private moments, I understand that some of what I've done as a reporter wouldn't pass muster with the students.

Chapter 56 Lora, The Girl With The Forward Look

Lora Biddle was mortified. During the summer of 1957, she went from flat-chested to generously endowed. It wouldn't have been quite so bad except that she was going into seventh grade.

That was the year the number three car company added exaggerated tail fins to the models it marketed as "Chrysler: The car with the forward look." "I became 'Lora, the girl with the forward look,'" she recalled. "I heard that forty times a day. I was very uncomfortable because I was stacked. I stood out at a time I didn't want to. I stood out and became suspect with the girls, so I spent a very lonely seventh and eighth grades."

Middle age brought Lora recurring cancer, radiation, newly curly hair, and a radical mastectomy that defied reconstruction. "As a teenager, I had wanted smaller boobs and naturally curly hair," she said. "And I got them … not how I asked, though."

In the fall of 1982, Anne Ballew, a long-time friend and then executive director of Hospice of Washtenaw County, dropped by The Ann Arbor News to ask me if I would do a short piece on the governor's proclamation of "Michigan Hospice Week."

Medicare was set to begin covering hospice, but care for the dying outside of acute care hospitals was still opposed by many in the Reagan Administration. I told Anne that a story on a proclamation would be meaningless, that the real story could be understood only through the eyes of someone Hospice was helping through the end of life.

Anne introduced me to Lora, thirty-nine, a retired Ann Arbor school teacher and divorced mother of two pre-teen daughters. She had been battling cancer for six years and had been told she had months to live. She was able to remain in her home with the help of hospice care.

I would pick up a decent bottle of red wine and a roast beef sandwich from Zingerman's Deli on many Fridays that fall and winter. Lora and I would share the meal, and then I would turn on the tape recorder. She said she wanted to leave a testimonial to her life — warts and all — that would allow her daughters to grow up to see their mother as a full human being. She wanted to thank Hospice, to help other people better relate to friends and loved ones who are dying, and to explain how she had to begin dying to learn how to live.

She died on March 20, 1983. I told her story in question-and-answer format, the best way to preserve her voice. It was spread over two days and took up nearly four full newspaper pages. As I wrote in the introduction, the story "made no effort to unblemish its heroine. It was her wish. She wore her scars with pride. They were part of the self she became. Besides, Lora hated plastic people."

Her candor was disarming. Following her mastectomy, it was months before Lora looked in a mirror. "I thought I was going to be physically ill," she said. She projected a tough exterior and underwent a "Looking for Mr. Goodbar" period of one-night stands. I asked if she could still turn heads. "No. I've turned his head fully dressed," Lora said. "He may know because I've told him of the surgery, but he has not seen, first of all, the place where there should be a right breast. I had a joke before I would go to bed with anyone, before I would undress. With my wonderful dry sense of humor, I would say, 'Now, if you feel like throwing up, would you please lean the other way.' I always got a laugh, but I never felt like laughing when I said that."

Lora said she had burned out on casual sex but was still struggling with depression and a dependence on pills. Four years after her first cancer episode, doctors found a lump on the left side of her neck. It was a malignant lymph gland, and her estrogen was enhancing the malignant growth. She went in for surgery to remove her ovaries. The surgeon found numerous growths throughout her abdomen. She wondered what she was being punished for. She blamed God. She contemplated suicide and accumulated enough Seconal to do the job. But she kept putting it off, finding excuses to live.

One excuse was her then seven-year-old daughter's enthusiasm for the TV program "Wonder Woman" starring Lynda Carter. "I saw it," Lora said. "It was so asinine and absurd. I decided I had a purpose in life. I was going to prevent her from watching the program."

On a more substantive note, she joined Al-Anon in an effort to rid herself of her pill dependence. There, she met Terry Dumas, a divorced father overcoming his own substance abuse problems. He became the love of the end of her life. And she became an in-home hospice client.

"That got me in touch with Nancy and Lloyd Williams," Lora said. "They were given to me as my friends from Hospice. They were an excellent choice, excellent! For a long time, they came by on a daily basis. Neither one had ever had cancer, but they have faced tragedy in their own lives. They lost a son in a car accident, and Lloyd had had a serious heart attack. "So they were not people who would say to me, 'Gee, I know how you feel.' But I know they can empathize, not only with my bad times but with my good, because they have come through the other side of a lot of anger and grief, just as I have."

They helped Lora learn two great lessons. First, it was not her job to entertain the friends who came to see her, to ease their grief at what was happening to her. The second was to let people help her rather than present a stiff upper lip and try to do everything herself. She learned how to visualize. She also learned how to like herself.

I asked her about Terry. "You don't have enough time," Lora said. "I've always read in various books about unconditional love, and never really believed it. I always thought it was for extra, super special people, and now I find myself experiencing it. He is a smart, wise, funny, strong person. All these things are to me abstract kinds of definitions of a person." He also helped rekindle her faith in God.

"I think I've got it made, I really do," she said toward the end of our interviews. "I love, and I'm loved by a really wonderful, wonderful man. My kids are relatively happy. They have a father who loves them and a stepmother who's trying very hard to love them. My legal papers are all in order. The estate is set up for my kids, and, quite frankly, sometimes, I am overwhelmingly tired. And I just want to get it over, you know, with a little bit of humor and some grace … that would be fine with me. "The point is to continue living your life the best you can. Cancer doesn't have to destroy lives. It certainly hasn't destroyed my life, although it may end my life earlier than something else."

Lora said she had come to think of her illness as "an invitation to make choices and live the kind of life that I wish I had been capable of living without having gotten cancer."

Lora Biddle died the way she wished, in her home at 916 Sunnyside with a visiting nurse and Terry at her side. I wrote her obituary, but I could not bring myself to attend her funeral. That was cowardly.

I have always been a good interviewer. I like most people who are not mean-spirited and can let my feelings show through. I look people directly in the eye, and the questions I ask give them the assurance that I understand what they are trying to tell me and will treat them fairly.
Empathy is a fine thing for a reporter, but I allowed myself to care too much for Lora. The downside was the pain I felt at her decline and death. The upside is that she became and remains a piece of who I am.

Terry Dumas applied several times to the St. John's Seminary in Plymouth, was initially rejected, finally accepted, and became a Roman Catholic priest. We played racquetball once. He wasn't very good.

Lora's ex-husband, Craig Biddle, asked to borrow the interview tapes. He returned them after several months. "Even in death," he said, "she got in the last word."

For years, people would tell me how much "that story" had meant to them. I would ask, "What story?" It would turn out to be the life and death of Lora Biddle.

Chapter 57 Indulging A Hard Edge

There is a scene in the film "Arachnophobia" where a deadly South American spider shrugs off every poison sprayed on it by village exterminator John Goodman, so he stomps it. Goodman hooks his fingers in his expansive belt and puffs up with pride as if to say, "I'm bad!" That resonated with me.

Walking into the Washtenaw County Courthouse one afternoon, I overheard two lawyers conversing quietly in a corner. One spotted me and said to the other, "Oh shit, there's Cain. I wonder who's going to get it now." I felt like hooking my fingers in my belt.

I never settled on whether I wanted to be the Detroit tough guy or the empathetic interviewer who chronicled Lora Biddle's dying discovery of life. Mostly, I just plunged ahead, but the Detroit in me would pop out from time to time.

I had been at The Ann Arbor News less than a year when the Detroit side of me provoked a reaction. Philip Power, heir to a serious fortune and owner of a suburban newspaper chain, and his wife, Sarah Goddard Power, a U-M regent and former State Department official, sat across the desk from my publisher, Timothy White. I had written what was, by Ann Arbor News standards, a sensational story on their adoption. They were not happy.

White never told me whether they explicitly demanded my firing or were just hoping that White would, in their opinion, do the right thing. But White had the back of his new hire. "You're the Charles and Di of Ann Arbor," he said, explaining that they wouldn't always like what was written about them. He didn't tell me of this visit for weeks in the quaint belief that I might feel threatened.

The couple (or their lawyer) had approached a young woman who was pregnant out of wedlock, was not interested in an abortion, and wanted her child adopted by a good family. The Powers, faced with what they saw as excessive delays under Michigan's oppressively bureaucratic adoption laws, arranged for the young woman to spend the end of her pregnancy in Hawaii. Following the birth, a Hawaiian probate judge handled all the legal work, and the family brought the newborn back to Ann Arbor.

Working from public records, I was able to estimate the size of the fortune to which the adopted infant was likely to be heir. I am certain it was better read and more talked about than anything else the paper had published in recent memory.

My gossipy invasion of their privacy was the kind of piece that hadn't previously made it into The Ann Arbor News. My thin justification for writing it was that the state's bureaucratic adoption laws would never be changed if they inconvenienced only the poor and not the rich and well-connected. I had come out of a different journalistic tradition than most of my colleagues at The News. The adoption story was a case of my simply plunging ahead. I'm less certain of my rectitude these days than I was at forty-one.

I don't know whether it was my reputation for being hard-nosed or a matter of trust, but the editors twice assigned me to the unpleasant task of fact-checking stories by colleagues that had been challenged by influential community members.

The first was an investigative piece by veteran reporter Chong Pyen about former Ann Arbor Mayor Lou Belcher. Belcher had complained to the editors that Pyen's story cast suspicion of wrongdoing over his business, which involved selling gray-market computer motherboards. Pyen's primary source was a disgruntled former employee. I concluded that Pyen's story was factually correct, but its slant gave too much credence to the ex-employee's accusations.

Belcher, his lawyer, Pyen, and I met with the editors to discuss the issue. I said no correction was warranted but that a clarification would be in order. Belcher's lawyer went into full bullying mode. I tried to talk him through the issue to no avail. Finally, I slapped my hand on the table and bellowed, "Are you a lawyer or a man!" He sputtered. Belcher told him to be quiet. The ex-mayor and I quickly worked out the language of the clarification.

Leaving the room, City Editor Dave Bishop said, "Cain, you are a real son-of-a-bitch. I'm just glad you're our son-of-a-bitch."

The second time the editors had me fact-check a colleague's story didn't end so well for me. Business reporter Rick Haglund had written an incredible story on Charles Gelman and the decline in the fortunes of Gelman Sciences, one of Ann Arbor's largest companies, with nine hundred employees and offices and manufacturing plants scattered around the world. The decline was attributed largely to Gelman's bizarre management style.

Haglund's story was based on on-the-record interviews, sworn statements, court suits, and Wall Street evaluations. It was solid in every detail. One of the more telling anecdotes involved one of Gelman's multi-day management conferences. He would dress up as a king or sometimes appear in his underwear and sit on a throne. His executives and senior managers would approach the throne individually. An aide dressed as a jester would make them get down on one knee and kiss Gelman's ring.

Gelman, who was famous for suing people who opposed him, demanded that The News retract and apologize for one item in particular that involved a fired vice president. According to the wrongful discharge lawsuit, a Gelman aide had intended to send Gelman a packet of pornography through the inter-office mail. It was in one of those reusable manilla envelopes where you cross out the last recipient's name and add the next. It was mistakenly delivered to the vice president, who opened it, saw the contents, and hurriedly sent it on to Gelman. But the vice president couldn't resist telling someone. Of course, it got back to Gelman, who fired the vice president, according to the suit.

I told my editors that, when Gelman came back in with his threats, they should promise him a clarification, identifying the material as "homosexual pornography." That was the Detroit in me. That's how you dealt with a bully, but all it accomplished was to earn me a stinging rebuke from my editors.

My punishment for being a smart ass was being assigned to write a story on all of Gelman's complaints against The Ann Arbor News. Gelman said he had founded and was head of the "Presidents Council" of Ann Arbor business executives and that the council was mad at The News. The only other member he identified was the equally squirrelly Domino's founder, Tom Monaghan. I was ordered to go out to Gelman's office, where I was to take a call from Monaghan, who was going to echo Gelman's comments against the paper. Monaghan's call was twenty minutes late, and the pizza man had only a vague idea of what he was supposed to say. I dutifully wrote up what the two men said, quoted White's response that the accusations were without merit, and defended Hagland's story as error-free.

Gelman ended with his reputation in tatters. Gelman Scientific had been discharging 1,4-dioxane — a probable carcinogen — into two unlined storage lagoons for years. Gelman filed multiple lawsuits in failing efforts to avoid accountability for the pollution, which got into the groundwater and spread through several neighborhoods in the Wagner Road area of Ann Arbor.

I had spent much of my early time at The Ann Arbor News seeking to avoid having to deal with either Gelman or Monaghan, but my editors had nailed me with both at the same time.

With one glaring exception, I rarely butted heads with my editors during my first decade at the paper. The exception happened when the editors called all the reporters to a conference room at the Campus Inn to announce that they were imposing standards for reporters. This was not well received.

The News had hired some seriously talented reporters by that time. But a couple of staffers, who had been with the paper for more than a decade, didn't measure up. My sense was that the new standards would be the basis for encouraging them to up their game or look for employment elsewhere.

When it was clear that the editors weren't going to back down on the standards for reporters, I said it was only fitting that there also be standards for editors. The reporters jumped on the idea. The editors reluctantly agreed and appointed News Editor Jeff Frank as chair of a committee to formulate them. I volunteered myself for the committee. Weeks went by, but Jeff couldn't be cajoled into calling a meeting. On my own, I drafted and distributed a set of standards for editors. The first line read: "It is the function of an editor to make a story better, not worse." Jeff never called a meeting.

I failed to learn my lesson from that episode. A decade after my retirement, the editor of the Asheville Citizen-Patriot, a former colleague from my Detroit News days, invited me to join the paper part-time as its writing coach at the beginning of the paper's new fiscal year.

The paper's computer had a feature called a writing trail, which allowed you to see the original copy turned in by the reporters and the changes made by the editors. It was clear to me that there would be little benefit in working with the reporters without also dealing with what the editors were doing or failing to do. At the beginning of the next fiscal year, the paper had a new editor. I proposed working with both reporters and editors. I was uninvited.

Chapter 58 Not Everything Academic Is Brilliant

Ann Arbor has always been a company town. The company is the University of Michigan, and The Ann Arbor News has been its cheerleader. The News was struggling to redefine its relationship to the elephant in the room, and an occasionally hard-nosed big-city reporter with an intimate understanding of the university seemed like a good fit.

My father had been senior faculty and a department chair. My mother was the founder of the U-M's Center for the Education of Women, and I grew up bartending their faculty cocktail parties. I had two turns as an undergraduate student, spent a year at the U-M on a National Endowment for the Humanities fellowship, taught writing in both the Department of Journalism and the Law School, and knew where many bodies were buried.

I was assigned to write some stories about the university and arranged for an interview with President Harold T. Shapiro. I had previously covered the proud and profane Detroit Mayor Coleman A. Young, who would roll you over unless you gave it back to him.

During that first Shapiro interview, I had joshed him as if he were Young. I saw his eyes glaze over. I immediately understood that I had massively misread the austere intellectual across from me. How could I cover the university if the top man had written me off as a fool?

I went to Provost Billy Frye, a friend of my father's, and confessed my stupidity. I asked him to brief me on some issue vital to Shapiro and then give me five minutes with the man. The issue was Michigan's Headlee Amendment, which threatened to seriously undermine the state's financial support of the U-M. The following week, Shapiro was scheduled to testify on the amendment before a legislative committee.

During the five-minute interview, my rapid-fire and penetrating follow-up questions to each of Shapiro's answers revealed that I knew almost as much about the implications of Headlee as he did. Shapiro did a double take. His look told me he was questioning if I really was the fool he had thought me to be.

I apologized and told the president what I had done and why. My gambit worked. Until Shapiro moved on to the Princeton presidency in 1988, I

was the one reporter whose calls he would take day or night. I didn't abuse my access by calling on trivial matters.
Shapiro, a Brahmin at heart, was a distinguished economist, excellent president, and fundamentally decent man. He was also socially stiff but accepted with good grace when I gently poked him in two subsequent stories.

I tagged along when he did a meet-and-greet with incoming freshmen at the West Quad dormitory, moving from student to student, asking each the same pair of questions: Where did they come from, and what did they hope to study? I wrote it up as if I were a critic giving a mixed review to a theater performance.

Midway through Shapiro's presidency, I invited City Editor Mike Maharry to do a joint interview for a lengthy profile of the man. His parents owned a gourmet Chinese restaurant in Montreal. From them, the university president had on his office wall an antique scroll with an elegantly painted, life-sized rendition of an ancient silk-embroidered Mandarin robe. We took a picture of it, spiced Shapiro's head on top, and titled the story "Shapiro: The Mandarin of Michigan." It was the perfect metaphor.

Most of my off-and-on coverage of the university was pretty straightforward, but I knew the administration would occasionally fret about what I would come up with next.

The tax-exempt university, for example, used to make an annual payment to the city to compensate it for providing the campus with police and fire protection. The university vastly expanded its campus cops as a full-fledged law enforcement department and sharply lowered payments, further straining the city's budget.

The university made the city's and the school's fiscal situation worse through its practice of buying property for most of its off-campus expansion rather than renting. Rental property pays taxes to the city, county, and schools. All of that disappears when the university takes the property out of private hands.

In one long investigative piece, I detailed how Liberal Arts Dean Edie N. Goldenberg effectively destroyed the Department of Communication, which she publicly branded a "weak sister." The department, which had been formed through the 1979 merger of the Department of Journalism and the Department of Speech and Communication, was an unhappy marriage between measurement-oriented political scientists and research psychologists on one side and the journalism faculty members more grounded in the humanities on the other.

Three retiring senior faculty members on the journalism side were replaced with six assistant professors. Students flocked to the department, which became a cash cow for the university. Outside faculty came to view Communications as a "gut major," although a study of grading practices suggested otherwise.

To remake the department, Goldenberg recruited UCLA's Neil M. Malamuth, a psychologist who was a trendy expert on pornography and sexual violence against women. One of his research projects involved putting penile cuffs on male students and measuring their reaction to dirty pictures.

I filed a Freedom of Information request to find out what the dean had to pay him to come to Ann Arbor. The tab included just under $200,000 for two years, a third-year sabbatical with $75,000 compensation, $30,000 for a lab assistant and expenses, $57,000 to remodel a lab for him, and an elegant university-owned Burns Park home at below-market rent. As the final part of the deal, he was allowed to bring an undergraduate student of from UCLA, Shirley Orion, who was to receive $16,864 as one of his teaching assistants and U-M Law School tuition waivers worth $35,198. One faculty member described Orion, who moved into the Burns Park home with Malamuth, as "looking like a young Sophia Loren and dressed like a nightclub entertainer."

Adjunct Professor of Communication Joan H. Lowenstein, assigned to supervise Orion, complained: "It is inappropriate for a department chair to make it look like its a smorgasbord, like the women are here for the pickings of the male faculty. He had trouble knowing what was appropriate and inappropriate behavior."

After failing to remake the department, Malamuth quit during his sabbatical, leaving the university to pay off the balance of his deal. Orion found a new friend and moved back to UCLA.

With Malamuth gone, Goldenberg sent in a new acting chairman, suspended the department's bylaws, declared the department's long-range plan “unacceptable,” and stripped it of control over its finances. It appeared that she was punishing the department for her mistake.

In one other major investigation, two reporters and I took apart the Board of Regents for the fiction they employed to evade the Michigan Open Meetings Act requirement that they conduct all their business in public. Even though the board was politically diverse, there was never any meaningful public disagreement. Virtually every vote was unanimous. The board members claimed they were acting legally by meeting secretly in small groups of less than a quorum to hash out their differences.
This came to a head when the regents met secretly in small groups to evaluate all the candidates for university president, ultimately making a 1988 pro forma public vote confirming their private selection of Academic Vice-President and Provost James N. Duderstadt, an unpopular choice with much of the university’s liberal arts faculty.

We pulled together the factual basis for The News’ attorneys, including Joan Lowenstein, to sue the university for violation of the Open Meetings and Freedom of Information Acts. The Detroit News and Detroit Free Press joined the suit. In 1993, the Michigan Supreme Court ruled, in a 4-3 vote, that the university had violated the acts. The case was returned to the Washtenaw County Circuit Court, which ordered the public release of all the secret search documents.

The documents revealed that the choice for president had come down to two men: Dudersdadt and Vartan Gregorian, who was then president of the New York Public Library. A majority of the regents favored Gregorian. But Deane Baker, R-Ann Arbor, the board's most conservative member, called Gregorian privately and threatened to make a public spectacle of his candidacy unless he withdrew. He withdrew, leaving Duderstadt the last man standing.

Duderstadt resigned in 1995, saying he had accomplished most of his goals. But we filed a Freedom of Information request for his letter of resignation. I wrote the story revealing that Duderstadt had quit because he felt he’d lost the regents' support.

My reward? I was assigned to cover the seemingly endless interviews and meetings that ended with the regents selecting former U-M Law School Dean Lee C. Bollinger as Dudersdadt’s successor. Bollinger had left Michigan to become provost of Dartmouth with the proviso that he could teach one law class at Dartmouth. When he emerged as a candidate, I flew to Hanover, New Hampshire, to sit in on his class. Bollinger was an old friend, so the assignment wasn't totally onerous.

I love the university. It's one of the world's great institutions, but my journalistic life would have been quite dull if I had had to treat the U-M with the same ponderous seriousness with which it regarded itself.

There was one graduation for which the University News Service flooded the newspaper with press releases that seemingly covered the upcoming event from every angle. Somehow, the news releases neglected to mention a secret, private reception, dinner, and program for individuals and companies that had given $1 million or more to the university. I doped out the menu and other details, including U-M graduate James Earl Jones as the dinner speaker, replacing U-M graduate Mike Wallace. I alternated paragraphs in my story with lyrics from Bob Dylan's "Million Dollar Bash," such as, "Come now, sweet cream, and don't forget the flash. We're all gonna meet at that million-dollar bash."

The bane of every reporter at The News was the annual "M Edition" welcoming students back to campus. It required us to generate dozens of stories to accompany an extravaganza of paid advertising. I was given a University News Service release boasting of famous Michigan folks ranging from Jerry Ford and Mike Wallace to Gilda Radner and Madonna, a trio of Nobel laureates, and a septet of astronauts.

I got to wondering what less-than-stellar personages also passed through the portals. It took a lot of digging, but I came up with Chicago thrill killer Richard A. Loeb, who joined Nathan Leopold to murder Bobby Franks, and David Henry Barnett, the only American-born Central Intelligence Agent ever caught selling out to the KGB. My favorite was Francois "Papa Doc" Duvalier, who had played a prominent role in Haiti-U.S. program of yaw eradication. He had caught the State Department's attention as a potential up-and-coming leader. The State Department sent him to the U-M to get a Master of Public Health degree. But Papa Doc was such an indifferent student that the dean couldn't bear to award him a degree. Instead, the school gave him a fancy gold-embossed certificate in Latin which, when translated, said in effect that he had attended.

I would have included Ted Kaczynski in the article, but the Unabomber's Michigan connection wasn't revealed until his arrest in 1996, long after my piece on infamous Michigan men. Nineteen years prior to Kaczynski's arrest, he earned his master's degree and Ph.D. in mathematics from the U-M and moved to California.

Between 1977 and 1995, Kaczynski sent sixteen bombs to various technology and academic figures, including U-M psychologist James V. McConnell, killing three men and injuring twenty-three. He promised to quit the bombing campaign if his manifesto attacking industrial society was published, which The New York Times and Washington Post did in late 1995. The bomber's sister and brother recognized the writing style as Ted's and informed the FBI after extracting a promise that the feds would try to arrest him without killing him.

The FBI put Kaczynski's rural Lincoln, Montana, cabin under surveillance in the hope of catching him red-handed while other agents across the country investigated his background and sought to determine whether he had acted alone.

About a week before his eventual arrest, I was tipped that he had been at the U-M, but I had to promise not to write anything until he was taken into custody. I went to University Microfilms for a copy of his doctoral dissertation titled "Boundary Functions" and interviewed every surviving member of his dissertation committee plus a couple of doctoral candidates in his old department.

They were unable to explain Kaczynski's math in terms I could understand, but they assured me that it was drop-dead brilliant. He had been able to solve a problem in geometry that had stymied one of his professors. What was even more remarkable was that his dissertation, which won an award as the best of the year, was actually a last-minute substitution that he had dashed off in a couple of weeks. He had been forced to abandon his earlier almost-completed dissertation when he discovered that someone at another university had just published the solution to his problem.

Kaczynski had taken only one course outside of the math department, physical anthropology, which was taught by Frank Livingstone. Frank had married my mother's former administrative assistant when my mother was president of the Michigan League of Women Voters. Livingstone recalled that Kaczynski was his only student during the grubby '60s who came to class in a sport coat and tie, the only one to whom he ever awarded an A+.

The Ann Arbor News copyrighted my piece, which ran as a sidebar to the Associated Press account of Kaczynski's arrest, and included a photograph of Livingstone and the grade book with the A+. The university mildly admonished Livingstone for violating the Unabomber's privacy. Frank didn't care.

Chapter 59 Socrates vs. The Jesuit

Father Keith Priestly was so delighted to have an English-speaking audience after spending ten years as a Jesuit missionary in Indonesia that he felt compelled to tell us everything he knew about his faith. I had no such excuse for my own long-windedness.

Pat and I had started dating during Vatican II while we were still in high school. When we married, I was required to vow to bring up our children as Catholic. Although utterly nonreligious, I became a student of the church on the theory that this would enable me to nudge our children toward the best of Catholicism and away from the worst. But even I had trouble following much of Father Priestly's homilies. I would look around during Mass at St. Andrew's Catholic Church in Saline and see the thousand-yard stares of parishioners zoning out.

During a Sunday evening church potluck, I took Father Priestly aside with the intent of going full Socratic on the Jesuit. I asked him how often he had a fresh insight into his faith. He said he didn't know. I asked him if one insight a month might be reasonable, noting that would be twelve a year, an impressive 120 new ideas during his decade in Indonesia. By this time, he had smelled a rat but agreed that number was plausible. I asked if it might even be one new insight a week, which would put him in the company of Summa Theologica, St. Thomas Aquinas' five-volume instructional guide to theology.

Father Priestly shook his head, unclear what I was leading up to. I noted that his homily of that morning had crammed five distinct ideas into 20 minutes, far beyond what a lay audience could absorb. Father Priestly, who was helping out in Saline while he worked on his Ph.D. at the U-M, said he got it. His homily the following Sunday was a model of one well-developed idea. The success of my Socratic exercise was short-lived. He was back to his old ways the following week.

Some months later, I got called on my own long-windedness. It came in the wake of Michigan Consumers Power's 1984 decision to abandon its unfinished Midland Nuclear Power Plant after wasting $4.5 billion. The plant, which was supposed to have achieved great efficiencies by selling its waste heat steam to Dow Chemical Company, was being built by Bechtel Corporation. Bechtel, the nation's largest construction company, had based its project professionals in Ann Arbor, making it a local story for The Ann Arbor News.

My part of the story was a long-running, billion-dollar lawsuit in Midland County Circuit Court in which Consumers, Bechtel, and Dow were each trying to affix the blame for the project's failure on each other. Most of Bechtel's engineers had left Ann Arbor for other projects around the world, so there wasn't much of a constituency for my stories. Nevertheless, I was intrigued by three normally secretive mega-corporations hanging each other's dirty linen out for others to see. I didn't ask myself how many readers of a family newspaper, even highly educated readers in a college town, really cared about the Nuclear Regulatory Commission's shifting standards on soil compaction. As the trial unfolded, I was writing overly long stories, making the classic reporter's error of dumping my notebook into print.

Mike Maharry, my city editor and best friend in journalism, took me to task. I saw immediately that he was right, felt mortified, and promised to do better. The testimony that day was from Consumers' former chairman, a patrician gentleman who remembered very little. I wrote a haiku that actually captured the essence of his testimony and transmitted it to The News. I turned off my phone and went to dinner. After dessert, I turned the phone back on, listened to several pointed complaints from Maharry, and transmitted a modest-length 15-column inch story I had written earlier.

I still wrote the occasional very long story, particularly when tracking the peregrinations of the Ann Arbor area's world-class-dope dealers, but otherwise tried to keep the Maharry admonition in mind.

Chapter 60 The "Barons Of Pot" Overreach

Ann Arbor is a town in which a substantial number of people consider the tars and nicotine of tobacco a greater evil than the cannabinoids of marijuana and believe that informing on pot dealers is, well, tacky.

Brothers Ned and Fred Shure, Ann Arbor's third generation of dope entrepreneurs, brought an estimated 200,000 pounds of Colombian marijuana through the city and environs in 1981, their peak year. But when the brothers ended up informing on some seventy-five friends, relatives, colleagues, and employees, they lost their Robin Hood allure.

Although I'd been exploring the city's dope underworld for eight months, I couldn't decide whether the rise and fall of the Brothers Shure was comedy or tragedy. So, I played it both ways. They needed a nickname, so I branded them the "Barons of Pot." Cathy Gendron, The Ann Arbor News' brilliant artist, created a full-color heraldic shield featuring easily recognizable caricatures of the brothers topped by a fleur de lis and a marijuana leaf. On the street, they were less charitably known as the "Deal and Squeal Brothers." Habitués of the trendy downtown restaurants they frequented inelegantly referred to them as the "Canary Brothers." When they finally ended up in federal prison, they were known as the "Rat Brothers."

There were several factors in the downfall of Fred Charles Shure, who had resigned as an associate professor of nuclear engineering at the University of Michigan, and his younger brother, Ned Garrett Shure, proprietor of Ned's Book Store in Ypsilanti.

While they knew they were breaking the law and tried to take precautions, they looked at Ann Arbor's casual attitude toward marijuana and convinced themselves that they weren't really criminals. They had no idea the extent to which the feds would play hardball. And the brothers never anticipated they would acquire their own "Boswell" (me) who would write story after story to keep them in the public eye, from first indictment to sentencing and beyond.

After their New Orleans indictment in April 1983, but before their attorney told them to keep quiet, I managed a brief interview with Ned Shure. "There are so many things that I'm innocent of that other people are not," he said. "I was never involved in anything other than that. It's a big country, and what gets blown out of proportion in one area [New Orleans] isn't viewed the same way everywhere. Now, if the whole federal system was in Ann Arbor … "

The Shures had paid more than $1.5 million for 40,000 pounds of Colombian marijuana from the freighter "Shady Lady," which had docked in New Orleans, and then they shipped the dope to Ann Arbor. But some of their agents in Louisiana got caught, rolled over, and the brothers were hit with a federal indictment.

Then in August, the U.S. Attorney in Norfolk, Virginia, issued a criminal information charging the brothers with contracting for 48,000 pounds of marijuana from the Colombian coastal freighter "Don Frank," which had sunk December 29, 1980, in a storm sixty miles off the coast of Cape Hatteras, North Carolina. They were left with several empty tractor-trailers, lost the front money they'd paid for the pot, and were out the $190,000 they'd laid out to rent a smaller boat to bring the drugs from the mother ship to shore.

"Those two boats were typical of them … make a million, loose a million," said Ann Arbor attorney Dennis Hayes, a friend of the Shures during the 1970s who ended up representing other pot dealers. "I heard they lost more boats than they brought in. Ned and Fred are from New York, Queens, a couple of bright, aggressive big-city boys who operate at a different level of metabolism than most people. I think the key to the direction they took was sibling rivalry: Ned was having more fun, and Fred joined him. The key to their downfall was the Peter Principle: They exceeded their level of incompetence when they started contracting for boatloads from Colombia."

Ann Arbor's first generation of marijuana smugglers were long-haired, dope-smoking, true-believing, pot-as-sacrament proselytizers. They brought back modest quantities of Mexican dope by car, camper, and pickup. The cottage industry thrived from the 1960s into the early 1970s. It was killed overnight when President Nixon clamped down on border traffic from Mexico.

With the little guys out of business, flamboyant blue-collar Ann Arbor-based combines emerged that were big enough to bring in boatloads from Colombia. There was pot world's late legendary Raymond Alan Suber, known as "Zoomer," a macro-veggie who was so opposed to all things cow that he insisted members of his dealing family wear cloth shoes. His organization merged with a second group headed by Paul Felix Jecura, known as "Hopper," who had a taste for fast boats, planes, classic sports cars, and gold.

Ross M. Parker, head of the U.S. Attorney's criminal division in Detroit, calculated that Suber and Jecura had imported 400,000 to 500,000 pounds of commercial-grade Colombian marijuana that they stored temporarily in rented and purchased farms in Saline, Manchester, Clinton, Gregory, Pinckney, and Stockbridge, as well as rural Oakland and Monroe counties. In addition to supplying the Ann Arbor market, their pot was transshipped across the country to New York and such places as Crested Butte, Colorado, and Ogallala, Nebraska.

Faced with a federal indictment, Suber spent nine months as a fugitive traveling around the country under the name "Ross Parker" before dying of a heroin overdose. Jecura, also a fugitive, was arrested in Sacramento, California, in early 1983, pled guilty in Ann Arbor to operating a continuing criminal enterprise, and was sentenced to a minimum of ten years in prison.

Meanwhile, the white-collar Shures had expanded their operation locally. Starting off with plane loads of Mexican pot in 1974, they ended up with boatloads of Colombian, bringing an estimated total of one hundred tons to Ann Arbor.

Unlike Suber and Jacura, Ned and Fred Shure lived outwardly modest lives while investing heavily in buying and restoring downtown Ann Arbor buildings. In their one extravagance, Ned Shure took a ninety-nine-year lease on the cavernous third floor over Mr. Flood's Party at 120 West Liberty Street. The brothers hired hippie craftsmen (cash only, no checks) to elegantly refurbish the area, including a Jacuzzi. The headboard in the bedroom was equipped with a silver spigot for spring water.

Ned's Bookstore became the first place in the county where college students could buy discounted texts. "They gave a lot of strange and unemployable people straight jobs," said Ann Arbor City Councilman Jeff Epton, who had worked at Ned's. "Broadly speaking, Ned and Fred were around the subculture but never really a part of it."

Shure money helped to keep Performance Network, Ann Arbor's professional Equity theatre, afloat. "Ned has supported a lot of hopeless and lost and useful cultural causes in the arts, music, and theatre," said Attorney Hayes. "At that level, he was real public-spirited."

Beyond their local operation, the brothers provided front money to a Virginia-North Carolina group that handled 190,000 pounds of marijuana and generated more than $40 million in gross revenues.

And in 1980-1981, the brothers provided financing for California connection Bruce Perlowin to bring seven boatloads carrying 75,000 pounds of high-grade marijuana from Colombia's Pacific coast into San Francisco Bay, according to Fred Shure's testimony in a Florida money-laundering case. But Perlowin, in lengthy prison interviews with me, said the total amount actually was between 159,000 and 162,000 pounds.

By the middle of 1983, the federal investigation into the Shures was still in its early stages. "It was agreed that we'd all tough it out," one of their distributors told me. "A number of people perjured themselves before the grand jury to protect Ned and Fred. But then the brothers turned around and made a secret deal for themselves. There isn't a lot of good feeling right now."

The collapse of the brothers' Louisiana, Virginia, and California operations gave the federal Organized Crime Strike Force in Detroit, which took over control of the Shures' fate, two massive hammers: They could charge them in federal court with operating a continuing criminal enterprise with a ten-year mandatory minimum sentence, or they could let Louisiana and Virginia try them in state court, where the brothers would face the possibility of life in prison.

Ned and Fred Shure hired former U.S. Attorney James K. Robinson. Under the deal Robinson cut with the feds, which wouldn't come to light until their plea and sentencing, the brothers would inform on everybody and account for every dollar. In exchange, they would pay a shade more than $1 million in back taxes, penalties, and fines, plead guilty, and face no more than thirty-five years in federal prison. The thirty-five years was for show. U.S. District Judge Charles W. Joiner ended up sentencing them to seven years each, which meant less than five years of actual time under federal guidelines.

I didn't have strong feelings about marijuana one way or another. But what drew me to the brothers was the scope of the conspiracies and the uniqueness of a big-time criminal who was also a brilliant U-M Ph.D. in physics and tenured associate professor in the university's Department of Nuclear Engineering. Fred Shure taught there from 1959 through 1981. I called up a copy of his doctoral dissertation, "Boundary Problems in Plasma Oscillations," one step toward the still-unrealized holy grail of limitless clean energy from laser fusion. I interviewed the remaining members of his dissertation committee at the university and several members of his department.

I also convinced two of the brothers' middlemen, Lyle Joseph Parks and Albert G. Papson, to talk to me on the record. Two others agreed to speak with me with a promise of anonymity, and I tracked the subsequent court cases of many of the Shures' colleagues.

The picture was not always pretty. One of the women the brothers turned against was Ned Shure's first wife, who was recruited as a courier after appealing to him for financial help. Another was a childhood friend to whom they had lent $10,000 and who felt he had a debt of honor when they came to him seeking help with a marijuana cargo.

My biggest frustration and my singular failure was my inability to follow the money. Based on the volume of marijuana the brothers handled, they should have had gross revenues of $100 million or more. But their expenses were high. They overpaid for just about everything, got ripped off left and right because they were not tough guys, and lost multiple loads.

Robinson's plea deal meant the Internal Revenue Service would not continue with its net-worth investigation. The government sought back taxes for only one year. So, was that a true picture of the brothers' wealth? Had they salted away money?

A retired local banker, who spoke to me on background, told me the brothers had used real estate transactions to launder some of their money. I discovered the Shures would form a partnership and name it with the address of the building they were buying. They would pay contractors under the table to rehab the structure, sell it at a profit, and pay capital gains, thereby laundering all the under-the-table payments.

I pulled the papers on every partnership in Washtenaw County whose name was the address of a building. I found half a dozen files that were the Shures' but only a couple of them had been signed out by the IRS, meaning the government had missed the others. But since the brothers' grand jury testimony, pre-sentence report, and the details of their plea deal were all covered by secrecy, I had nothing against which to compare my discoveries.

I poked and prodded, trying without success to break loose some of that secret information. The feds had a massive incentive not to help me. If I could prove the Shures had lied to the government, it might have unraveled the convictions they were piling up.

Fred Shure would later testify at the Tampa, Florida, trial of a money launderer that the brothers had made $1 million from their real estate transactions and the bookstore and had kept both totally separate from their marijuana activities.

That wasn't true. In addition to the apparent real estate money laundering, they used the bookstore to generate fake W2 forms so some of their dealers would appear to have a legitimate source of income as employees. If the brothers had listed the fake salaries on the bookstore's tax returns, it would have inflated the expenses of running the business and thus reduced their taxes. But tax returns are secret, and I was stymied again.

After serving slightly more than a year at the federal prison camp in Duluth, Minnesota, the brothers appeared before Judge Joiner asking that their sentences be cut in half. They complained that the other inmates treated them unkindly, branding them the "Rat Brothers."

Strike Force Attorney Martin E. Crandall, who had negotiated their deal, did not oppose their request. He termed their cooperation "exceptional, extraordinary," adding that the government received "substantial, unexpected dividends" from their cooperation. Joiner took their request under advisement. I moved on to a pair of subsequent, even larger drug conspiracies, one of which had ties to the CIA and the Reagan Administration's Contra resupply, and forgot to check back on the judge's decision.

Several years later, after the brothers had served their sentences, I was having dinner with my wife at a restaurant in Saline. Seated several tables away were Ned and Fred Shure, their wives, and brother-in-law Jack Barenfanger, who had been their chief lieutenant and had also served a prison term.

Toward the end of the meal, Fred Shure had to walk past our table to get to the restroom. He kept his head turned sideways to avoid making eye contact with me and stumbled over a chair. I didn't try to speak with him. He was yesterday's news

Chapter 61 "Mad Dog" Merkle And The Pot Genius

TAMPA — Bruce Perlowin, the bearded and pony-tailed master drug smuggler from California by way of South Florida, was risking additional years in federal prison by defying U.S. Attorney Robert W. "Mad Dog" Merkle. Merkle, who had defied Attorney General John Mitchell by prosecuting Panamanian dictator Manuel Noriega, a CIA asset, was known as a hard-ass even by U.S. attorney standards. Perlowin was using me to jerk Merkle's chain. Or, perhaps I was using him. Either way, we were both playing a somewhat risky game.

Merkle had put Theodore "Ted" Koury, former board chairman of Red Carpet Inns International, Inc., on trial for his role in laundering monies from the joint marijuana smuggling operation of Perlowin and Ann Arbor "Barons of Pot," Ned and Fred Shure. The Shures had rolled over on some seventy-five of their friends, relatives, and colleagues, managing to avoid having to testify. The Detroit Strike Force attorneys used the threat of their testimony to induce Shures' former colleagues to plead guilty, making them offers too generous to refuse. If one of the Shares did end up testifying and a defense attorney could show he lied to the feds, it could unravel a lot of convictions.

Merkle had a reputation for not playing ball with anyone, including the Detroit Task Force attorneys. He called Fred Shure as a witness against Koury. The Ann Arbor News let me fly to Tampa to hear what Fred Shure had to say.

When the Shures cut their deal to become government witnesses in exchange for reduced prison time, Perlowin told me he knew his time was up. He pled guilty to operating a continuing criminal enterprise and was serving a mandatory minimum ten-year prison sentence. He rejected a deal for less prison time that would have required him to testify against others. Sometimes, there actually is honor among thieves.

Someone had sent Perlowin a copy of the profile I did on the Shures in late 1983. Perlowin called me from prison at my Ann Arbor News office. I did a subsequent profile of the brothers' California connection based on what ended up being two extended jailhouse interviews.

Merkle had the U.S. Marshal's Service transfer Perlowin from California to Florida even though the former drug dealer had said he was unwilling to testify. If Perlowin continued his refusal to testify, Merkle threatened to prosecute him for contempt of court. That would add additional years to the front end of his ten-year sentence. He held firm.

Perlowin and I reconnected during the Koury trial. At the end of each day of testimony, Perlowin would call me from the Hillsboro County Jail. I would review the day's testimony, and Perlowin would offer his sometimes contradictory version, which I would write up for the next day's paper.

Perlowin had begun his smuggling career in the early 1970s, bringing about 100,000 pounds of marijuana into South Florida. But it was becoming an unhealthy place for pot smugglers as Colombian and Cuban "cocaine cowboys" sought to take over their smuggling operations to move cocaine.

Perlowin sold his redwood furniture business and pot operation. With cash in hand, he moved to San Francisco. He hired private investigators to analyze every major West Coast marijuana bust in the previous ten years so he could avoid the mistakes others had made.

He wasn't interested in Mexican marijuana, which was then considered pretty low-grade. He also concluded that it would be too risky to bring marijuana from Colombia's Atlantic coast through the Panama Canal and up the coast to California or overland from the Gulf of Mexico.

The growers of higher quality "Punta Roja" (red point or red bud marijuana) in south-central Colombia had trouble getting their product to market. Perlowin and the growers split the cost of a DC-3 that would fly bales of product over an Indian village on the Pacific Coast that could not be reached by rail or car. "They'd kick the bales out of the plane as it flew over the beach," Perlowin recalled. "We hired the entire village to gather, store, and secure the marijuana.

"Meanwhile, we would outfit a boat for whatever was in season — rig for tuna in tuna season, rig for black cod when that was in season — and send the boat to Costa Rica to refuel, get provisions, and wait for the radio message that all the stuff was on the beach and ready to pick up."

The genius of the operation was that Perlowin had purchased a 1,000-foot pier in San Francisco Bay, which was hidden from radar on Alcatraz by the

Richardson Street Bridge. The pot boat would join the fishing fleet as it returned to the bay, offloading at its secure berth.

A fanatic for developing backup systems, Perlowin, who was manufacturing houseboats at the pier, moored one of his houseboats at the mouth of the Sacramento River. As yet another backup, he bought six nineteen-foot Zodiac speedboats that could have offloaded to any beach in Northern California.

Perlowin had everything in place but lacked the front money for loads. He heard from a friend that two Ann Arbor brothers were hoping to use a helicopter to offload marijuana in California. It was a strategy Perlowin knew had failed in Florida. He offered himself as the Shures' backup. Two days later, Ned Shure called.

Their basic deal was that the brothers would pay half of all Perlowin's smuggling expenses in exchange for a 37.5 percent share of the pot.
The U.S. Coast Guard initiated a series of random offshore interceptions and nabbed one of their mother ships. For the most part, however, the smuggling came off without a hitch.

I needled Perlowin that, if Secretary of Defense Robert McNamara had turned to him rather than the "best and the brightest," the U.S. might have won the Vietnam War. He acknowledged the compliment but didn't think it was funny.

There were problems, however. Perlowin said his Colombian connection had to move the pickup point for their first boatload. Perlowin's people packed the marijuana bales by burro across fast-moving mountain streams. "Those streams swept away several burros, and the rest of the load got soaked," Perlowin said. When they finally got the marijuana to San Francisco, they bought or rented three homes, closed the windows, spread out the pot on every floor with the help of Ned and Fred Shure, and turned up the thermostats as high as they would go.

Fred Shure testified that they salvaged six thousand pounds. Perlowin told me they'd actually succeeded in drying sixteen thousand pounds. I did a boat-by-boat comparison between Fred Shure's testimony about the seven boatloads they brought in during 1980 and 1981 and Perlowin's interview totals. Perlowin said Fred undercounted by seventy-five thousand pounds.

Nevertheless, Perlowin said he did not believe the Shures had salted away large amounts of money. "None of us were violent, and the Shures, in particular, had difficulty collecting from people who wouldn't pay," he added. When they finally parted, each ended up claiming the other owed $500,000.

"In 1981, we had a pretty intensive need for money, and they had a real hard time coming up with it," Perlowin said. "I also learned that they had to borrow money from one of their distributors to finance the next-to-last boat we brought in together in 1981."

For his end, Perlowin sought front money from two big-time California cocaine dealers who turned out to be undercover federal agents. But he said it wasn't until he learned that Ned and Fred Shure had rolled over that he pleaded guilty. On the other hand, Fred Shure testified that he and his brother didn't decide to plead until they were given access to seven thousand pages of transcripts of Perlowin's conversations with the undercover agents.

I liked Perlowin, didn't have much use for the Shures, but didn't know who was telling the truth. I didn't have a lot of affection for Koury, either. During a break in the trial, I joined the defendant and his lawyer for lunch in the Keys. They thought it was funny to stick me with the bill. At the conclusion of the Tampa trial, Koury was convicted of money laundering. "Mad Dog" Merkle decided there was no need to prosecute Perlowin for contempt of court and returned him to federal prison in California. I flew back to Ann Arbor.

Perlowin ended up serving nine years. Upon his release, he remained in California, cut his ponytail, shaved off his beard, became one of the West Coast's leading advocates for marijuana legalization, and established himself as a pot entrepreneur. His Facebook page boasted that he had earned more than $100 million in profits during a thirty-year career that began with nickel bags in high school. "I am CEO of Hemp Inc., and I am passionate about products made from hemp," he wrote. "My vision is to create eco-villages and improve the world."

But the federal Securities and Exchange Commission charged Perlowin, one of the leaders of the pot penny stock bubble, with fraud for allegedly selling hundreds of millions of unregistered shares in Hemp Inc. The stock price dropped from $2.99 to four cents a share.

Chapter 62 A Billion-Dollar Doper Scams The Feds

When you are the partner in a billion-dollar cocaine and marijuana smuggling operation based mainly in Brighton, Michigan, you have unusual ways of dealing with adversity.

Commercial pilot Michael Bernard Palmer and fellow pilot Kenneth Jason of South Lyon, Michigan, landed Palmer's Beechcraft Queen Air on a fallow field near Santa Marta, Colombia, in 1985. As they began loading eighty-pound bales of marijuana, Colombian National Police helicopters came screaming over the treetops, shooting up the plane.

The pair surrendered when Palmer couldn't get the Queen Air's engine started, and they were hauled off to the Colombian federal prison in Valledupar, where they remained incarcerated for three-and-a-half months, Jason recalled in a 1988 jailhouse interview.

Jason said Palmer kept assuring him they could leave anytime but first wanted his passport back and a promise from Colombian authorities that he could continue making drug flights from Colombia to the United States.

Palmer regularly arranged to have marijuana, cocaine, and local women delivered to them in prison and just as regularly drank himself to oblivion on Chivas Regal scotch, said the fellow pilot. He added that Palmer made periodic trips to Bogota and Medellin and was visited several times in prison by Colombian drug lord Oswaldo Morales.

Leigh Ritch of Grand Cayman Island, the drug conspiracy's "Mr. Outside" to Palmer's "Mr. Inside," would later tell the U.S. Senate's Foreign Relations Subcommittee on Terrorism and Narcotics that a $60,000 bribe was paid to Colombian authorities to secure Palmer's and Jason's release. Other members of the smuggling network remember far higher amounts being paid.

Palmer's fiancee, Cindy Fitzgerald, an Eastern Airlines flight attendant, and Jason's wife, Cindy, made several trips to Valledupar. Cindy Jason told me the pair were freed with the aid of General Alverro Valencia Tovar, former head of the Colombian Army, whom she described as "a funny-looking little guy with a big house." They stayed in the big house during their visits.

Palmer, a Delta Airlines pilot flying out of Miami for twelve years, maintained a safe house in Ann Arbor under an alias. He stored the largest of his drug planes, a DC-6, with legendary fuel dragster Connie Kalitta at Willow Run Airport. Palmer made or organized as many as two hundred drug flights, mostly from Colombia to Michigan.

While everyone else charged in the drug conspiracies ended up in prison, U.S. Attorney Roy C. "Joe" Hayes decided that the indictment of Palmer should be dismissed "in the interests of justice." Justice had nothing to do with the dismissal. Palmer had managed to play the Drug Enforcement Administration against the Federal Bureau of Investigation. He involved himself with the Central Intelligence Agency, the State Department, and the Nicaraguan Contra resupply effort run out of the National Security Council by Lieutenant Colonel Oliver North. He also set up two massive drug stings. In short, he made himself toxic.

Bill Spindle, a young reporter with The News, and I began working the Michigan end of the story in June 1986 with the federal indictment of Michael Paul Vogel of Brighton Township. Vogel was charged along with Michael Palmer and seventeen others. Spindle and I struggled in a futile effort to pin down the role of Kalitta and the Connie Kalitta Flying Services. I continued on the story through the 1988 subcommittee hearings in Washington chaired by then-Senator John Kerry.

Spindle and I interviewed more than a dozen members of the drug conspiracy and their lawyers, as well as most of the assistant U.S. attorneys around the country who had pieces of the action. We also collected hundreds of pages of court filings. The News published some two dozen major stories, but we were never able to prove that the government let Palmer bring in drugs in exchange for his help with the Contra resupply or that the CIA pulled strings to get the indictment dismissed.

U.S. Attorney Hayes called the Vogel network the largest he had ever seen, saying it employed more than one hundred people and imported an estimated one million pounds of marijuana, of which 566,000 pounds came to southern Michigan.

All of the defendants, except for Tom "The Bomb" McGowan of rural Howell, were invited to surrender through their attorneys. McGowan, who had two prior federal drug convictions and the reputation as Vogel's enforcer, was targeted by the FBI's Special Weapons and Tactics team.

McGowan was sleeping in the buff when he was awakened in pre-dawn by a noisy parade of black SWAT vehicles roaring up his long farm driveway. According to one of the FBI agents, he grabbed his stash of cocaine, jumped in the shower, and was trying to flush it down the drain as he was confronted by SWAT officers with a shotgun, carbine, and a snarling German shepherd. "Happy feet," said one of the agents. They recovered about a pound of water-soaked cocaine.

The FBI also seized three airplanes from Willow Run Airport, property near Brighton, a variety of cars and trucks, Ritch's condo in Grand Cayman Island, and the Dillworth Hotel in Boyne City.

According to affidavits and federal indictments, three marijuana flights had come into Willow Run. The documents also contend that Vogel, under the alias "Joseph Gallagher," had used Kalitta planes to fly millions of dollars in drug money to Florida. Using warrants of seizure, the feds grabbed three vans, two Lear Jets, and a Mitsubishi MU-2 from Kalitta.
The warrant said the pilots flying "Gallagher" were given specific instructions not to log the flights, not to question their passenger about his business, and to pay for everything in cash.

However, neither the FBI nor Spindle and I could prove that Kalitta had actual personal knowledge of the illegalities, despite a three-and-a-half-year investigation. The closest we came was a major story we published under the headline "The Case of the Suspicious Red Stripe." Zantop Airlines, by far Willow Run's largest and busiest air freight hauler, painted all of its planes with a distinctive red stripe. We interviewed airport workers, who told us Kalitta had personally instructed them to paint an identical red stripe on Palmer's DC-6. That allowed the plane to be flown in and out of the airport without attracting attention. Kalitta Vice President Tom Warner said he and Kalitta had been cooperating with the Drug Enforcement Administration (not the FBI) and that the repainting could have an innocent explanation. He refused to say what that explanation might be.

In the end, Hayes didn't feel he had a strong enough case to seek an indictment against Kalitta, and Kalitta went to federal court in Ann Arbor in a successful bid to get his property back.

Meanwhile, Palmer, at his 1986 federal court bond hearing, testified that he worked for Vortex Aviation and Southern Air Transport. Southern Air was identified in the congressional Iran-Contra committee report as a CIA front. On behalf of Vortex, Palmer had signed a contract with the State Department to make "humanitarian" flights to the Contras as well as "clandestine missions."

Once freed on bond, Palmer tried to cut deals with several FBI offices around the country but was rebuffed by each. He had better luck with the DEA in Brownsville, Texas, and spent eighteen months working undercover for them even as he was doing State Department flights.

Three months after his indictment in Detroit, Palmer got the DEA's okay to fly 20,000 pounds of marijuana from Northern Mexico into the southern United States. But there was an unexplained screw-up, and 16,000 pounds ended up on the streets of America.

Palmer's second sting was more successful. He came up with $1.4 million of unexplained origin and arranged for 128,000 pounds of marijuana to be shipped on the freighter "Madrid" into Port Arthur, Texas, in August 1987. This time, the feds were waiting. In his final sting that September, Palmer turned to his old DC-6 to fly 574 pounds of cocaine and 17,387 pounds of marijuana from Colombia to the Grosse Ile Airport, south of Detroit, again into the waiting arms of the feds.

On Oct. 19, 1987, U.S. Attorney Hayes sent one of his assistants before U.S. District Judge Ralph Freeman to get all the charges against Palmer dropped. Hayes told me that he had personally authorized the dismissal. "There was absolutely no Washington influence, never any communication from the CIA or any other government agency," Hayes said. "The decision was local, only involving those who work here in drug enforcement."

I was stunned by his outright fabrication. Shortly before the last two stings, the Justice Department had pulled together a secret meeting that included the key players from the FBI, DEA, and U.S. Attorneys with offices in Michigan, Texas, and Colorado. They were joined by Palmer's lawyer, a former federal strike force chief. The purpose of that meeting, according to later congressional testimony, was to "broker Palmer's fate."
The News interviewed five of the men who were either at the meeting or were briefed immediately afterward. They all told essentially the same story: There was a grudging agreement to let Palmer try to lure his long-

time supplier, Colombian drug lord Oswaldo Morales, to Panama or Costa Rica, where U.S. agents could snatch him. There was no mention of the CIA, but there was a tacit understanding that Palmer would go free. The Morales ploy failed. The FBI agents who built the case against Vogel, Palmer, and other members of the drug conspiracy were privately furious at Hayes for seeking the dismissal.

Miami defense attorney Ronald C. Dresnick, who represented one of the main figures in the Grosse Ile sting, mounted what he called the "DeLorean defense," echoing the strategy by which John DeLorean was found not guilty of cocaine charges after a federal court jury agreed with the defense's assertion that the federal government's conduct was even more reprehensible than the former auto executive's.

Dresnick argued that the federal government set up the stings as an excuse to drop the charges against Palmer so he wouldn't testify about the CIA's drugs-for-guns conduct. The defense attorney was able to raise suspicion but could produce no credible evidence. His client was convicted.

Senator Kerry's subcommittee tried to take a bite from the same apple at hearings I covered in Washington in the spring of 1988. Vogel, who had pled guilty to drug charges and was serving a twelve-and-a-half-year sentence, testified that, from 1974 through 1980, he was the primary distributor for the fugitive smuggler Jerry Carroll. He said he and Palmer handled forty-five to fifty plane loads of pot for the Carroll organization. Vogel and Palmer then formed their own organization later in 1980 and did 44 to 48 small loads, mainly with planes based at the Hillsdale Airport, plus two large DC-6 loads to Willow Run. He said he made $12 million from his deals with Palmer, whom he described as his boss. He said Palmer made three to five times as much per load.

Vogel was not able to cast any light on Palmer's role in the Contra resupply but did testify that Palmer had bribed a U.S. Customs agent who had regular access to the El Paso Information Center (EPIC) computer used to keep track of all planes and boats the government suspected of smuggling. That allowed their planes to avoid seizure. He said Palmer also had a friend in the Coast Guard who helped them avoid having any of their boats being intercepted at sea.

Palmer also testified before the Senate committee, but only after he was granted immunity. He told dramatic stories of his smuggling adventures and admitted to helping maintain CIA planes used in the Contra resupply but flatly denied any government or personal wrongdoing.

Palmer said he broke with Vogel when Vogel bragged about trying to get Teamsters Union friends to assassinate one of their associates. "It signaled to me that they [his drug associates] were no longer a bunch of fun-loving Jimmy Buffett types going down in song and legend," said the drug pilot.

Palmer successfully sparred with Senator Kerry whenever the subcommittee chairman tried to pin down the exact nature of what the ex-smuggler had done for the CIA and the Contra resupply operation. I talked with a disappointed Kerry at the end of Palmer's testimony. "I don't think we know the full extent of everything that took place," he admitted.

Chapter 63 State Shrink Seduces Pedophile Killer

HOWELL — Ronald Lloyd Bailey, a slightly-built twenty-six-year-old pedophile with dusty blond hair, was facing trial for the kidnapping, rape, and murder of the junior high school-age son of an Ann Arbor News circulation supervisor.

Dr. Jose Tombo, the Phillippine-born psychiatrist in charge of Northville State Hospital's male young-adult ward, had seduced Bailey when he was a patient on the ward. Or, perhaps Bailey had manipulated Tombo for favors.

Bailey's defense attorneys initially hoped to convince the jury that their client hadn't killed thirteen-year-old Shawn Moore. When that approach appeared hopeless, their alternate strategy was to argue that Bailey wasn't criminally responsible because of his prior sexual abuse at Tombo's hands.

Into this morass, fellow reporter Tina Lam and I double-teamed an investigation into Tombo, also exposing the Michigan Department of Mental Health's lackadaisical approach to investigating earlier sex abuse allegations against the psychiatrist. Reporter Amy Smith and I did tag-team coverage of Bailey's month-long trial while trying to comfort Shawn's distraught parents, who sat in the front row of the visitor's section throughout.

There was a hard edge to our stories.

On August 31, 1985 (Labor Day), Shawn took a break from yard work with his father after a lawn mower broke. He rode his ten-speed to the Pump 'N Pantry for a can of root beer, returning along Whitmore Lake Road in Green Oak Township, north of Ann Arbor. Three witnesses saw him being grabbed off his bicycle by a man driving what was later confirmed to be a new AMC Jeep Renegade.

Armed with a computer printout of every Renegade owner in southeast Michigan, law enforcement task force members interviewed Bailey, a Livonia resident, four days after the kidnapping. Two tipsters broke Bailey's initial alibi, but the three kidnapping witnesses failed to pick him out of a lineup.

Undercover officers tailed Bailey as he fled Michigan to a trailer park outside of Ocala, Florida, where his girlfriend lived. The girlfriend's father told officers he had lent Bailey the key to his one-room hunting cabin outside of Gladwin in north-central Michigan.

At 4:30 a.m. on September 13, State Police Detective Sergeant Paul Bowers found Shawn's nude, partially decomposed body off a dirt track, partially hidden by foliage, and just two-and-a-half miles from the cabin. Forensic investigators said they found one of Shawn's fingerprints in the cabin.

Bailey had disappeared from the Florida trailer ahead of the police. For two days, he eluded 225 officers — some on horseback, others with bloodhounds. He emerged from the woods, mosquito-bitten, with his arms raised in surrender. "I'm Ronald Bailey," he told a startled off-duty corrections officer. "I'm tired of running. I'm hungry. I give up."

Two weeks later, Tina Lam and I met with Bailey lawyers Raymond A. Cassar and Charles A. Murphy in their Farmington Hills office. In an on-the-record interview, they told of Bailey's accusations against Tombo. But toward the end of the interview, the lawyers said they changed their minds and wanted it off the record. "Too late. It was on the record, and you can't take it back," I said with a sudden fury that left me stunned at myself. "We will print it!" I'm not sure we would have carried through on the threat, but Murphy gulped and said, "Okay."

It turned out that we didn't need to quote the lawyers at all. Their accusation led us to a thirty-page report compiled by State Police Sergeant Wayne Bullen in 1980, five years before the murder. The report, which we obtained under a Freedom of Information request, detailed accounts from staffers and former patients accusing Tombo of having sexual contact with Bailey and at least five other patients since 1974.

We tracked down one former patient, who said the sexual contact with Tombo took place both in an outpatient clinic run by the hospital and at the psychiatrist's Northville apartment. "I wanted it to stop," he told us. "I knew it was wrong."

The young man, whom we agreed not to name, had told his family about the sexual abuse. We talked with his mother, who related that, for Christmas, Tombo had given her son a new corduroy suit, herself a tablecloth and perfume, and gave her son's aunt a shower cap. When the young man again began hearing voices and was readmitted to Northville, the family insisted that a different doctor treat him.

Under direct questioning, Dr. Rowan Sanders, Tombo's supervisor, told the State Police's Bullen that a patient had accused Tombo of having sex with him on the ward in 1977 or 1978. The patient also told Bullen that Tombo had masturbated him during a physical examination, but the hospital's Office of Recipient Rights had said the psychiatrist had "merely conducted a very thorough physical examination."

The Michigan Psychiatric Society also launched an ethics investigation of Tombo in 1979 after a patient's family brought their son to Dr. George Newman of Dearborn. The young man told Newman that Tombo had had oral sex with him several times. Newman, who became society's president in 1985, said its investigation of Tombo was dropped after Tombo resigned from the society. Newman told us he did not make a formal complaint to the hospital because the family hadn't asked him to and that he didn't do it on his own because of patient confidentiality. I wanted to grab him by the lapels and shout in his face, "You gutless coward, look at the harm you could have prevented!" But reporters never do that. You write the dry facts and hope that the reader comes to share your outrage.

Dr. Newman had been interviewed by Bullen for the 1980 State Police report. According to the report, Newman told Bullen he believed the patient and said he would be willing to testify. The patient himself told Bullen that Tombo had threatened not to help the young man unless he had sex with him. Bullen sought a warrant charging Tombo with criminal sexual conduct, but the cowardly Wayne County Prosecutor's Office turned it down because of a question of consent and the mental state of the victim. That was bullshit, of course. There was no public outcry to force their hand, and they didn't want to get bogged down in a complex, messy case.

Neither Northville Hospital nor the Michigan Department of Mental Health asked for a copy of Bullen's report until we raised the issue with department chief C. Patrick Babcock five years after the report was issued. Tina and I laid this all out in a front-page copyrighted story on October 6, 1985. Babcock finally requested a copy of Bullen's report, said he was reopening the case against Tombo, and was sharply critical of his department's "too casual" handling of the matter five years before.

It also turned out that Tombo, in a failed effort to cover his tracks, had called Alfred Bailey, Ronald's father, shortly after Ronald's arrest, asking that the senior Bailey not publicly mention a trip to Windsor the psychiatrist had taken with the young man in the late 1970s.
Several days before our copyrighted story appeared, Tombo met with Al Bailey and Ronald's lawyers and denied having had any sexual contact with the young man.

Tina and I wanted to talk directly with Ron Bailey, but officials ruled that his parents and his lawyers were the only ones allowed to visit Bailey, who was being held in the Livingston County Jail to await trial. Tina and I, together with a Detroit Free Press reporter, asked Al Bailey to take a list of written questions to his son.

Al Bailey met with us after seeing his son and read his hand-written answers to us. Ronald Bailey acknowledged having sex with Tombo in a hospital examining room and said the two "exchanged oral sex" during the trip to Windsor. We published that story on October 10, reporting also that the mental health chief had suspended Tombo pending an investigation by Attorney General Frank Kelley.

In researching the October 10 story, we were able to document that there were two initial investigations in early 1978 by the hospital itself and its Office of Recipient Rights into Bailey's allegation that Tombo spent 15 minutes masturbating him in an exam room. Those charges were ruled "refuted." In addition to the investigations we had reported on the previous week, it turned out there were three more probes of a 1980 sex abuse allegation. All except for the Bullen's probe were both superficial and quickly concluded. Tombo's only punishment was a six-day suspension for a nonsexual violation of hospital rules. The hospital, however, did remove Tombo from treating young adult males.

Ann Arbor News photographer Larry E. Wright got a superb surveillance photo of Tombo prior to his suspension from Northville. I took it around to a couple of suburban Detroit gay bars and a gay dance club. While the people I approached were more than willing to help, no one recognized him.

Bailey, following his release from Northville, had lived in Florida for three to four years. Amy Smith flew to the Ocala area but was unable to find any new information about him. One of the places she checked was a gay bar known for the rough trade. Amy phoned the newspaper office from Florida and was asked what the bar was like. "Full of bad-ass butt-fuckers," she told the stunned editor. You go wherever the story takes you.

The massive publicity of the Shawn Moore murder prompted Wayne County authorities to take a look at Bailey in connection with several unsolved sex crimes. As a result, he was charged with the June 1984 kidnapping and sexual assault of a fifteen-year-old Redford Township youth and the July 16, 1984 kidnapping and slaying of Kenneth Myers, fourteen, of Ferndale. Both those cases were put off until the conclusion of Bailey's trial for the Moore murder, which began in early September 1986.

The Ann Arbor News was an afternoon paper, which meant we could get updates into the paper as late as 11:30 a.m. Amy and I would write an overnight story after each day of the trial. Then, the following morning, we would alternate calling in updates to Assistant City Editor Adeline Adams, who managed to keep everything straight and flawless.

Defense attorney Murphy acknowledged in his opening statement that Bailey had killed Shawn Moore but said he should be found not guilty by reason of insanity. He branded Tombo, who had been in charge of treating Bailey for nearly three years, a "Frankenstein" psychiatrist, suggesting that Bailey was his creation.

"He ran that ward like a Nazi concentration camp for one purpose, to gratify his deviant sexual desires, his craving for young, blond, blue-eyed boys," said the attorney. "This young man was a sick young man, to begin with, but if he had any hope of becoming sane, it was destroyed by Dr. Tombo."

Despite the admission to the killing, the prosecution put on fifty-one witnesses to build a convincing case that Bailey had, indeed, kidnapped and murdered Shawn Moore.

The defense called Ronald Bailey's father, Al, who testified that, when his son was thirteen, he was sent to Northville's Hawthorn Center for a year for abducting and fondling an eight-year-old boy. When he was fifteen, he abducted, choked, and fondled another boy. That was when he ended up being sent to Northville, where he came under Tombo's care.

Ronald Bailey took the stand, testifying at length about being instructed in "voodoo" by Tombo, by being ordered to call Tombo "Master," and being compelled to have sex with him. Bailey also admitted to kidnapping and sexually assaulting nearly three dozen boys in Michigan and Florida. When Ronald Bailey cried, it was for himself.

Bailey's attorneys repeatedly tried and failed to subpoena Tombo, who had been fired from Northville the previous year and moved to an inner-city Detroit apartment. They turned to Dr. Joel Stanley Dreyer, who owned a psychiatric clinic in Southfield that was heavily advertised on television. Dreyer had called the attorneys, volunteering to be their expert witness.

Dreyer claimed that Tombo forced Bailey into sexual atrocities that pushed him into the final stages of schizophrenia, where he disassociated. This "allowed him to act out as if he were Tombo and seek out young boys." He said Bailey "thinks he is a sorcerer and a demon" and didn't know it was wrong to kill Shawn Moore. Dreyer formally diagnosed Bailey as suffering from "pseudo-psychopathic schizophrenia," a diagnosis that the medical literature says "has fallen into oblivion."

Even the jurors seemed embarrassed by Dreyer's bizarre testimony. Dreyer looked directly at the jury as he spoke. The jurors looked away.

Prosecution psychologist Dr. Harley Stock and psychiatrist Dr. Lynn Blunt, both of the state's Center for Forensic Psychiatry in Ypsilanti, testified they had administered a series of tests that demonstrated convincingly that Bailey was faking mental illness. They diagnosed him as a "borderline personality and homosexual pedophile with sexual sadism," all exceptionally serious disorders. However the state's two experts insisted that Bailey was not mentally ill and could resist his urges.

On October 1, the jury found Bailey guilty of kidnapping, first-degree premeditated murder, and first-degree felony murder. When he was sentenced to life with no parole, both the judge and prosecutor used the occasion as a platform for oratory.

Tombo appealed his firing but lost a binding arbitration decision.
Both Bailey and Tombo left me feeling unclean. There was no kindness in our portrayals of either man. Amy, Tina, and I coldly skewered each example of official incompetence that we encountered, and there were many. It was all we could do.

Chapter 64 Exposing A Deadly, Fetid Nursing Home

YPSILANTI — Prospect Park was an inverse inferno. In Dante, the punishments worsen as you descend from one circle of hell to the next. At the fetid Prospect Park Convalescent Center, conditions deteriorated as you ascend.

I wandered the second and third-floor halls of the nursing home, dropping in to chat with several patients. It was February 1987, cold outside but swelteringly hot inside the square, brick former Beyer Memorial Hospital.

Two of the bedridden patients on the third floor, who had kicked their sheets aside, asked me to open a window for them. Parts of the fourth floor, however, were freezing cold. The staff had opened windows in a failed effort to dilute the odor of urine, which was so strong it left your eyes smarting.

Only once in four decades of newspapering had I encountered anything nearly as rank: The boys' bathroom at Copernicus Junior High School in Hamtramck in 1972. In the bathroom, the toilet bowls sat unenclosed against one wall. The toilet paper dispensers and sinks were against the opposite wall. In protest, the kids peed repeatedly on the aging cast-iron radiators.

At Prospect Park, the fourth floor was where the nursing home warehoused most of its patients suffering from dementia, its incontinent patients, and patients whose families rarely visited.

I returned with a photographer the following Friday afternoon. On the fourth floor, one aide was helping a patient use the toilet with open doors to both the bathroom and hallway. The rest of the staff was in the break room.

I went into a day room where there were eleven unattended patients. All but two were either asleep or staring into whatever unimaginable void their lives had become. Eight were strapped into chairs or wheelchairs, including three who were safety pinned into large diapers that desperately needed changing.

I recruited two of The Ann Arbor News' younger reporters — Chong W. Pyen and Paul Judge — to help research and write a massive series, "The Trouble With Nursing Homes." We evaluated each of Washtenaw County's ten nursing homes, interviewing staff and administrators, patients, families, state inspectors, members of patient advocacy groups, and University of Michigan gerontologists. We collected hundreds of pages of state inspection reports. We tracked down not only former nursing home employees who felt freer to talk but also physicians and other medical staff who had treated nursing home residents who had been hospitalized as a result of injury or neglect.

The administrators at Prospect were particularly vexed with me because I had become a notary public. That allowed me to collect and notarize waivers of confidentiality, giving me legal access to patient records that they were no longer able to keep secret. One of the first I found included treatment notes dated February 29, February 30, and February 31, 1987.

I wrote the cover stories for each day, choosing Prospect Park for myself. The place had several times more violations than any home in the county. Behind each violation was a fragile, elderly man or woman being abused or neglected. As with the earlier Bailey-Tombo cluster fuck, you translate your cold fury into words. It's what journalists do. Reading over my clips to write about Prospect Park, I got mad all over again.

There was stroke victim Lenore Beiderman, seventy-eight, who developed two out-of-control urinary tract infections, blood poisoning, and a softball-sized bedsore that turned gangrenous. A registered nurse who treated her at Beyer Hospital before she died there said she came to the hospital dirty and malnourished.

Mary Cannon, also seventy-eight, hated the indignity of using a bedpan but usually could not find an aide to take her to the bathroom. Her best friend, Josephine, was helping her to the bathroom. Mary, shaky on her four-legged walker, stumbled. Josephine fell on top of her, breaking Mary's leg. Mary remained at the nursing home through two full shifts before someone called an ambulance to take her across the street to Beyer. She died four days later when the fracture triggered a blood clot that lodged in her lungs, according to the death certificate.

Harold Benner was different. He lived. The fourth-floor patient was wandering around at 4:30 a.m. on January 6, looking for something to eat.

The midnight nursing supervisor, who was taking a cigarette break, told him the kitchen was closed. She gave him a cigarette but did not see him back to his room.

At 6:10 a.m., Ypsilanti police found him on the shoulder of Ecorse Road, unconscious and suffering from severe hypothermia, and took him to Beyer Hospital. He was wearing a plaid shirt and slacks but no shoes, socks, or underwear. When he was sufficiently recovered, the hospital returned him to Prospect Park. I asked the nursing home's new administrator why Benner was allowed to wander. He replied that he wasn't running a prison.

Then there was Erna Howett, seventy-two, dying and in intractable pain from cancer throughout her body, a nasty lesion on the side of her neck, a pair of bedsores on her coccyx, and an unhealed, displaced fracture of her left arm. She had filed suit against the nursing home, alleging twenty-six instances of abuse, neglect, and professional malpractice. She had exceedingly fragile bones and suffered several breaks at the Prospect Park. The most recent incident occurred when two aides took her by her arms to the bathroom rather than put her in a wheelchair. That snapped her left arm.

Her treatment plan called for her diaper to be changed every two hours to keep her dry, but that rarely happened. She complained a lot. During her eighty-one-minute deposition, the nursing home's bottom-feeder attorneys kept trying to get her to admit she was a difficult patient, as if the abuse and neglect were her fault. "When I have a messy bed, for instance, my body doesn't function according to schedule, and I get bawled out," she said. "I simply get broken-hearted and sometimes cry because of what they say to me. I don't want to cause anybody extra work and stuff."

You want to cry because no one should die like that, but your eyes are dry. You want to strangle someone, but that doesn't help. So again, you write with cold, merciless precision because that's all you can do.

The horror stories that I tracked down and put in print were the human side. A broader but less personal view was offered by the twenty-seven pages of deficiencies that the state found during its annual licensing review six weeks before our visits.

Dr. Tamra D. Martin of Dexter Village Family Physicians, who had conducted the medical review of Prospect Park's Medicaid patients, wrote:

"I was very dissatisfied with the quality of physician and nursing [care] as a whole. The information available for the R-19 forms [which includes patient histories] was inappropriate. Many diagnoses were obviously inappropriate."

The inspectors found that computer-generated standardized care plans were not updated to reflect each patient's actual documented needs. A review of twenty records found that seven failed to address documented problems. They evaluated thirty-three patients with indwelling urinary catheters, concluding that about half were inappropriate.

Using catheters meant the staff could avoid time-consuming continence training and rehabilitative nursing and didn't have to take them to the toilet. But they didn't even do an adequate job with the time-saving catheters. In a number of instances, Beyer Hospital staff reported treating Prospect Park patients who came to them with dirty catheters and painful urinary tract infections.

During an earlier survey, forty-two of 173 patients had developed bedsores. Some patients will develop bedsores despite immaculate care. But the number and severity at Prospect Park were overwhelming evidence of both poor preventive care and inadequate treatment.

On the day of the latest inspection, breakfast was fifty-five minutes late, and lunch and dinner were each forty-five minutes late. Patients on physician-ordered restricted diets received the same food as everyone else, and substitute food was not offered to patients who were not eating. I tracked down a former food service supervisor who said she had conducted a one-month survey the year before, documenting that eighteen to twenty-two trays a day from each floor were being returned to the kitchen with the food largely untouched.

The last day I was there, a middle-aged woman complained that her mother was "wet to the eyeballs while the staff was down the hall smoking … pathetic. And Saturday's meal was bologna on dry bread, no butter, no nothing."

I did find one sixty-three-year-old dialysis patient who had been sent over from the Veterans Administration Hospital who said, "They treat you real good here. I am well pleased here, well pleased. They treat you as good as you treat them."

I should have come back in six months to see, but I was reasonably sure that only marginal improvements would have been possible. The reason is that the state simply didn't pay enough to provide decent care for poor people on Medicaid. "Nursing homes represent a two-class system of care. That is very clear," said Ruth Campbell, a senior social worker at the University of Michigan's Turner Geriatric Clinic. "There is one level of care for those who can afford it, another level for the poor and the middle-income people whose money has run out."

Prospect Park and two other of Washtenaw County's ten homes accepted Medicaid patients. At the time of the stories, they were reimbursed at the rate of only $15,000 to $16,000 a year per patient. All three were for-profit enterprises, and state inspection reports showed they consistently ranked as the worst in the county.

To get admitted to one of the better-rated non-profit homes, a patient had to be able to guarantee they could pay $18,250 to $32,000 a year for two years before going on Medicaid.

The chronic shortage of decent nursing homes for poor patients left state inspectors in a no-win situation. They could fine a home for its violations, but the money would come out of the pot for patient care. If they revoked the license of a Medicaid home, there would be nowhere else for the patients to go.

For a reporter, you write such stories as "The Trouble With Nursing Homes" in the hope that, over time, enough people will come to recognize the need and lean on their legislators to do the right thing. It often feels like you're whistling past the graveyard, but you keep going.

As I wrote the first draft of this chapter for "Relentless," Senate Republicans were working on a revised plan to repeal the Affordable Care Act and replace it with something that would strip hundreds of billions of dollars from Medicaid. That would mean only the rich could afford to grow old. At least that measure failed.

Although it sounds trite, most of the reporters I have worked with believe that part of our mission is to "Afflict the comfortable and comfort the afflicted." A year after the nursing home series, fellow reporter Phil Cackley and I got to do a slight bit of afflicting.

Washtenaw County Probate Judge John N. Kirkendall, at the request of the Evergreen Hills Nursing Center, had appointed Detroit attorney Arlond R. Reid as guardian and conservator of 19 of the nursing home's residents. As reports of funny business began to surface, Cackley and I spent a lot of time talking to a very angry judge and the four local attorneys whom he appointed as special guardians to review Reid's conduct. We pored over the records that the attorneys pulled together.
Under Medicaid, a nursing home resident at that time was allowed to keep $32 a month from Social Security, with the rest being paid to the home for his or her care. But Reid allowed former Ypsilanti Township resident Paul Wilcox an average of only $3 a month for clothing and amenities, charging Wilcox's estate $1,320 in guardianship fees and leaving his ward a zero balance when he died.

One Reid accounting showed he bought 65-year-old Frederick Freewald a $10 Christmas gift from K-Mart using the man's own money, charged a half-hour shopping time to the estate, and billed the estate for the one hour he spent at the Evergreen Hills Christmas Party.

"Reid is taking from their need," said Ann Arbor attorney Priscilla Cheever, whom the judge had named as Robert Livingston's special guardian. "He can't get his chewing tobacco or stamps to mail his poems out to magazines. Some people can't even get slippers.

"These are people who have been poor all their lives," she added. "At Evergreen, they have a bed, one drawer in a nightstand, and a locker with two pieces of clothing. He is denying them the little pleasures they might have had at the end of their lives. Their money is being used to provide a quality of life for an attorney."

In the end, Reid agreed to repay $12,100 he had improperly deducted from the estates of eighteen of nineteen Evergreen patients. There were no established standards for what guardians could charge, so Judge Kirkendall said he couldn't ding him for more.

I was reminded of the initial rule of the revolution: "First, kill all the lawyers." I don't mean that literally, and there are many fine lawyers. But there are times when the sentiment does resonate.

Chapter 65 Too Many Failures Enable A Rapist

Growing up in Inkster's LeMoyne Gardens public housing project in the middle 1970s, you were either a chump or a punk. Ervin Dewain Mitchell, Jr., was a chump. "He was someone that kids half his size would hit up the side of his head for his lunch money 'cause he'd never fight back," recalled Craig, a friend from the old days.

"Back when we were young, I'd never seen him fight no guy. I would get in his face, and he would back down. He was a coward with no manhood. One guy Ervin hung out with was such a nerd no one else would hang out with him. He mostly hung out with the younger brothers. The girls never liked him."

Craig and I talked on Super Bowl Sunday, 1995. He asked me not to use his last name so his own past wouldn't catch up with him. He turned off the television and sent his common-law wife into the other room to feed their infant son. "I used to pop him up the side of the head, bang, pow!" Craig said. "Maybe that got to him."

Nearly two decades after high school, Mitchell would extract, in the most terrible way, revenge for being bullied when he was young. Beginning in 1992, he attacked from behind, beat, and raped three women he had stalked on the streets of Ann Arbor.

Then, in the early afternoon of May 7, 1994, he ambushed Christine Gailbreath, who was walking along a lightly wooded path behind Ann Arbor's main U.S. Post Office on West Stadium Boulevard. He repeatedly beat, raped, and then murdered the thirty-two-year-old woman. The cause of death was listed as "Blunt impact to the head with injuries to the brain and manual strangulation."

Until that murder, the Ann Arbor Police Department had withheld the fact that a serial rapist was loose in the city, earning the fury of women who rightly felt the secrecy had put them at added risk. Then, the police earned the enmity of much of the African-American community with their heavy-handed investigation, including demanding DNA samples from young and middle-aged Black men who couldn't prove their innocence.

The first of Mitchell's Ann Arbor assaults occurred shortly after breakfast on September 28, 1992. A 47-year-old woman was taking a walk through

Eberwhite Woods on the south side of Liberty Street when a man jumped her from behind, repeatedly bludgeoned her with his fists, and raped her.

Then, on September 2, 1993, there was an incident that, had the police done their job properly, would have prevented the evil that came after. A woman walking down Liberty fought off a would-be purse snatcher. "Homer," the Ann Arbor Police tracking dog, followed the assailant's scent to the home where Mitchell lived with his girlfriend and her mother. Mitchell told officers his shoes were wet because he had gone out to rent a movie. His girlfriend gave him an alibi for the actual time of the attack. The police didn't bother to investigate further.

The third proven assault occurred a month later, at 10:30 p.m. on October 1, 1993, when a twenty-three-year-old University of Michigan student, who was walking down Longshore Drive, was repeatedly punched around the head and face and raped.

The fourth was at 2 a.m. on November 1, 1993, when a forty-year-old woman, returning to her apartment in the 800 block of Miller Avenue, was beaten and raped.

DNA extracted from the assailant's sperm confirmed that those three rapes and the rape murder of Gailbreath were all committed by the same man. There were as many as a dozen other attacks on women that bore similar hallmarks but no proof they were done by the same man.

The Ann Arbor Serial Rapist Task Force was formed that included officers from the city, the U-M Department of Public Safety, the Washtenaw County Sheriff's Department, and the Michigan State Police. Officers logged interviews with 730 suspects, all of them Black men who had been either named in tips or simply stopped on the street because they were Black males of approximately the right age. Officers sent out 160 DNA samples for testing. Some were given voluntarily by men wishing to prove their innocence. Most, however, were demanded by the police, including ten for which they had to get warrants.

Despite the massive publicity, a $100,000 reward, and the heavy police presence, there was almost certainly one other attack by the same man. A thirty-one-year-old woman walking on the path alongside Community High School was beaten unconscious and raped. She was unable to provide a clear description, and too little DNA was recovered to analyze.

In the end, it wasn't police work that captured Mitchell. On Christmas Eve of 1994, a woman walking along Dexter Avenue was assaulted by a Black male wearing white gloves who hit her and attempted to steal her purse. Early on Christmas Day, cab driver Michael DeCamillo, who had read a description of the assailant in The Ann Arbor News, saw a man wearing white gloves walking along North Main Street. He radioed his dispatcher and followed the man, Ervin Mitchell. Officers arrived to make the arrest. His DNA matched the three rapes and one rape-murder victim.

Reporter John Barton had been doing the police beat stories. Marianne Rzepka and I were assigned to investigate Mitchell. I headed for Inkster. In addition to his high school buddy, Craig, I tracked down the school's attendance officer, Henry Hughes, Jr., who said Mitchell wasn't a problem student, just an absent student. "I spent a lot of time dragging him back to school," he said. "I could never get a parent to show up for him, though."

Garnet Hegeman, who was the Inkster High School principal in the 1970s, remembered Mitchell as a loner. "Even once he was in the building, we had difficulty getting him to attend class. He would try to hang out in the bathroom or hallway, always by himself."

Mitchell, the oldest of three boys, was born in Ann Arbor but spent most of his childhood and young adulthood in Inkster. He lost track of his father, who had been in the Army in Germany throughout Mitchell's teen years. Mitchell's mother, Doris Jones, had long ago remarried and remained in Inkster, where she was raising the two eldest of Ervin Mitchell's six children. She politely refused to talk about her son and had not been out to visit him in jail.

Mitchell's first adult encounter with the police had come in 1982 when he climbed through the bathroom window of a seventy-three-year-old Inkster woman's house. She heard a noise and called the police. Mitchell, with a nylon stocking over his head, threw the woman onto her bed and sat on her legs while he bound her with duct tape. The police showed up, rang the doorbell, and caught him crawling back out the bathroom window. He later pled guilty to burglary and was sentenced to three years' probation.

Two years later, he had been caught in a dope house raid but was let off with a fine, according to Inkster police records.

On October 12, 1985, he had been accused of beating and raping the estranged mother of two of his children. He was arrested five days later, released on personal bond, and ended up convicted only of misdemeanor assault and battery. The reason for the reduction was not clear from court records. He was sentenced to six months probation.

A year later, Mitchell had crawled through the second-floor bedroom window of the estranged mother, beat her up, and fled with her house keys. Two days later, a neighbor spotted him crawling through the basement window of the woman's house. He was arrested and charged with assault and battery, malicious destruction of property, and two counts of illegal entry. He failed to show up for court, was caught by Inkster police two years later, pled guilty to one count of assault and battery, and was sentenced to nine days in jail. With credit for time served, he was released.

In 1992, Inkster police arrested Mitchell on suspicion of rape and sent a sample of his blood to the Michigan State Police DNA lab for comparison with the fluid recovered from the rape. However, the State Police said the sample from the rape was too small to provide a valid comparison. Inkster police refused to release any other information to me, claiming the case was still under investigation.

Since the state had the Mitchell DNA sample from 1992, it should have been available to compare against the semen samples from the Ann Arbor rapes. There was no explanation why that was not done.

Relocating in Ann Arbor, Mitchell took up with Angela Moore and moved in with her and her mother, Carol Hopp. It was Moore who gave Mitchell an alibi when the Ann Arbor Police tracking dog followed a scent to Hopp's house following the September 1993 attempted strong-armed robbery.

In addition to accepting Moore's alibi, the investigating officers either didn't bother to check Mitchell's criminal history or neglected to follow up on the earlier assault and rape accusations. Mitchell refused to give a DNA sample and was not served with a subpoena for his DNA.

Following the Eberwhite Woods rape, police told The News' Barton that Mitchell was given a polygraph that he did not flunk. The paper apparently never looked further into that dubious claim.

I tracked Mitchell through a series of short-term jobs in Ann Arbor. Angela Moore did get him a job at the Old Fashioned Soup Kitchen, where she worked. Mitchell presented himself as a chef, but owner Tim Abraham said, "He had no idea how to cook." Abraham kept him on as a dishwasher but fired him four months later after his work deteriorated and he got into a dispute with another employee.

Marianne Rzepka's end of the story was several lengthy jail-house interviews with Mitchell. I fed her all my material, but Mitchell denied everything she threw at him, even when there were court records contradicting him.

The mother of two of his children wanted to visit him, but Mitchell refused to grant permission. "There is no reason for her to come see me," he said. "She ain't seen me in nine years. Why she'd want to see me now? Is this some kind of publicity or something?"

He was asked about the four other women who had each borne him one child. "Sometimes, when you fall out of love, you just want to go," he said. "And when I wanted to go, it seemed they would have a baby." He called it their tactic to keep him around.

But Mitchell never turned his back on Moore, the woman he called his alibi. Despite being behind bars, he arranged to have flowers sent to her on Valentine's Day. "I try to keep her in good spirits," he said. "I've still got a heart."

Mitchell went on trial in late May 1995 in front of Washtenaw Circuit Judge Donald Shelton, who sequestered the jury throughout the 16-day trial because of the massive daily newspaper and television coverage. Relying heavily on the DNA evidence, the jury convicted Mitchell of one count of first-degree murder and four counts of rape. He was sentenced to life in prison.

The story doesn't end there. Blair Shelton, thirty-seven, a part-time janitor at the Greenhills School, had been stopped and interrogated seven times by the Ann Arbor Police because he was a Black male who was older than a teenager, younger than a senior citizen.

Shelton had been fired from his other part-time job at T.J. Maxx after Ann Arbor Police Detective Mick Schubring told his employer he was a suspect in the murder and rapes. Shelton said he was intimidated into giving police a DNA sample. He was rehired by the clothier two weeks later but was eventually forced out of the job because of ongoing suspicions. Following Mitchell's conviction, Shelton asked for the return of his DNA sample, but the police refused.

As it happened, Kurt Berggren, a member of the Ann Arbor Chapter of the National Lawyers Guild, sometimes played evening pick-up basketball games at Greenhills. Shelton told him his story.

Berggren drafted a complaint charging the Police Department and Detective Shubring with violating Shelton's Fourth Amendment constitutional rights against illegal search and seizure as well as his Fourteenth Amendment rights of equal protection and due process of law. The lawyer argued that the police conduct targeting Black males also violated the state's Elliott-Larsen Civil Rights Act, adding in counts of slander, invasion of privacy, gross negligence, and emotional distress.

Two other members of the Ann Arbor chapter, Richard Soble and Michael Steinberg, asked to join the suit. It was filed in Washtenaw County Circuit Court on November 13, 1995. Soble argued the case, which was assigned to Judge Kurtis T. Wilder. The city refused to settle, and the case dragged on for three years until the judge, a conservative Republican, surprised the attorneys by ruling in favor of Shelton. The city decided against appealing.

All 160 Black men got back both their DNA samples and associated paperwork, and Wilder issued an injunction barring the Police Department from similar conduct in the future. Shelton kept the two vials of blood in his refrigerator as a reminder of his travail.

The Mitchell saga left me shaken. I used to half-joke that police were Darwinian agents of natural selection, that they culled the criminal population of its stupidest members, leaving the smarter and more careful lawbreakers free. Mitchell was neither smart nor careful, yet his predation lasted a dozen years and didn't end until a newspaper-reading cabbie noticed his white gloves.

Chapter 66 Spicing Up The Police Briefs

There is an uncomfortable truth that reporters and editors are loath to admit: The vast majority of what we write and shovel into the news columns of our daily papers is insufferably dull. I don't exempt myself from that indictment.

Some folks who were raised on newspapers keep reading out of habit, but they tend to be older now and are dying off faster than they are replaced. You may read about the proposal to raise the speed limit on your street because you have a stake in that issue, but pass on a story about something across town. There are sensational stories where you hang on every word, but they are few and far apart.

It can be pretty dull for the reporters as well, and that recognition would occasionally send me in search of the "Hey Maud!" story. "Hey Maud" was the term the late Jim Treloar, my last editor at the old Ypsilanti Press and later a colleague at The Detroit News, used for the kind of story that would compel a reader to call out and share with "Maud" or anyone else nearby.

The police briefs, which most of us at The Ann Arbor News took turns writing, were dull to write and dull to read. For the most part, they were the daily recitation of burglaries, car crashes, vandalism, and cats stuck in trees. To me, that made them the perfect vehicle for adding some unexpected spice.

One of my favorites was a brief on the flashing of a midnight-shift worker at a service station on South Main Street just off I-94. I suspect she had been flashed at some time in the past and had stewed ever since on how she wished she had reacted. This time, according to the Ann Arbor Police report, she pointed down at the flasher and said, "Tee hee hee. If I had anything that small, I'd keep it hidden." He whipped his coat closed and ran out the door.

Then there was this one: "Fifteen Washtenaw County Sheriff's deputies participated in the burning of a small roadside patch of marijuana north of Dexter yesterday afternoon. Eleven of them stood downwind." That last fact wasn't in the report itself. I had relied on the gossip of the deputies, who were manifestly unhappy when they saw it in print.

Twice, however, I ran afoul of former City Editor Dave Bishop, who had been appointed as reader representative or ombudsman for The News. Bishop was a nice guy, but he had been kicked upstairs to clear the way for Rick Fitzgerald's appointment as city editor. He often had to reach for things to write about.

I had written a brief about a motorist who had been driving inbound on tree-lined Washtenaw Avenue. A gust of wind had snapped a large overhead branch whose pointed end crashed through the windshield and impaled him, killing him instantly.

Bishop wrote a column about my police brief, concluding that I was too graphic and should have just said, "killed by a falling branch." I had been struck by the horror and randomness of the death and had sought to communicate that sense to the readers. Soft-playing death, such as saying someone has "passed away" or "gone to join his ancestors," is an affectation of an earlier time.

The second time Bishop took me to the woodshed was for a short piece I had labeled "Fat kid grazing." He said the reference was "fattest" and disrespectful of hefty people. A mother, with her grade-school-age son in tow (the police report called him fat), were in a store in the Arborland Shopping Center that sold bulk candy. It was mid-afternoon, and they hadn't eaten lunch. The kid took a Milk Dud out of one of the bins and popped it into his mouth.

The store manager went ballistic, called the police, insisted that the kid be charged with larceny, and demanded that the mother reimburse the store for the retail cost of the entire bin's contents. I had identified the manager by name but not the mother or son. The one-paragraph piece was a hit-job on the manager for being a colossal jerk.

The kid should have been able to go to school and tell the story of his encounter with the manager, but he couldn't after being labeled as fat in the newspaper. I agreed with Bishop on this one.

Chapter 67 I Jerk My Publisher's Chain

Ann Arbor News Publisher Timothy White called me at home three days after I had named his son on the front page for his role in the pre-graduation smoke bombing at Huron High School. White said his wife wanted to know why I'd singled out Todd.

The Ann Arbor Police had set a trap for The News on the smoke bombing affair. My putting Todd on the front page had avoided the trap and been an act of mild journalistic courage but wrong-headed.

White's nighttime call to me was also wrong, and laying his displeasure off on his wife was cowardly. I was angry, and my reaction was stupid. I told him that I had actually done Todd a favor. The six other seniors involved had all admitted their roles and been held out of the graduation ceremony. Todd had lied, claiming he was not the lookout and was allowed to walk with the rest of his class. His name would have been mud among his friends, I said, but his naming in the story meant he could say that he, too, had paid a price.

Moreover, I told White that he now had the perfect shield against local advertisers who frequently tried to pressure him to influence news coverage. I said he could point to that article as proof of how independent the news operation was from the business side. All of this was perfectly true, but you don't piss on a man's shoes and tell him it's a warm summer rain.

This was before the now-universal policy against printing the names of juvenile suspects. I had little sympathy for Todd for not being a stand-up guy, but my wife and eldest daughter properly raked me over the coals for singling out Todd by name.

There was no reprisal against me from White, but he forgot the principle about the independence of news operations. In May 2000, after he had moved on to a much bigger job, White was forced out as publisher of The San Francisco Examiner, a Hearst Newspaper, by a firestorm of criticism. In court, he had been compelled to admit that he had offered to trade favorable news coverage of Mayor Willie Brown for the mayor's support of Hearst's purchase of the rival San Francisco Chronicle.

The Todd story was the unexpected outgrowth of our long suspicion that the Ann Arbor police were censoring the incident reports we received each morning. I was temporarily assigned to the police beat with orders to catch them. I did.

There was a small group of young Black men who were carrying out a large number of unarmed robberies of White male U-M students in and around campus. They would punch and kick each student they waylaid, running away with their wallet and watch. But there was no mention of race in the reports we were allowed to see and no indication that it was a single group carrying out the assaults. Our lawyers took the information I had uncovered and, under threat of suing the department, negotiated full access to all reports that would not compromise ongoing investigations.

On the first full day of the agreement, the department handed me a large stack of investigative reports on the smoke bombing. The reports spelled out Todd's role. If we chose to ignore it, we would be hypocrites for demanding openness for others while hiding our own dirty laundry. Rather than ask my editors what I should do, I simply wrote the story the way I thought it should be and presented it to them. I figured it would be harder to censor a story that was already written. They passed it into the paper.

Chapter 68 I Censor Myself

Unlike the journalistic corruption that caused me to leave The Detroit News, the only censorship I encountered at The Ann Arbor News was self-imposed.

I got interested in tapping into the possibilities of Ann Arbor's University Microfilms (now Pro-Quest), incorporated in 1938 by Eugene Power, father of Phil Power, the founder and chief benefactor of the Center for Michigan's pioneering online Bridge Magazine. University Microfilms had assembled a library of virtually every doctoral dissertation in the world. Printed copies were then available for about $5 each. This incredible repository has grown to more than three million dissertations and master's theses, as well as 125 billion digitalized pages of various other publications.

My idea was to order up the dissertations of five famous Americans whom you wouldn't think of as having earned doctorates and see what insights I could derive from their early writing.

My first was Senator George McGovern, who was crushed by Richard Nixon in the 1972 presidential election. The former Methodist divinity school student earned his Ph.D. in history from Northwestern University in 1953 for his 450-page account of the 1913-1914 Colorado Coal Strike against the Rockefeller interests. His sympathetic treatment of the miners, including a recounting of the Ludlow massacre, revealed much about the development of his liberalism.

Next was W. Michael Blumenthal, President Jimmy Carter's secretary of the treasury from 1977 to 1978. The dissertation for his 1956 Ph.D. in history from Princeton dealt with labor relations in Germany's post-World War I Ruhr. It confirmed Blumenthal's genius. What told me more about his character was that when he was a teen, his family had bribed his father out of a German labor camp. They fled to Japanese-occupied Shanghai, where they were confined to a ghetto until they could emigrate to California.

The third was Sally Ride ("Ride, Sally, Ride"), who, in 1983, was the first American woman in space. She earned her Ph.D. in physics from Stanford in 1978, writing about the interaction of x-rays in the interstellar medium. Like Blumenthal, she was awesomely smart, ending up as a professor of physics at the University of California-San Diego.

On the other hand, Bill Cosby Jr.'s 1977 doctorate of education from the University of Massachusetts-Amherst was an embarrassment. Its title, "An Integration of the Visual Media via Fat Albert and the Cosby Kids into Elementary Curriculum as a Teaching Aid and Vehicle to Achieve Increased Learning," sounded like a joke on the educational establishment from a man who had flunked 10th grade three times before dropping out of high school. Cosby would later get his GED and graduate honestly from college.

His doctoral dissertation, however, was even more vacuous than its title. It seemed clear to me that the university had held its nose in giving the degree to its most prominent fundraiser. It gave me a pretty good idea of Cosby's character even before the first of the three dozen women went public with their sexual abuse allegations.

It was Dr. Martin Luther King's 1955 doctorate from Boston University that gave me fits. It was the late 1980s when I read and then reread his dissertation: "A Comparison of the Concepts of God in the Thinking of Paul Tillich and Henry Nelson Wieman." If you are a writer or a careful reader, you develop an ear for the voice of various authors, how they use words, their patterns of sentence structure, how they translate their thoughts into words, and how they describe things. It is obvious, for example, that Paul's letters in the New Testament were written by more than one person.

Try as I might, I couldn't reconcile Dr. King's dissertation with any of his speeches or writings during his ministry and civil rights campaigns. What could I say, "It doesn't sound right to Cain's ear?" I wasn't about to write an article mentioning my suspicion about the most admired Black man in America. This was pre-Internet, and I could think of no way of proving what I suspected. I wasn't about to write an article that didn't include my suspicions of plagiarism. In frustration, I simply gave up on the whole project and went on to other things.

In late 1990, The Wall Street Journal broke the story of King's suspected plagiarism. The following October, a Boston University board of academic inquiry concluded that Dr. King had lifted major parts of his 1955 dissertation from the 1952 dissertation of fellow BU student Jack Boozer but declined to revoke his degree.

I was disappointed in King, but I understand that saints aren't necessarily saintly from head to toe. I was disappointed in myself for not being able to land the story.

Chapter 69 "Baby Jessica" Custody Turns Ugly

BLAIRSTOWN, Iowa — Not since "The Murders," the unsolved execution-style slayings of elderly farmers Charles Plucar in 1977 and Amos Jellison in 1981, has anything so bestirred this town of 672 people as the Schmidt-DeBoer battle for the custody of "Baby Jessica."

When Richard Gere came to Blairstown to shoot the cemetery scene for "Miles From Home" in 1987, it made the 125th anniversary edition of the town's history. But the three ladies who went out to see him came back disappointed, and no one recognized the Hollywood star when he stopped in at the Blairstown Cafe for breakfast.

When Mayor Elmer Eichhorn and a buddy from the American Legion shot Jody Burdick's dog "Rudy" early in the summer of 1992, the sixty-eight-year-old city hall was packed for three successive monthly town council meetings. Burdick said she lost her job at the independent Coon Creek Telephone and Cable Company in part because of her outspokenness.

The murdered farmers, the movie star, and the dead dog were mere sideshows compared to the town's preoccupation with the efforts of the former Cara Clausen, daughter of one of the town's best-loved citizens, and her delivery truck driver husband, Dan Schmidt, to gain custody of their biological child from would-be adoptive parents Robby and Jan DeBoer of Ann Arbor.

I flew out to Blairstown in early February 1993 as the custody hearing before Washtenaw County Circuit Court Judge William F. Ager, Jr. was set to resume. The hearing was being broadcast live on cable television's Court TV.

"The town gets really quiet during the trial," said Blairstown resident Nancy Stults. "The people are really into this." The VCRs were running for those who were off to work in Marengo, Belle Plaine, the Amana Colonies, or twenty miles east in Cedar Rapids. At Terry's Place, just up Locust Street from the cafe, the overhead television was switched to the hearing for folks who flocked in for Barb Norton's luncheon special.

Ann Arbor, a town of high culture and higher education, views itself as a marvelous place to raise children. The residents, for the most part, were overwhelmingly and passionately behind the media-savvy DeBoers, who were represented gratis by attorney Suellyn Scarnecchia of the University of Michigan's Child Advocacy Clinic.

Really, who from Ann Arbor would choose to raise their child in a place like Blairstown? It was typical of the tiny hamlets that popped up every ten miles or so as the town's namesake, John Insley Blair, pushed the tracks of the Chicago and Northwestern Railroad west of the Mississippi in the early 1860s.

This was the kind of place where folks pulled up their grape arbors at the beginning of Prohibition rather than risk giving in to temptation. Pay phones were still a dime.

Expert witness Thomas Horner, a U-M child psychologist, had testified the previous week that the hostile battle between the DeBoers and the Schmidts, who lived in a rented one-bedroom bungalow in Blairstown, would become "town versus town, state against state." He got it wrong.

I had come to Blairstown expecting that the folks there would be solidly behind Dan and Cara, as they were universally known, but that was not the case. For example, the couple had stiffed the ladies of the American Legion Auxiliary whom they had hired to cater their wedding. The ladies were unforgiving.

I started out deeply conflicted over the custody battle, which had already dragged on for two years, and was becoming a national cause celeb. I saw Cara and Dan Schmidt as flawed human beings, but I also realized that Robby DeBoer brought much of her agony upon herself, publicly picking at her sorrow like an inflamed scab.

I took a newsman's refuge. I didn't have to decide. My job was to write as insightfully as I could about the people and issues so that the readers would have a basis for drawing their own conclusions.

Baby Girl Clausen, as she was listed on the birth certificate, was born in Cedar Rapids on February 8, 1991. Unmarried at the time, Cara listed a false name as the father. On February 10, she agreed to a private adoption and signed away her parental rights. Three weeks later, she told Dan Schmidt that he was the actual father. Dan, who had not given up his parental rights, went to court on March 27, asking the Iowa judge to award him custody of the infant.

However, the DeBoers' attorney had already gotten the courts to give the Ann Arbor couple custody pending completion of the private adoption, and the DeBoers had returned to Ann Arbor with the girl they named Jessica. Cara said she had been led to believe that the DeBoers' attorney was representing her interests as well.

The DeBoers could have given up Jessica as soon as Dan asserted his parental rights, but they would later say they didn't necessarily believe he was actually the father and didn't want the baby girl to go into foster care pending a determination.

A DNA test confirmed Dan as the father, and on December 27, the Iowa District Court ordered that Jessica be given to her birth father. The DeBoers refused, saying they were going to appeal the court decision.

In April 1992, Dan and Cara were married in Blairstown. Finally, on September 23, the Iowa Supreme Court ordered that the child be returned to the father. It reaffirmed its ruling on November 22, and the Schmidts drove to Ann Arbor to pick up their daughter.

The DeBoers again refused, and their attorney asked Judge Ager to take jurisdiction. On January 5, 1993, Ager agreed to make a determination of what would be "in the best interests of the child" and scheduled the televised hearing for early February.

"I am very overwhelmed and thankful that someone is deciding our daughter has rights, that she has a life, that she is a human being," said Jan DeBoer. Dan Schmidt countered: "I am very disappointed, devastated really … We want her home with us. Where children belong is with their roots."

The story was too expansive for a lone reporter. Ann Arbor News veterans Julie Wiernik, Susan Oppat, and I worked on the main stories. Chong Pyen and Maryann Rzepka also contributed stories. Photographer Larry E. Wright and I flew out to Iowa.

Larry and I didn't even get out of the Cedar Rapids Municipal Airport before being drawn into the controversy. Car rental agents Laurie Tipton and Janet Johnson, discovering we were from Michigan, wanted to know why we weren't as passionate in favor of the DeBoers getting custody as most Iowans.

Because they couldn't watch the hearings while they were working, Johnson said they had stay-at-home friends who would call them if anything interesting happened during the hearings. Johnson, whose own effort at a private adoption had fallen through, said she was a "true believer" in the DeBoers' cause.

Kathryn Kubichek, an Avon Lady for thirty-five years, told us that being from Blairstown made her a bit of a celebrity whenever she went to regional Avon meetings in Cedar Rapids. "The other sales ladies have no use for the Schmidts," she said. "Someone will always have fresh tidbits of something negative Dan may have said or the supposed reason why Cara had lost a job several years before."

Kathryn, her sister-in-law Evelyn Kubichek, and three other American Legion ladies sat down with us to explain that Dan and Cara had asked them to cater their wedding reception for 320 guests the previous April. But the Schmidts had refused to pay for the food ordered for the 195 guests who hadn't shown up.

Irene Hannen recalled that Cara, as a teen, would lie on the carpet, forcing guests in the Clausen home to step over her. She said that Cara was a young woman her mother couldn't control.

Added Nancy Stults: "When she got pregnant, she was twenty-eight years old, a woman who did her own thing, who lived her whole life just like she wanted, but now they make her out like Snow White, and that's what makes me so mad. "She's lying about how close-knit her family is and what a churchgoer she is. Why bring in God? Now, she says she wants to be a Sunday school teacher. Why didn't she do that way back?"

Marlene Kimm's story helped shape the feelings of her fellow Legion ladies. "I gave up my child when I was nineteen, gave him up at birth," she said. "I had lost my job. I had no place of my own to live. I would think of him every year on his birthday. Would I go see him? No. I loved him. I never would have uprooted his life. It is selfish to think of your feelings, not his. It tears me up to think the other little girl [Jessica] could be torn away from the only parents she knows, her life torn apart. I sent $10 to the Jessica fund."

I asked the Legion ladies whether they believed in redemption, forgiveness, second chances. "You still have to pay the consequences of what you do," said Stults, answering twice for the group.

We found no women in town who would speak up for Cara and Dan. The men were more circumspect, largely because of their high regard for Cara's father. L. H. "Shorty" Clausen had spent fourteen months in Stalag Luft 3 after the Germans shot down the B-24 he was co-piloting.
"Shorty and his wife are really swell people," said Mayor Eichhorn. "The girl, as far as I know, is fairly decent, although I lost track of her when she left Blairstown to go to work ten years ago. "Where the mistake was made, I don't know. I can't blame the people in Michigan. I guess I don't want to get involved. Everybody has a different version of who is right and wrong."

Shorty stopped in for coffee at the Blairstown Cafe. "I've been watching the trial when I can," he told us. "There are people in town who think they should leave her [Jessica] where she is. I don't know how many. My friends don't talk about it when I am around."

In a stunning ruling on February 12, 1993, Judge Ager said he was "acting in the best interests of the child" in awarding custody of Jessica, then two years old, to the DeBoers. He declined to give the Schmidts visitation rights and begged them not to appeal his ruling. "Think of the possibility of saying 'Enough!'" the judge wrote.

In denigrating what he saw as the Schmidts' fitness as parents, the judge cited testimony that Cara did not get prenatal care until the last month of her pregnancy. He noted that Dan had never seen the thirteen-year-old daughter he had fathered in a previous relationship and, for nine years, had not seen his sixteen-year-old son. Ager, who, in his decision, cherry-picked information negative to the Schmidts, added that taking Jessica from the DeBoers would cause her short-term and possibly long-term emotional damage.

Schmidt attorney Marian Faupel of Ann Arbor, filed for an expedited appeal. Six weeks later, the Michigan Court of Appeals overturned Ager. It ruled that the DeBoers, as "third parties," had no legal standing to sue the birth parents of a child for custody of the child.

On July 2, the Michigan Supreme Court, in a 6-1 ruling, affirmed the Court of Appeals decision and said that the Iowa Supreme Court awarding of custody to the Schmidts must be obeyed.

The U.S. Constitution explicitly holds that each state must give "full faith and credit" to the court rulings of other states, the bedrock principle that makes America a nation rather than merely a loose coalition of states. The DeBoers had an impressive bevy of legal talent on their side, but I thought their efforts to finesse the Constitution were lame.

For example, Jan and Robby DeBoer argued that "psychological parents" should have the same standing as biological parents and that a child should have independent legal rights in the determination of what would be in the "best interests of the child."

Robby appeared on "Larry King Live," complaining that "Jessica is being treated as luggage" and begging the U.S. Supreme Court to hear the case. In late July, the high court, by a vote of 6-2, refused to block the Michigan Supreme Court order.

In hopes of easing the transition, the Schmidts met several times with the DeBoers and Jessica, whom they named Anna. But during the actual hand-over at the Ann Arbor Police Station on August 2, Robby DeBoer let out a primal scream. That set off Jessica/Anna. Television captured and endlessly rebroadcast shots of the hysterical child being strapped into the child seat in Schmidt's darkened van. The fact that Robby had caused the hysteria was largely lost.

The already bitter situation took yet another ugly turn in late September with the made-for-television ABC movie "Whose Child Is This? The War for Baby Jessica." Susan Dey portrayed Robby DeBoer as a kind of upscale Madonna whose life was fulfilled with the adoption of Jessica.
Detroit Free Press columnist Brian Dickerson described the movie as a "deceitful production that canonized the DeBoers and reduced Anna's parents to hillbilly caricatures living in a hubcap-studded trailer."

Robby DeBoer added to the drumbeat with a 288-page lament titled "Losing Jessica." In a dust-jacket letter to Jessica, she wrote: "We are about to venture into a dark place, to turn back the pages of your life. It will be a sorrowful journey, full of pain, looking into the inner core of what happened, somehow trying to explain it to you." Robby launched a national book tour in the summer of 1994, telling one television interviewer, "I wrote the book for Jessie. I wanted to fill the emptiness in her heart."

The DeBoers had privately adopted a newborn boy in June 1994, just before beginning her tour of agony. I have no doubt that Robby DeBoer was genuinely heartbroken over losing Jessica, but I never understood how she could consider the book, tour, and movie in the child's best interests.

Pam Lewis, the Schmidts' Iowa attorney, estimated that the DeBoers received approximately $1 million in compensation for their story's movie, book, and magazine syndication. I and other Ann Arbor News reporters tried to question the DeBoers about the money. We were stonewalled. In addition to their various sources of Jessica-related income, the DeBoers launched "The DeBoer Committee for Children's Rights," which grew into a national advocacy group with fifty-seven chapters in thirty-seven states.

Faupel, who represented the Schmidts, said they received $150,000 from "Inside Edition" for their side of the story but added that it didn't pay much of their legal bills. Faupel told me she had to borrow $50,000 to keep her law office afloat.

Cara and Dan had a second child, Chloe, who became Anna's playmate and best friend. Lucy Biven, the court-appointed neutral therapist who oversaw the transfer, visited the Schmidt home twice during the year following the transfer. "I expected short-term difficulty, but I've been very surprised at how good it's been all along," said Biven. "She [Anna] likes to talk. She's friendly, very possessive of her sister, affectionate, a little bossy sometimes."

The adults didn't fare as well. Dan and Cara divorced, splitting custody of their daughters. Robby and Jan also divorced, citing tensions over the long-running custody battle, but later remarried.

A decade after Anna was returned to Iowa, Detroit WDIV-TV reporter Paula Tutman flew out to Blairstown to spend a day. She portrayed Anna as a self-possessed twelve-year-old who adores her parents and her nine-year-old sister, makes friends easily, and sings every Sunday in the Lutheran Church whose congregation once looked down on her parents. Tutman's tape shows a bemused Anna leafing through a copy of "Losing Jessica." I doubt if that scene was Robby's expectation when she wrote the book.

I had not realized how deeply the "Baby Jessica" story had affected me until after I had retired. Pat and I moved to the mountains outside of Asheville, North Carolina. We became volunteer guardians ad litem. As officers of the court, we ended up representing twenty-one abused and neglected children who had been removed from their homes by the Department of Social Services. We were able to ensure that none became the object of a tug-of-war.

Chapter 70 Two Women Build A Good Life

Benjamin, five, and Jessica, three-and-a-half, called Nancy Quay "Mom" or "Mommy." Ben and Jesha, as they were more informally known, together with some of the kids in the neighborhood, called Sherry Marcy "Poppy," also the nickname some of her female relatives had given her.

They lived in a trim gray house with a white picket fence at the corner of South Seventh and Sunnyside in Ann Arbor's Old West Side neighborhood.

Inside, there were more toys than you could shake a stick at, more books than two dozen shelves could hold, an Isuzu Trooper in the driveway, a cat named "Snacks," an organic garden, and a compost bin made from old newspaper pallets. "We are a standard middle-class family," said Sherry. "We just happen to be two women."

Nancy and Sherry had been friends for eleven-and-a-half years and a couple for nine when I met them in the fall of 1993 and did a lengthy feature story for The Ann Arbor News. The headline was "Portrait of a Family." It was an important time for them. They lived in Ann Arbor because of its reputation for tolerance and registered under the city's Domestic Partnership Ordinance. But they were facing a test.

Nancy and Sherry were so open and thoughtful, so involved in the neighborhood, church, and charity, so apple pie normal in so many ways that you might forget they were lesbians or decide it was irrelevant.

The family was accepted in the neighborhood, but Ben was ready to start kindergarten at the Oak Trails Montessori School in Superior Township, and Jesha was heading for pre-school at the adjoining Children's House. "Our responsibility as parents is to see that our children aren't blindsided by the outside world," said Nancy. "We are the only parents they know. They are not born with any feeling that it's wrong to be different or knowing that their family is different. So we teach them of all the differences, Mommy and Daddy, Mommy and Poppy, Dad and Grandma, single mothers, widowed spouses, and elderly couples."

It was an important time for me as well. Pat and my eldest son is gay. While we are comfortable with that, I wanted the assurance that a good life, well lived, was possible for him and others. I hoped it would become the norm.

Nancy and Sherry became that for me. Looking back after more than three decades, it's heartening to realize that Ben and Jesha had grown up to become marvelous adults. My story of their family was well received, but the next Ann Arbor News reporter after me ran afoul of our editor. More on that later.

There was a lot of learning going on about what it meant to be gay. One of Nancy and Sherry's favorite stories was about Dan, a third-year University of Michigan medical student from Birmingham, Michigan, who, as part of his education, was sent out to do a case study on an unconventional family.

He composed himself on the couch in the living room, opened his notebook, and asked, "What is the presenting problem?" "We laughed," said Sherry, "and then gave him the 'Just look around' treatment. Dan later wrote us a letter essentially thanking us for broadening his horizons."

Nancy and Sherry had purchased their house nine years earlier (joint tenants in common with full rights to the survivor), resurrected the old practice of post-Art Fair block parties for the twenty-eight households on the Sunnyside cul-de-sac, and became Neighborhood Watch co-captains. Some people figured them out early. Others took longer.

"We had a Christmas open house in 1985," said Nancy. "We didn't know whether to make it a gay party or a straight party, so we invited both. Of the 106 people we asked, more than eighty showed up. We only had one bedroom at the time. The other two were fixed up as an office and a dressing room. Anyone uncertain about us had their uncertainty answered."

In many of the lesbian families in the Ann Arbor area, the children were the product of earlier heterosexual unions that failed. But starting in the mid to late 1980s, the trend for lesbian couples in established unions was to conceive their own children through artificial insemination.

In this couple, Nancy became the biological mother because she was younger. It made economic sense for Sherry to continue with her career. They sent a picture of Sherry to the Oakland Women's Health Collective in California in hopes of finding a donor who looked like her so their children would bear the closest possible physical resemblance to both moms. They used one donor, making Benjamin and Jessica full siblings.

"When we had kids, we suddenly made sense to the families in the neighborhood," said Sherry. "They were more comfortable with us because they understood us as a family." There were twenty-seven children in the cul-de-sac and seven mothers at home during the day. Five of them, including Nancy, organized and shared supervision of a playgroup. It was a neighborhood in the old-fashioned sense that everyone knew your name, and the kids would dart into each other's houses with scarcely a knock.

The same year I wrote the story on Nancy and Sherry, the U-M changed its nondiscrimination code to include sexual orientation. Fellow Ann Arbor News reporter Kim Clarke did a series of follow-up stories about being gay on campus.

There was push-back. Ed Petykiewicz, our editor, hadn't said anything to me about my earlier story, but he told Kim he thought her stories were too gay-friendly and demanded that anti-gay voices be included.

Kim resigned from the newspaper's diversity committee, which was dedicated to seeing all voices covered. "That's when Ed said that, if I was implying he was anti-gay, I'd best find another place to work," she recalled. Kim quit the paper to become the U-M's director of bicentennial communications.

Petykiewicz proved to be an outlier. Broad acceptance of gays and lesbians has been the fastest and most profound social change in the history of the nation. At hundreds of local papers across the country, there were reporters like Kim and me who wrote stories portraying gays and lesbians as human beings and neighbors. I would like to think we made a difference.

One measure of change: In 2013, Nancy and Sherry were married in a civil ceremony in Rochester, New York, an event featured in The New York Times. In another measure the following year, the U.S. Senate voted 97-0 to confirm Judith E. Levy, another openly gay friend from Ann Arbor, as a U.S. District Court judge for the Eastern District of Michigan. It didn't mean the whole Senate had suddenly become gay-friendly. She was part of a package of nominees. That same year, she married Janet Jackson, her partner of nearly three decades, in a civil ceremony. They have three children.

Judy told the story of her journey that December at the Unitarian-Universalist Congregation's fifth annual interfaith service of affirmation. As a favor for the program organizer, I wrote up an advance of her address for The Ann Arbor News. Judy and I had been Facebook friends, but she canceled her account so that attorneys appearing before her couldn't use her posts as grounds to disqualify her from hearing their cases.

Nancy and Sherry remain friends of mine on Facebook. They have lived a good life together and raised a pair of spectacular children. I still feel good about being able to tell their story.

Chapter 71 When I'm My Own Worst Enemy

In sixth grade at Angell School in Ann Arbor, our teacher momentarily left the room. Several girls went up to the chalkboard, drawing cartoon figures. When no one would tell the returning teacher who did it, she called the principal.

Miss Dorothy Buckley assumed the boys were to blame and lined us all up. We would have died rather than rat out the girls. She told us to hold out our left hands and went down the row, whacking each of us with a wooden ruler. I freaked out and unthinkingly grabbed and broke her ruler over my knee. I horrified myself. I had never before defied an adult. My mother was called in and promised to impose suitable punishment. All I got was the mildest admonition.

I have had a visceral dislike of bullies for as long as I can remember, but it wasn't until my final year at The Ann Arbor News that it got me in trouble.

As fifty-four-year-old Sue Ellen Curtis lay dying of a stab wound to her heart and a slashed throat in their rural Dexter Township home, she begged her husband, Bill, for help. But William Hall Curtis Sr. had something more important to do. He ran to the kitchen to get the keys to his 1986 maroon Cadillac so the killer, twenty-five-year-old Todd W. Plamondon, could escape.

Moments after Plamondon sped out of the neighborhood, a woman from across the street entered the house and cradled Sue Ellen's head in her lap, pressing a towel to her throat while Bill Curtis called 911. Joyce Ancypa said Curtis recited the Lord's Prayer while rescue squad members were trying in vain to save his wife's life.

Plamondon, a Ypsilanti resident who sold his body to men to support his crack cocaine addiction, was arrested and arraigned on charges of first-degree murder and armed robbery on April 4, 1991, three days after the killing.

I wrote a story on April 6 that detailed extensive earlier contacts between Curtis and Plamondon. Curtis would acknowledge the relationship but maintain his innocence, claiming the killing was a robbery gone wrong. The Washtenaw County Sheriff's Department insisted that Curtis was not a suspect.

I would later learn that Curtis, only two-and-a-half weeks after the murder, had applied to ADP Data Processing, Sue Ellen's employer, for a double indemnity life insurance payment under the terms of her pension. Prudential Insurance obtained a heavily redacted copy of the death certificate and incident report from the sheriff's department, but the department did not supply the company with a requested copy of my stories. In a telephone conversation, a Prudential representative confirmed to me that the sheriff's department had also failed to disclose that Curtis was, indeed, a suspect in his wife's murder. Prudential paid Curtis $86,000 on June 24.

I knew from Plamondon's attorney that the young man had met Curtis three or four years earlier through a mutual friend. Beginning in February 1991, Curtis and Plamondon had spent ten afternoons of beer and conversation at Ypsilanti's Cross Street Station. It was allegedly during these meetings that Curtis paid Plamondon for sex, supplied him money to buy drugs, and promised him $5,000 for killing his wife. Curtis also gave him a straight razor.

The sheriff's department was being opaque about the investigation it was conducting, and the Washtenaw County Prosecutor was making no comment. I arranged for an Ann Arbor News photographer to get a good surveillance headshot of Curtis. Then, I dove into the paper's photo archives, looking for comparable glossies to assemble a photographic lineup to show to potential witnesses. I was short of the number I wanted until I came across a headshot of the paper's editor, Ed Petykiewicz.

I took the expanded photo array around to the Cross Street Station and the Dexter-Chelsea area bar, where Curtis bought Plamondon four or five beers before driving him out to the Curtis home on Cottonwood Lane. I found an employee at each establishment who said they might have seen Curtis with a young man, but the identifications were too tentative for me to use.

I bragged to a fellow reporter about my use of Petykiewicz's photo. The story of my stunt spread like wildfire through the staff. Former City Editor Dave Bishop, who was serving as the paper's ombudsman, took me aside and said I should tell Petykiewicz myself before someone ratted me out.

I walked into Ed's office, laid his photograph on his desk, and said I owed him an apology. I expected an explosion, but he was preternaturally calm when he asked me if I had been trying to prove him a murderer or a homosexual. I assured him neither. It wasn't until later that I realized the profound insecurity and paranoia behind his question.

The authorities weren't confident enough of their evidence against Curtis to arrest him until five months after the killing. He was convicted of first-degree murder and robbery based mainly on Plamondon's testimony and sentenced to life in prison. Plamondon pled guilty to second-degree murder and was also sentenced to life in prison.

The photo incident was only one of multiple confrontations I had with Petykiewicz. When he was on your case, he would ask a hostile question, follow it up with another hostile question before you completed your answer, then another and another. I considered him a bully, blamed him for driving my two best friends from the paper, and handled our relations poorly. I felt my mental acuity slipping when I had to deal with him.

My father had died of pneumonia after a twelve-year battle with Alzheimer's. I was fifty-seven, too old for early-onset Alzheimer's, but I was scared. In 1998, I went to my doctor at the U-M's Briarwood Family Medicine Center and outlined my fears. Twenty minutes into the appointment, the doctor asked me to repeat the first five minutes of our conversation. I did, pretty close to word for word. He said I was suffering from chronic stress, not Alzheimer's.

Pat and I reviewed our finances. The News held a modest retirement party for me at a local pizza place. Ed didn't attend.

In early March 2009, just over a decade after my retirement, Ed announced his retirement. Several days later, Ann Arbor News owner Booth Newspapers announced that The News would cease to exist as a daily newspaper. Most of the staff was fired. Some were offered new jobs at a fraction of their former pay. Ed stayed on during the transition, helping the staff as much as he could. I give him credit for that.

The News has continued to publish a slim newspaper twice a week, mainly existing as an online presence with scant local news. It's a pattern repeated across the country as communities lost much of the glue that held them together and public officials were freed from someone looking over their shoulders.

I took my life in a new direction, relegating Petykiewicz to a passive memory.

Chapter 72 Life After Newspapers

With the influx of cocaine cowboys from Cuba and Colombia, South Florida was becoming an increasingly unhealthy place for Anglo marijuana dealers. In 1980, Richard Riggs packed up his belongings, drove to Asheville, North Carolina, got a Buncombe County map, and headed into the mountains north and west of town. His quest was to find a hidden cove where he could safely grow an acre or so of pot.

Sandy Mush, an unincorporated community fifteen miles and 150 years from Asheville, was home to Frank and Lois Black, children of families that had settled in the dead-end valley prior to the Civil War. In 1940, Frank purchased two-and-a-half acres of bottomland sandwiched between Sandy Mush Creek Road and the Sandy Mush, a 20-foot-wide rushing mountain creek. On the far side of the creek, the property included a 19-acre hidden cove cut into the side of Early's mountain. The small mountain was named for Jubal Early, the most incompetent of Robert E. Lee's generals.

Frank started building a two-bedroom cabin out of wormy chestnut lumber taken from trees killed by the blight that eradicated most numerous hardwood east of the Mississippi. The following year, the Tennessee Valley Authority started construction of the Fontana Dam on the Little Tennessee River in the far western part of North Carolina. Frank signed on as a welder for the next three years. The Blacks found a couple to move in and finish the cabin while they were away.

Upon their return, Frank planted two acres of tobacco and constructed the most poorly built barn in Sandy Mush to hang his tobacco and house his chickens (I wrote a paper on the tobacco barns of Sandy Mush). He built a cinderblock garage where he did welding on cars and farm equipment. A heavy smoker, Frank died of lung cancer in 1972.

Lois told me she had quit grazing cattle in the hidden cove because she was afraid of crossing the fast-flowing creek. She said she was also increasingly afraid of living alone. When Richard Riggs showed up and offered her cash, she sold the property and moved into a trailer next to her son's house on North Turkey Creek on the opposite side of Early's Mountain.

Richard moved into the cabin and began scouting the cove for where he would plant. About halfway up the cove, there was a small copse of hemlocks, their lower branches reaching the ground and functioning like the sides of a room. Richard parted the branches. Inside was a moonshiner's still, all set up and ready to go.

"I left a note saying this was where I was planning to locate my spring house," Richard told me. "I went back several days later. The still was gone." Then he started getting anonymous calls accusing him of stealing the still. Richard denied it, but the caller didn't believe him. The caller said: "We're building a grudge on you, building a grudge on you!"

Richard had visions of the Hatfields and the McCoys. He put a target on the side of his barn. Every time he heard a car driving down Sandy Mush Creek Road, he would take his rifle out on the cabin's side porch and shoot at the target, trying to convince passersby that he was "Deadeye Dick." Several weeks later, a neighbor called and said no one was coming after him anymore. Richard told me he had never been able to find out the identity of the moonshiner.

It was a convoluted road that took Pat and me to Sandy Mush. When we were still in our 50s, Pat asked me where we should go when I retired. She suggested North Carolina as a possibility even though she had never been there. The research took me all of 15 minutes. The coast was Cape Fear and hurricanes. Raleigh-Durham and Chapel Hill in the Piedmont were culturally and socially attractive but expensive and hotter than hell in the summer. Why leave Ann Arbor? That left the mountains. Asheville was the only place with an international airport and a first-class hospital.

Pat thought retirement would be several years off, but we went ahead and hired a Realtor. We told him we wanted property on water within an hour of Asheville. That was somewhat problematic because there were no natural lakes west of the fault zone that defined the edge of the Blue Ridge Mountains. All the property along the French Broad River, which passed through Asheville, was either already built up or inaccessible. The Ivy tributary was a flat meander and ugly. That left the Sandy Mush. The Riggs' place had just come on the market. Our Realtor made an appointment to visit the property.

Richard had married, fathered a son and daughter, farmed marijuana for about a decade, divorced, remarried, gave up both growing and smoking, failed to make an adequate living carving birds and other critters from laminated wood, and decided he really belonged back in South Florida. He accepted our bid on the property in late 1997.

I surprised Pat with my decision to retire the following year. I was the only Cain without a college degree. I enrolled in Eastern Michigan University in Ypsilanti because they didn't have a foreign language requirement, and they allowed me to design my own program (social science and American culture, grounded in the History Department).

Unlike my three earlier ventures into university degree programs, where I crashed and burned, I reinvented myself as a fanatical student. I completed the final two years of my bachelor's degree and all the coursework for a master's in under two years, posted a 3.9 GPA, and still found time to teach a feature writing course in Eastern's Department of Journalism.

I focused every course I could on Southern Appalachia. Armed with a tape measure, camera, and notebook, I traveled around Sandy Mush interviewing people with interesting barns. That produced an undergraduate paper that I ended up delivering at a national conference on folk architecture. Its opening line: "The social history of Sandy Mush is written in its tobacco barns."

Professor of Historiography Richard Goss had me pegged as a promising student and sought to motivate me to go "all in" on a research paper that would be more than half the grade in his course. He told me about Prof. Robert H. Woody, his mentor at Duke University and a distinguished Civil War historian. Prof. Woody had been waiting for a student good enough to research how supply chain problems crippled the Confederate war effort. It was a challenging project that the professor had wanted to do himself but could never find the time. Goss took it on for his Ph.D. dissertation, and it launched his academic career.

Reflecting on the 1791-94 Whiskey Rebellion in Western Pennsylvania, I decided to do a paper on the political influence of Western North Carolina's numerous moonshiners. I learned a great deal about moonshiners but could find no evidence of significant political influence. In newspapering, you walk away from a story that doesn't pan out. Not so in academe. I ended up with my only A-. Nevertheless, I asked Dr. Goss to serve on my master's thesis committee.

I did my thesis on cultural change in the southern mountains, figuring my reporting skills would give me a leg up. I conducted 27 oral history interviews, mostly with elderly men and women whose ancestors had settled in Sandy Mush prior to the Civil War. I asked them what they felt they had lost of the old ways, what they sought to hold onto. I transcribed the interviews, which became part of the University of North Carolina Asheville's oral history collection.

One of the first people I interviewed was Larry Cook, who had dropped out of school in 6th grade to operate his first still, which, coincidentally, he had dug into the side of the cove I had purchased from Riggs. I told Larry about the missing still that Riggs had spotted under the hemlocks. "Oh, that was my uncle Gaither Surrett's," he said. Gaither had a reputation for making the worst moonshine in Sandy Mush. Larry and I figured a chronically drunk Gaither had found Riggs' note, moved the still to a new hiding place, and had forgotten he'd done it.

Beekeeper Jim Hannah, another interviewee, was the youngest and only survivor of eight brothers whose father resettled in Sandy Mush from the Cataloochee Valley in Tennessee when the federal government established the Smoky Mountains National Park. Pat and I accompanied Jim to the annual reunion of families that had been forced out of Cataloochee in the 1930s. Jim knew about half of the 300 people who gathered around the old white clapboard church in the valley. Most were the sons, daughters, and grandchildren of those who'd been forced to leave, and they wanted to keep alive a sense of the old times.

I found an article in the South Atlantic Quarterly in which Prof. Woody recounted his participation in the 1950 Cataloochee reunion that was attended by about 150 people. He predicted that the reunions would die out with the passing of the old settlers. He was wrong. I included that as a footnote in my thesis, hoping that Prof. Goss would notice that I quoted his mentor. He did and was amused at the length I'd gone to gently jerk his chain.

I hired Larry Cook, who ran a small excavating business, to build a bridge across the Sandy Mush, cut a road up the cove, dig a half-acre spring-fed bass pond, and level a section of the cove wall for a house.

We were still living in Lodi Township outside Ann Arbor when a storm came through, knocking over two large black walnut trees in our black yard.

I found a man with a portable bandsaw mill who turned the trees into 2,000 board feet of lumber. With all that lumber, I needed a trailer. To haul it to Sandy Mush, I needed a truck. To mill the wood for the 3,500-square-foot house we were building, I needed a wood shop, which I set up in the cinderblock garage.

Meanwhile, Larry came across a long-disused sorghum mill built by the Chattanooga Plow Company in 1881, which I helped him restore. He planted a quarter acre of sorghum, chased away a family of beavers that had been feasting on the crop, and organized the first of five annual molasses "workings."

I joined some two dozen men gathered on a fall Friday afternoon to harvest the sorghum. From that evening through midday Sunday, the sugar cane-like sorghum was fed through the mill as mules owned by another friend turned it. The sugar juice was piped into a rectangular container and cooked down by a factor of seven. It yielded 200 quarts of molasses. The nights were fiddle and banjo music, clogging, and white liquor.

Sunday afternoon was a potluck that featured smoked pork butt, out-of-season deer, wild turkey, and Larry's mother's hot-out-of-the-oven biscuits smothered in molasses. Two-thirds of my oral history interviewees took part in the working. Several brought grandchildren to show them something of the old ways. The story of the working was the thread of my master's thesis. For me, academia was journalism plus footnotes.

During one of the molasses workings, Larry said he would give me a quart of moonshine if I would take some photographs for him. I made sure I had at least one picture of everyone who participated and gave Larry two copies of each, one for himself and one to give away. Larry forgot about the moonshine, and I wasn't about to remind him. A year later, he showed up at our house with an entire case of white liquor. He asked me not to tell Pat because he didn't want her to think poorly of him.

We settled into life in the mountains, were active in Pat's church, and spent several years as guardians ad litem, representing children who had been abused or neglected and removed from their homes by social services. I dove into woodworking with a passion, also made jewelry, and sold my crafts at weekend art shows throughout North Carolina.

A crew from the French Broad Electric Membership Corporation, a non-profit utility formed under the REA during the Depression, came down the mountain opposite our cabin, dropping trees for a power line. They just left the fallen trees. A year later, a friend and I took our chainsaws and reclaimed about 3,500 board feet of cherry. We did his living room, dining room, and entrance hall in 5-1/2 inch wide, random length, tongue-and-groove cherry, pegged ends in black walnut, and I took the rest of the wood.

Another friend's great-great-grandfather returned from the Civil War in 1867 and built a small barn. It became horribly deteriorated over the decades. The friend asked me to help clean up the site. About 15% of the wood was salvageable. I took half.

We sold the big house up the cove after renovating and expanding the farm cabin. I removed two sides of the cabin, which were wormy chestnut.

Pat wanted to be closer to the kids and grandkids, so we sold the cabin and bought a condo in downtown Ann Arbor, plus a 1926 bungalow with a freestanding garage and back room. Our youngest son and his wife got the bungalow. I got my shop and a place to store the cherry, wormy chestnut, and vintage barn wood that I brought north. I make and sell a variety of crafts at the Sunday Artisans Market in Ann Arbor's Kerrytown, which is also an opportunity for me to tell old stories and collect new ones.

My one frustration in retirement is coming across situations crying out for good reporters, crying out for local news outlets, and knowing there aren't the advertising dollars to support them. There are some hopeful online ventures, but they are shadows of what's been lost.

I was mentored by great editors and reporters from earlier times and was fortunate enough to work during the closing decades of the last golden age of local and regional journalism. My hope is that the successes and failures I've written about in "Relentless" will be both a window into the past and an encouragement for future journalists. And for non-journalists, I hope you enjoy the stories.

In ending "Relentless," I can't do better than Edward R. Murrow's nightly radio sign-off from London during the Blitz: "Good night and good luck."

Author's Bio

Stephen Cain was born in 1941 in Bronxville, New York, to a scientist father and college English teacher mother. He spent his early childhood in Tennessee. Moving to Ann Arbor in 1950, he was raised alongside his father's graduate students and would bartend at his parent's faculty cocktail parties. He dropped out of college three times and, without a degree, taught a feature writing course at the University of Michigan and Eastern Michigan University. He co-directed a legal writing seminar at the U-M Law School.

He followed the old-fashioned route to reporting, going from the weekly South Lyon Herald to The Grand Haven Daily Tribune, then The Ypsilanti Press, hitting his stride as an investigative reporter at The Detroit News, and won a year-long National Endowment for the Humanities Fellowship for Journalists at the U-M. He quit The News after it censored his investigative piece on the Teamsters international vice president who controlled the distribution of the paper, finishing his career at the mid-sized Ann Arbor News. Along the way, he won three dozen news writing awards, was twice nominated for a Pulitzer, and was inducted into the Michigan Newspaper Hall of Fame. He retired in late 1998, completed the final two years for his bachelor's, and went on to get his master's at Eastern Michigan University. He and his wife, Pat, live in Ann Arbor.

Made in the USA
Columbia, SC
07 July 2024

3dc0f072-2f2d-4499-b8c7-4987d061af29R02